LONDON BUS FILE

89

KERS

KEN GLAZIER

Capital Transport

INTRODUCTION

This is one of a series of handbooks, each of which contains a complete list of all buses and coaches owned by London Transport during a period of between four and six years, together with a brief description and history of each type covered. Vehicles which either joined or left the fleet during the period under review are listed with additional columns showing the dates on which they were formally taken into or removed from stock. These refer to the dates when ownership changed and, in the case of buses taken out of stock, do not necessarily coincide with the day a vehicle left London Transport's hands physically. Vehicles sold were often despatched before the paper work was completed and some vehicles were stored for a time after being sold. Where a body was scrapped before its chassis, the day on which the body was scrapped is deemed to be the date the complete vehicle was written off. For vehicles bodied by manufacturers other than London Transport, the date into stock is the date when the completed vehicle was first received from the body builder. The chassis will have been owned for some time before this as the normal procedure was for the chassis to be delivered formally to London Transport, either physically or as a book transaction, before being sent for bodying. For vehicles bodied at Chiswick, the date into stock is the date when the body was officially recorded as having been mounted on the chassis.

Most of the double-deck buses acquired by the new Board were inherited from the LGOC and its associate companies and they were therefore much more homogeneous than the single-deckers. The LGOC NS class and the Tilling O class petrol-electrics were in the process of being withdrawn when the Board took over and this was continued, alongside the early replacement of open top and solid tyred vehicles and the non-standard Daimler, Dennis, Guy, Leyland LB, Maudslay and Sunbeam buses. Other types cleared out included the DST, DL and LS and the acquired Leyland Titans in the TD class, most of which were in store at the end of 1939. New vehicle deliveries were dominated by the STL class which was gradually improved over the years until its successor, the RT, blossomed in 1939. The 100 STDs were the only significant challenge to the dominance of the STL, although the Board did try five AEC Qs none of which survived the decade in service. The next phase of vehicle replacement, involving the withdrawal of the ST class, had just started when it was interrupted brutally by the Second World War.

London Transport continued to use and add to the vehicle class codes and numbering already established by the LGOC, but between 1933 and 1935 vehicles allocated to the Country Bus and Coach department did not have fleet numbers. During those years the responsibility for licensing, maintenance and overhaul of the green fleet was in the hands of Reigate who continued the practice of LGCS, and it was not until Chiswick took over these tasks that numbers were allocated. This happened when the bus first visited Chiswick and any vehicles which did not survive long enough to do so were never numbered. This explains why many in the ST, STL and TD classes were apparently numbered out of sequence. The rule adopted when allocating the numbers was that, generally, they should be in the alpha-numerical order of the registration numbers, which is why batches of identical STs were broken up and why ST 1139, the oldest, had the highest number. In contrast, acquired buses which were allocated to Central Buses were normally numbered in the order that they were taken over.

These books would not have been possible without the unstinting help of Dr Andrew Gilks, from whose private collection the bulk of the information concerning dates has been derived. He has also done much donkey work, beyond the call of duty, in sorting out a great deal of the detail regarding specifications of individual buses. One important point needs to be made here. No vehicle records were kept by London General Country Services from its formation in 1932, nor by its successor the Country Bus and Coach department between 1933 and 1935. For these years it has been necessary to rely on the records kept in the Peter Wilson archive and on those published by the PSV Circle

First published 2001   ISBN 185414 249 6

in its supplements LT6 and LT6A. This data varies in detail but is all that is available and we must be grateful that these sources exist. Even so, there are a few vehicles whose fate cannot be traced for certain after 1932 and which may or may not have been taken over by the LPTB. These are acknowledged in the text. Thanks are also due to Brian Bunker, John Gent, Malcolm Papes and David Ruddom for providing so many of the illustrations from their personal collections and to the photographers of the time, who are acknowledged separately in the body of the book. The two names that appear most often are D.W.K. Jones and J.F. Higham, without whose pioneering work we would all be much the poorer.

CONTENTS

K	4
S	5
O	6
PS	8
NS	9
L	28
D	29
LS	30
TD	32
DH	44
LT	46
ST	60
DL	74
DST	78
STL	80
Q	110
STD	114
RT	118
Minor Types	120

Title page
The last buses bought by City were three Leyland Titanics which were delivered in March 1933 but their Dodson bodies with open staircases and projecting cabs looked more like something built four years earlier. They compared unfavourably in this respect with Westminster's Sunbeam Sikh, which had a handsome modern body from the same Dodson stable, and the contemporary STLs but the chassis specification, which included an 8 litre oil engine, was right up to date. This photograph of TC 2 at Hanwell seems to have been the only one taken of any of the class during their short career with London Transport. The TC class is among those listed under Minor Types. D.W.K. Jones

Front cover
Country Bus Q 5, one of four double-deck Qs bought by London Transport, two for the country area and two for the central area. Painting by Barry Pearce

K

The K had been a landmark in double-deck bus design when it first appeared in 1919 as it was the first forward control model, in which the driver sat beside the engine. Although nearly all of the type had been withdrawn by the spring of 1931, ten remained in service on route 90 until June 1932 because of a weight restriction on Chertsey Bridge. Fifteen were still in stock, delicensed, when London Transport was formed. Apart from K 424 which was retained for the museum collection, they were scrapped in 1934.

Chassis:	AEC 301	
Engine:	AEC 4-cylinder 4.4 litre 30 hp petrol	
Transmission:	3-speed chain gear with multi-plate clutch	
Bodywork:	originally LGOC, Brush, Dodson, Short Bros. or Strachan	
Capacity:	O24/22RO	
L.T. codes:	not allocated	
Built:	1919–1921	
Number built:	1132 (double- and single-deck)	
Number in stock	1.7.33: 15; 31.12.39: nil Last in stock: 23.4.34	

K		Date out of stock	K		Date out of stock	K		Date out of stock
25	LU8274	16.4.34	719	XC8279	12.4.34	924	XC9725	16.4.34
194	LU8411	16.4.34	746	XC8295	11.4.34	931	XC9729	13.4.34
424	XC8059	*	825	XC9771	19.4.34	949	XC9754	23.4.34
632	XC9711	20.4.34	888	XC8464	17.4.34	969	XC9769	19.4.34
700	XC8396	20.4.34	897	XC9757	18.4.34	1121	YP6684	18.4.34

* Retained for museum collection.

Although not one of the fifteen that survived into LPTB ownership, K 606 was among the last to be withdrawn from service and was typical of a class which had changed little in the twelve years since its first appearance. This photograph, taken in March 1931, shows it at Chertsey, where the weight restriction on the bridge prevented the use of heavier buses and prolonged the life of the class until June 1932. H.C. Casserley

S

The S-type was an enlarged version of the K, introduced in 1921 following an increase in the maximum permitted gross weight from 7 to 8½ tons, a concession which had been sought by the LGOC. It was nearly two feet longer than the K, at 24ft 8¼ inches, with a wheelbase of 14ft 11ins. This enabled the double-deck version to have fifty-four seats, only two short of the figure which was later to be the standard for nearly thirty years up to the 1950s.

Replacement of the main S-type was completed by the LGOC with the ST and LT classes and the only double-deckers still in stock by July 1933 were in the London General Country Services' fleet. These are believed to have been used to support the PS-type operating on route 410 but all were withdrawn in 1934. They did not receive numbers in the S series.

Chassis:	AEC 401
Engine:	AEC 5.1 litre 35 hp petrol
Transmission:	3-speed chain gear with spur reverse
Bodywork:	Short Bros.
Capacity:	O24/28RO
L.T. codes:	not allocated
Built:	1922

Number in stock 1.7.33: 15   31.12.39: nil   Last in stock: 26.10.34

S		Date out of stock	S		Date out of stock	S		Date out of stock
	PC9317	* 26.10.34		PC9319	* 26.10.34		PC9321	* 26.10.34
	PC9318	* 26.10.34		PC9320	* 26.10.34		PC9322	* 26.10.34

* These dates are taken from the Peter Wilson archive. No official records were kept for these vehicles.

Six S-type double-deckers came into the LPTB fleet from London General Country Services, all Short Bros bodied open-toppers dating from August 1922 but they were soon withdrawn. PC9321 (East Surrey number 94) has met this fate and is parked in a yard awaiting disposal. It originally had solid tyres but in common with the rest of the East Surrey double-deck fleet had been fitted with pneumatic tyres at the end of 1928, and a lower skirt panel added. The radiator was cast with the East Surrey name as these six vehicles were owned by the company, rather than being on loan from the LGOC.
D.W.K. Jones

O 29 was one of an original 166 Tilling Stevens TS7 petrol-electrics bought by the LGOC in 1923–24 for operation on its behalf by Thomas Tilling, 61 of which passed to London Transport. Although pneumatic tyres had been fitted to some of the type, O 29 still had solids when photographed in Duncannon Street, Charing Cross, after the formation of the Board, its lines contrasting starkly with the Bluebird LT behind. D.W.K. Jones

O

The TS7 was the last of the Tilling-Stevens models taken into stock in quantity by Thomas Tilling Ltd, who had favoured petrol-electrics since 1911. The 166 buses which originally comprised the double-deck element of the O class (there were also 12 single-deckers), were all owned by the London General Omnibus Company and operated on its behalf by Thomas Tilling Ltd. The petrol-electric system was powered by a petrol engine driving a dynamo which supplied power to an electric motor which in turn powered a worm and wheel live rear axle through a prop shaft. It was claimed by the manufacturer to be jerk-free and buses carried a notice to that effect. Their 48-seat open-top bodies were built at Tilling's own factories in Lewisham and Lee.

Withdrawal of the TS7s had started in November 1932 with the arrival of the new STLs and by 1st July 1933 there were 61 remaining in stock. Forty-five were licensed for service and were allocated to Catford and Croydon garages for operation on routes 1C, 59B and 254. As these vehicles were owned by the LGOC, they passed into the ownership of the LPTB on vesting day but the licensed buses were placed on formal loan to Thomas Tilling which remained an independent company for the time being. They remained with Tilling until either withdrawn or returned to London Transport when the business was acquired on 1st October 1933. The replacement of all but three was effected by the allocation of former LGOC STs to Catford between July and November 1933 and the transfer from there to Croydon of some Tilling examples. The three survivors were at Croydon where they worked on route 254 which went under a low bridge in Croham Road. They were replaced on 29th January 1934 by the former Pickup open-top STLs.

Chassis:	Tilling-Stevens TS7
Engine:	Petrol electric: 4-cylinder 30 hp petrol engine driving a 20KW dynamo
Transmission:	Gearless
Bodywork:	Tilling
Capacity:	O26/22RO
L.T. codes:	Not allocated
Built:	1923–1924
Number built:	166
Number in stock	1.7.33: 61 31.12.39: Nil Last out of stock: 17.4.34

All were taken into stock on 1.7.33, having been owned by the London General Omnibus Company, but remained formally on hire to Thomas Tilling until the company was acquired by the LPTB on 1.10.33.

O		Date out of stock	O		Date out of stock	O		Date out of stock
10	XN7310	* 30.8.33	37	XN7337	26.3.34	144	XR744	* 30.8.33
13	XN7313	18.7.33	38	XN7338	9.4.34	146	XR746	11.8.33
15	XN7315	* 4.9.33	39	XN7339	16.11.33	148	XR748	21.9.33
16	XN7316	12.7.33	40	XN7340	14.11.33	149	XR749	6.7.33
18	XT8779	* 4.9.33	41	XN7341	15.11.33	150	XR750	11.4.34
21	XN7321	17.4.34	42	XN7342	18.11.33	151	XT8773	8.8.33
22	XN7322	14.4.34	45	XN7345	15.11.33	152	XT8774	11.8.33
23	XN7323	26.3.34	48	XN7348	30.10.33	153	XT8775	* 25.9.33
24	XN7324	13.4.34	50	XN7350	18.11.33	154	XT8776	8.8.33
25	XN7325	* 6.4.34	51	XP2351	20.11.33	155	XT8777	29.3.34
26	XN7326	6.4.34	54	XP2354	31.10.33	157	XT8779	4.9.33
27	XN7327	6.4.34	57	XP2357	16.11.33	159	XT8781	29.3.34
28	XN7328	* 6.4.34	60	XP2360	21.11.33	160	XT8782	12.7.33
29	XN7329	* 5.4.34	63	XP2363	9.4.34	161	XT8783	* 11.4.34
30	XN7330	4.4.34	66	XP2366	20.11.33	162	XT8784	15.1.34
31	XN7331	9.4.34	69	XP2369	11.4.34	163	XT8785	* 15.1.34
32	XN7332	6.2.34	70	XP2370	6.2.34	164	XT8786	7.4.34
33	XN7333	10.4.34	72	XP2372	5.2.34	165	XT8787	12.4.34
34	XN7334	2.2.34	81	XP2361	11.4.34	166	XT8788	* 10.4.34
35	XN7335	5.2.34	96	XP2396	5.4.34			
36	XN7336	5.4.34	110	XR710	* 30.8.33			

* – O 10, 15, 18, 110, 144 and 153 were returned to LPTB in exchange for O 25, 28, 29, 162, 163 and 166 which went on loan to Thomas Tilling.

A Tilling TS7 with pneumatic tyres at Camden Gardens, Camden Town on route 59B, one of the last major routes on which the O-type operated. D.W.K. Jones

PS

The PS was a more powerful version of the S and was bought in some numbers by the East Surrey Traction Co. between 1924 and 1927. Most had been withdrawn by the time the LPTB was formed, leaving only eleven still in stock, their open top bodies being suitable for operation under the low bridge at Oxted on route 410. They were all withdrawn and disposed of in 1934 when the new lowbridge 'Godstone' STLs were delivered. As they were withdrawn before Chiswick took responsibility for Country Buses, they were never numbered by London Transport.

Chassis:	AEC 502 (except PD9018: 507)
Engine:	AEC 5-type 4-cylinder side-valve 6.8 litre 45 bhp petrol
Transmission:	3-speed chain gear with spur reverse
Bodywork:	Short Bros. (PF9018); Ransomes Sims & Jefferies (remainder);
Capacity:	O26/22RO (PE8309, 8310); O24/26RO (PF9018); O24/24RO (PD1355, 1358, 1359, 1363, 1368, 9754–9756)
L.T. codes:	Not allocated
Built:	1926 (PE8309, 8310); 1927 (PF9018); 1924 (remainder)
Number acquired: 11	
Number in stock 1.7.33: 11	31.12.39: Nil
	Last in stock: 1934 (exact date unknown)

	Date into stock	Date out of stock		Date into stock	Date out of stock		Date into stock	Date out of stock
PD1355	1.7.33	1934	PD1368	1.7.33	1934	PE8309	1.7.33	1934
PD1358	1.7.33	1934	PD9754	1.7.33	1934	PE8310	1.7.33	1934
PD1359	1.7.33	1934	PD9755	1.7.33	1934	PF9018	1.7.33	1934
PD1363	1.7.33	1934	PD9756	1.7.33	1934			

The eleven PS type double-deckers still in service in July 1933 were kept for operation on route 410, as their lower clearance was needed for the low bridge at Oxted. Seen here at the Reigate 'Red Cross' terminus, PD1358 (formerly East Surrey 130) was new in June 1924 and had Ransomes Sims and Jefferies bodywork. J. Higham

There were 144 open-top NSs in the Central Bus fleet, some of which survived until the end in the original 1923 condition with solid tyres but with anachronistic drivers' windscreens. NS 520, which seems to be in some sort of trouble on this fine summer day, was one of these. Side lamps (known then as 'police lights') were fitted to all buses but headlamps were only to be found on buses used on specific routes, usually those using unlit country roads. E.G.P. Masterman

NS

The NS was a major landmark in the history of motor bus design and could justifiably claim credit for establishing the basic layout of all front-engined double-deck bus chassis for the succeeding forty years. It was a development of the S-type of 1920 and took the design a significant stage further by having a double reduction rear axle. This enabled the frame behind the front axle to be cranked so that the lower deck floor level and the height of the whole vehicle could be dropped by nearly a foot. Behind the rear axle, the frame was even lower, which meant that the platform was low enough to be reached with a single step, compared with two on earlier buses. This level was not bettered, nor always even matched, on production buses until the arrival of the Bristol Lodekka in the 1950s. The lower centre of gravity also made the chassis suitable for mounting with a covered top body. NS 1 was fitted with a detachable top cover when it was first built, to test the reaction of the Metropolitan Police but their approval was not forthcoming and over 1700 entered service as open toppers. Four Short Bros-bodied examples built in the summer of 1925 were fitted with purpose-built covered top bodies and operated experimentally on route 100 (Elephant & Castle–Epping Town) from August that year. This led to approval being granted for more general operation, although still subject to strict control of the routes on which they could be used. A further 16 for East Surrey and National were built with open tops but the remaining 580 built new from March 1926 onwards all had top covers and 1684 of the earlier deliveries were so fitted during 1926 and 1927. During 1932/1933 fifty covered top vehicles were converted back to open top for use on private hire work and as grandstands for Epsom Races.

The mechanical specification of the majority of the NSs mirrored that of the S-type, including a similar 4-cylinder engine and standard LGOC 3-speed chain gearbox. However, the first 300 or so originally had AEC constant mesh gearboxes and there were at least five different types of box tried at various times. NS 1–1605 had AEC chassis manufactured at Walthamstow but between September 1924 and June 1928 the chassis were built-up at Chiswick using AEC mechanical components. All NSs up to NS 2296 were fitted with solid-tyred wheels when new but in July 1928 authority was given for pneumatic tyres to be fitted and a total of 56 of the new 422 model were ordered and placed in service in 1928 and 1929 (NS 2297–2346 and 2372–2377).

Pneumatics had been pioneered for double-deckers on the LS class in 1927 but the Metropolitan Police resisted their use on the NS for a time because of the extra width needed to accommodate the 'balloon' tyres on their large rear wheels. These were the first new NSs from AEC since 1924 and were built at the new factory in Southall. The original order had been for 75 but this was reduced to 50, which accounts for the missing numbers. The last six were a later order. The 422 chassis was improved in a number of ways, notably in having a more powerful engine, the AEC A128, which developed 57 bhp. It was visually distinctive too in having an ADC-style radiator, although with 'GENERAL' lettering, replacing the style which had been in use for the past 18 years. The bodies also differed from earlier buses. Apart from being wider, they had two half-drop sliding windows on the front of the upper-deck, instead of the standard three-window arrangement and the opening windows on each side of both saloons slid vertically, rather than horizontally. Internally they were fitted with improved seating. The seating capacity was reduced to 50 to keep the complete vehicle within contemporary weight limits. Between July 1928 and March 1934 1251 solid-tyred NSs were fitted with pneumatics, including 53 LGOC-owned open-top buses operated on its behalf by East Surrey Traction Co. and National Omnibus and Transport Co. The seating capacity was reduced to 50 on all conversions before 1932, after which the new weight regulations allowed the capacity to remain at 52. NS 2378 was a 422 demonstrator with pneumatic tyres which was acquired for the East Surrey fleet in 1929 but did not receive its number until after its acquisition by London Transport.

The Country Bus NSs all had pneumatic tyres and 35 of the 56 were open-toppers. Although not numbered by LGCS or Country Buses, PE8825 was NS 1743 and carried a plate with the embossed number painted over. It was one of ten which had been owned in its own right by East Surrey and was fitted with headlamps for operation on country roads. It was one of a number of double-deckers allocated to Grays to replace a multiplicity of vehicles operated by Eastern National and a number of Independents on the intensively served Grays–Purfleet road. Non-standard route and destination boards lend the bus a makeshift air in the early days of route 372. J.F. Higham collection

This nearside view of NS 1612 (again with number painted over) gives a good indication of the lines of the body, whose basic design was inherited from the S-type. The height of the single step to the low slung platform which had been such a pioneering feature of the NS in 1923 was to remain much the same on most buses until the 1960s. Snook & Son; D.A. Ruddom collection

None of the class had a driver's windscreen when built, even those with covered tops, because the Metropolitan Police were opposed to them on safety grounds. There were some less than wholly satisfactory experiments in 1929 but it was not until May 1931 that Police approval was secured for their general use. Between then and early 1933 a total of 1983 windscreens were fitted to LGOC vehicles but because LGCS and, for the first two years London Transport's Country Bus department, did not keep vehicle records, the number of their vehicles converted is not known. All LGOC NSs without windscreens had been withdrawn by August 1932.

One other important variation of the NS class was the special design developed for operation through Blackwall tunnel, an experimental body being built early in 1927 and mounted on NS 2050. It had a narrower body than the standard type, which meant that the seats had to be longitudinal. On the upper deck, the seats were arranged in 'knifeboard' fashion back-to-back along the centre of the saloon. It also had an enclosed rear platform, the first double-decker so fitted in London. A production batch of 24 similar vehicles entered service between October 1927 and January 1928. During 1928 the knifeboard seating on upper decks of these 25 was replaced by individual 'bucket' seats set at an angle, which reduced the total capacity from 46 to 44. A further batch of six tunnel buses had open staircase bodies with domed roofs to fit the profile of the tunnel which removed the need for sunken gangways and allowed a conventional upper-deck seating layout to be adopted. They were mounted on older overhauled chassis and took numbers scattered through the series. Because of the narrow roads in the tunnel and the propensity for wheels to rub against the kerbs, with one exception these NSs retained their solid tyres until withdrawn in 1937 and were the last solid-tyred buses to run in London service. The exception was NS 2213 which was fitted experimentally with reinforced pneumatics in April 1935. The experiment was successful, which enabled the tunnel STLs which replaced them to operate normally on pneumatics.

There were 1,077 NSs which were never fitted with pneumatic tyres but a large proportion of these did receive top covers, either when new or after the regulations changed in 1926. NS 827, seen on the stand at Roehampton Village, was one of a number whose withdrawal was delayed while Chelverton Road garage was rebuilt to provide enough headroom for pneumatic-tyred vehicles. J.F. Higham

Twenty-one Country Bus NSs had covered tops, all with pneumatic tyres, enclosed windscreen and headlamps. NS 1033, unnumbered until 1935, was one of 25 allocated to the National Omnibus and Transport Co for operation on behalf of the LGOC in the north and north-east country areas. It is at New Barnet Station in April 1935. D.W.K. Jones

The London branch of Tilling and British Automobile Traction operated 33 of these green-liveried 409-type AEC NSs on route 24 from a garage in Rochester Mews (Camden Town; code AQ). NS 2387 is at South End Green, Hampstead, in the short period it continued to operate under LPTB ownership, these solid-tyred vehicles being among the first to be withdrawn by the Board. On these, the nearside route number board was carried on the side panels above the front lower deck window, rather than behind the glass of the short central window as on the LGOC type and the front board at the bottom, rather than the top, of the window. D.W.K. Jones

The bodies built for the last series of NSs in 1928 had the front of the upper deck divided into two large windows with the route number stencil on the canopy, instead of the earlier three-section arrangement with two smaller windows separated by the route number display. These and the opening windows on the side of the saloons were of the drop-down instead of the horizontally sliding type. NS 1770, seen at Wanstead, would have had the earlier style when new. J.D.P. House

NS 2232 was one of the original batch of enclosed staircase 'clerestory' buses with domed roof profile built for operation through Blackwall Tunnel. It is passing The Two Brewers, Perry Hill in June 1936. Malcolm Papes collection

The rears of the tunnel NS bodies were tapered to avoid the risk of them striking the tunnel wall on the series of sharp bends in Blackwall Tunnel. The back end of NS 2220 is seen in Athol Street garage next to STL 400. The tunnel NSs had roller blinds at the back, where boards would have been inaccessible to the conductor, but standard stencils and boards at the front. London's Transport Museum

The reason why the tunnel buses were called 'clerestory' is that the upper deck was arranged with seats down the centre, originally as a bench, knifeboard style, and later with these angled bucket seats. The inward leaning sides, domed roof and curved rear end are shown clearly in this photograph. London's Transport Museum

The supplementary batch of six bodies for tunnel operation had open staircases and a conventional seating layout on the upper deck. The body design was based on the new style introduced in 1928, with vertically sliding windows and two, instead of three, windows at the front of the upper deck. On this style of body the route number stencil returned to the front canopy, as can be seen on NS 1590 at Bromley-by-Bow. J.F. Higham

Apart from the mainstream NSs delivered to the LGOC, a total of 58 were allocated to the East Surrey Traction Co. and the National Omnibus and Transport Co. and a further ten were owned by East Surrey. There had been some exchange of vehicles within the Group when some of the outer London routes changed hands and by the time London General Country Services (as successor to East Surrey and National) was acquired by the LPTB, it owned a total of 56, of which 35 were open top and 21 covered. Among the open-toppers were the three former East Surrey-owned 409s (NS 2347–2349) and the 422 type former demonstrator NS 2378. The only other NSs to come into London Transport's ownership were 33 ADC 409 type dating from 1927, formerly owned by Tilling & British Automobile Traction (numbered NS 2379–2411 by LPTB). These had covered top bodies and solid tyres.

Withdrawal of the NS class had started in 1932 and by the time the LPTB took over, 183 had been scrapped or sold. Many others were delicensed awaiting disposal but, with over 2000 still in service, the class was still to be seen in all parts of London and the Home Counties. The programme continued uninterrupted by the formation of the LPTB, who scrapped their first (NS 882) on 3rd July 1933, the last LGOC example having been NS 46, on the last day of the company's existence, 30th June. London Transport gave priority to the withdrawal of open-top and solid-tyred vehicles. The last open-top NSs in the Central Area were withdrawn at Old Kent Road garage on 11th April 1934, their retention at that garage being dictated until then by a low roof in the shed. The last non-tunnel bus solids were withdrawn on 18th July 1935. These had remained in service longer than they might otherwise have done as they were allocated to Chelverton Road garage which did not have sufficient headroom to accommodate pneumatic-tyred buses until it was rebuilt. The first group of pneumatic-tyred vehicles was withdrawn on 31st July 1935. By June 1936 the number owned had fallen to 1032 but the Board decided that the rate of replacement should be accelerated and completed in 1937, so it authorised the purchase of an exceptionally large number of new buses for that year. Among the new vehicles were the tunnel STLs which replaced London's last solid-tyred vehicles at Athol Street in April 1937. The very last of the class to run in passenger service was NS 1974 which made its last journey on the short peak hour route 166, leaving Aldwych for Bank and West Green garage at 7.27pm on 30th November 1937. The distinctive lines of this classic bus were to remain visible in various parts of London for at least another decade in the guise of mobile staff canteens, twelve being so converted. Others were used as tower wagons and tree loppers and one became a trolley wire lubricating vehicle.

Chassis: AEC 405, 406, 407, 408 or 409; or ADC 422
Engine: AEC 4-cylinder 5.1 litre 35 bhp petrol; or 4-cylinder 5.1 litre 57 bhp petrol (422 type)
Transmission: LGOC 3-speed chain gear (but see text)
Bodywork: LGOC, Brush, Ransomes, Sims & Jefferies or Short Bros.
Capacity: O28/24R; H28/24RO; H26/24RO or (tunnel buses) H22/22R and H24/22RO
L.T. code: not allocated
Built: 1922–1928
Number built: 2385 (1805 built as open top, 580 covered top)
Number in stock: 1.7.33: 2202 (including 179 open top)   31.12.39: Nil
Notes: NS 1738 was a single-deck coach prototype of the AW class. It did not survive to pass to London Transport.
NS 1953 was acquired by LGOC from Hull & District Motor Services.
NS 2051–2053 never operated in London but were sold to Greyhound Motors of Bristol.
NS 2231 was acquired by the LGOC from Mr Antichon in Yorkshire as a single-decker. It was fitted with a standard LGOC double-deck body.
In all cases the NSs were taken into stock on 1st July 1933, acquired from LGOC, LGCS or Tilling & British Automobile Traction.

NS		Date out of stock	NS		Date out of stock	NS		Date out of stock
1	XO1019	7.3.34	54	XN7031	29.12.33	114	XN7067	18.3.37
2	XR1442	28.12.36	55	XN7016	13.4.34	115	XO1005	8.2.35
3	XO9273	20.7.37	56	XN7003	31.10.36	116	XO1046	24.2.37
4	XO9268	23.3.37	57	XN7017	20.6.34	ot 117	XO1030	19.11.34
5	XN7005	8.2.34	60	XN7032	27.10.37	118	XN7060	17.4.34
6	XN1799	7.5.36	61	XN7018	8.2.35	119	XN7073	27.5.37
7	XN1776	17.11.33	62	XN7096	17.1.34	120	XO1047	16.7.37
8	XN1796	1.9.37	63	XN7019	20.1.34	121	XO1006	5.7.33
9	XN1780	20.4.34	64	XN7041	15.6.36	122	XO1012	11.6.35
11	XO1004	4.4.34	66	XN7033	24.2.36	123	XN7061	3.2.37
12	XN1792	30.7.37	67	XN7034	18.4.34	124	XN7088	21.2.34
13	XN1786	s 13.5.36	68	XN7021	3.2.36	125	XN7068	31.3.37
14	XN7006	4.9.35	69	XN7062	27.7.33	126	XO1036	8.1.34
15	XN1787	14.1.36	70	XN1086	27.10.36	127	XN7074	29.4.36
18	XN1788	13.4.34	71	XN7047	2.4.36	128	XO1013	25.1.35
19	XN1794	12.3.35	73	XN7035	14.7.33	129	XN7089	26.4.34
20	XN1789	30.4.36	74	XN7042	8.1.34	130	XO1037	2.1.35
21	XN1797	27.7.33	75	XN7027	1.9.33	131	XN7090	26.11.34
22	XN1790	11.9.35	76	XN7023	20.8.34	132	XO1007	13.7.33
24	XN1767	8.1.34	77	XO1020	14.7.33	133	XN7082	1.4.36
25	XN1745	30.8.33	78	XN7063	10.2.37	135	XN7083	6.11.34
26	XN1798	31.5.34	79	XN7056	23.1.35	136	XO1014	4.8.37
27	XN1773	30.3.37	80	XN7040	26.7.33	137	XO1015	2.11.36
28	XN1770	6.3.37	81	XN7052	c 8.11.37	139	XN 7076	20.3.37
29	XN1766	30.12.36	84	XN7024	21.12.36	140	XO1060	11.12.36
30	XN7007	21.3.36	85	XN7025	16.4.34	141	XN7077	20.3.37
31	XN1774	19.4.34	86	XN7079	5.7.33	142	XN7099	17.5.34
32	XN1778	12.10.34	87	XN7081	23.11.35	144	XO1038	3.1.34
33	XN1769	13.4.34	88	XN7038	11.2.35	145	XN7078	5.2.35
34	XN7008	28.3.36	90	XN7064	12.4.34	146	XO1021	22.2.34
35	XN7080	15.1.34	91	XN7054	18.5.34	147	XN7092	14.7.33
36	XN1775	1.2.34	93	XN7098	16.4.34	148	XO1039	24.3.34
37	XN7051	14.5.34	95	XN7070	17.12.34	149	XN7093	21.1.35
38	XO1028	26.9.34	96	XN7075	15.4.36	150	XO1061	15.2.34
39	XN1785	30.3.36	97	XN7094	14.12.34	153	XO1095	17.4.36
41	XN7010	10.10.36	98	XN7071	1.9.33	154	XO1055	25.5.37
42	XN1768	22.10.34	99	XN7057	4.12.34	156	XN7084	3.12.36
43	XN7028	s 13.5.36	100	XN7055	11.2.36	157	XO1023	20.5.35
44	XN7001	8.3.37	103	XN7065	13.10.36	158	XO1017	10.5.34
45	XN7030	18.3.36	105	XN7058	9.5.34	159	XO1031	7.1.35
47	XN7026	19.4.34	106	XN7100	20.10.36	161	XO1009	25.7.33
48	XN7011	16.1.37	107	XN7095	4.3.36	162	XO1078	13.1.34
49	XN7012	7.2.34	109	XO1002	2.11.34	163	XO1032	15.6.37
50	XN7013	4.5.36	110	XN7087	9.11.34	164	XO1024	24.4.34
51	XN7014	23.5.34	111	XN7097	6.12.34	165	XO1033	28.3.34
52	XN7015	19.3.37	112	XN7059	1.3.34	166	XO1010	6.4.34
53	XN7002	23.6.37	113	XO1003	17.5.34	167	XO1063	8.10.36

NS

NS		Date out of stock
168	XO1025	22.5.34
169	XO1056	5.3.34
170	XO1018	23.11.33
171	XO1034	3.12.36
172	XO1096	23.1.35
173	XO1026	s 16.4.37
174	XO1048	23.1.35
175	XO1049	25.2.37
176	XO1040	24.2.37
178	XO1071	6.2.34
179	XO1011	17.1.34
180	XO1027	5.4.34
182	XO1064	25.1.25
183	XO1072	22.3.37
184	XO1057	8.10.36
185	XO1079	8.1.37
186	XO1035	31.10.34
187	XO1065	21.4.36
188	XO1066	20.10.36
189	XO1051	16.8.37
190	XO1029	c 12.11.37
ot 191	XO1052	23.1.35
ot 192	XO1041	19.9.34
193	XO1042	5.2.34
ot 194	XO1053	2.6.34
195	XO1043	19.1.37
197	XO1044	8.2.37
198	XO1098	2.11.34
199	XO1045	22.10.34
200	XO1080	1.1.34
201	XO1073	2.4.37
202	XO1068	6.6.35
203	XO1081	22.1.35
ot 204	XO1058	6.9.34
205	XO1088	10.3.36
206	XO1069	5.6.36
207	XO1099	30.4.35
ot 209	XO1086	22.10.34
210	XO1074	3.3.35
211	XO1059	24.5.35
212	XO1084	13.11.34
213	XO1085	15.2.36
214	XO1106	7.1.35
215	XO1108	14.3.34
216	XO1087	19.11.36
217	XO1075	4.11.36
218	XO1076	12.7.33
220	XO1125	6.3.37
ot 221	XO1100	3.10.34
222	XO1107	26.3.36
223	XO1089	6.2.37
224	XO1111	14.12.34
ot 225	XO1090	24.8.34
226	XO1091	20.8.37
227	XO1112	27.5.37
cb 228	XO1110	22.7.35
cb 230	XO1093	8.1.36
231	XO1103	23.1.35
232	XO1101	14.12.34
233	XO1094	9.11.36
234	XO1120	30.1.37
ot 235	XO1102	19.6.34
236	XO1121	16.10.36
238	XO1122	7.4.36
239	XO1126	27.8.37
241	XO1105	25.1.35
242	XO1123	26.8.37
243	XO1082	21.10.36
244	XO1113	13.1.37
245	XO1114	27.2.37
246	XO1117	29.12.36
247	XO1127	5.11.34
249	XO1109	31.1.35
250	XO1083	s 13.3.37
251	XO1142	21.1.35
252	XO1133	14.12.34
253	XO1118	16.7.37
254	XO1128	11.7.36
255	XO1138	1.2.34
256	XO1124	11.6.35
257	XO1129	22.12.36
258	XO1134	27.2.34
259	XO1130	8.7.37
ot 260	XO1140	30.11.34
261	XO1131	19.6.36
262	XO1143	23.10.34
263	XO1115	28.7.33
264	XO1135	1.11.34
ot 265	XO1144	26.9.34
266	XO1141	31.10.34
267	XO1136	9.3.36
268	XO1145	27.11.36
269	XO1146	15.5.35
270	XO1153	7.3.36
271	XO1154	15.1.37
272	XO1147	25.5.37
273	XO1152	14.12.34
274	XO1148	11.1.37
275	XO1155	4.1.35
276	XO1119	25.2.37
277	XO1137	2.3.34
278	XO1156	14.6.37
279	XO1157	4.3.37
281	XO1159	26.2.37
282	XO1149	22.12.33
283	XO1160	7.5.37
284	XO1171	25.6.36
285	XO1177	11.12.36
ot 286	XO1161	10.10.34
287	XO1193	25.4.34
288	XO1150	16.1.37
289	XO1139	s 1.3.37
290	XO1167	14.1.35
291	XO1168	11.12.34
ot 292	XO1162	31.8.34
293	XO1178	12.7.33
294	XO1151	2.11.34
295	XO1163	26.6.36
296	XO1179	7.12.33
297	XO4001	6.3.37
298	XO4026	20.7.33
ot 299	XO1164	20.11.34
300	XO1194	23.5.35
ot 301	XO1170	20.12.34
302	XO4027	25.10.37
303	XO1173	27.1.34
305	XO1180	16.1.34
306	XO1181	24.12.33
307	XO1176	5.11.34
308	XO1175	20.8.36
309	XO1182	20.4.37
310	XO1166	11.1.35
311	XO1183	20.1.37
312	XO1174	29.10.34
313	XO1184	13.2.37
314	XO1184	29.5.34
315	XO1185	21.1.37
316	XO1185	11.3.36
317	XO1187	10.12.36
318	XO1188	8.5.34
319	XO1169	16.5.34
320	XO1189	22.1.35
321	XO1190	29.5.35
ot 322	XO4005	13.12.34
323	XO1195	17.4.34
324	XO1200	6.4.34
325	XO1196	22.6.36
326	XO1191	8.7.37
ot 327	XO1197	16.1.35
328	XO4085	21.3.34
329	XO4003	3.4.36
330	XO4004	20.6.36
332	XO4007	9.4.34
334	XO4008	30.11.36
335	XO4009	17.8.37
336	XO4028	27.2.35
337	XO4002	28.7.37
338	XO1199	30.10.34
ot 339	XO4010	20.7.34
340	XO4029	19.7.37
341	XO4011	14.1.35
ot 342	XO4093	18.2.35
343	XO4019	c 22.11.37
344	XO4030	12.11.36
345	XO4012	13.8.37
346	XO4020	24.8.37
347	XO4031	17.10.36
ot 348	XO4021	3.8.34
349	XO4013	10.11.37
350	XO4014	5.5.36
351	XO4053	3.2.36
353	XO4032	30.10.34
354	XO4015	1.3.34
355	XO4033	8.3.35
356	XO4023	27.5.35
357	XO4016	6.12.34
358	XO4068	9.12.33
359	XO4017	29.6.36
360	XO4024	16.6.36
361	XO4069	22.12.33
362	XO4034	9.11.37
363	XO4025	8.5.36
ot 364	XO4064	6.9.34
365	XO4006	17.2.37
366	XO4052	10.12.35
367	XO4035	11.6.36
368	XO7605	6.6.35
369	XO4082	14.5.35
ot 370	XO4038	4.3.35
371	XO4054	30.10.36
372	XO4074	14.5.35
373	XO4036	13.3.36
374	XO4056	31.12.36
ot 375	XO4039	3.1.35
376	XO4063	1.2.35
377	XO7606	5.6.34
378	XO4060	27.3.36
379	XO4061	22.3.34
380	XO4059	15.6.36
381	XO4040	20.1.34
382	XO7616	25.1.35
383	XO4041	28.2.34
ot 384	XO4042	3.9.34
385	XO9249	27.4.37
386	XO9243	12.2.36
387	XO9254	30.1.35
388	XO9248	22.5.37
389	XO9269	19.6.37
390	XO9260	6.2.34
ot 391	XO9241	18.12.34
392	XO9263	18.12.34
393	XO4037	19.3.34
394	XO9259	20.5.34

NS		Date out of stock	NS		Date out of stock	NS		Date out of stock
395	XO9242	19.4.34	470	XO7620	11.6.35	544	XO9283	2.8.35
396	XO9255	22.6.37	471	XO7634	24.4.34	545	XO9217	19.5.37
397	XO4055	24.5.37	472	XO9211	16.3.34	546	XO9246	14.6.37
ot 398	XO4066	24.8.34	473	XO7669	18.5.34	547	XO9208	7.12.34
399	XO4043	22.4.37	474	XO7619	2.11.34	548	XO9205	18.6.35
ot 400	XO7642	21.6.34	475	XO7658	3.9.34	ot 549	XO9225	15.10.34
ot 401	XO7604	17.10.34	476	XO7667	20.4.34	550	XO9226	2.1.34
ot 402	XO4070	19.6.35	478	XO7630	14.3.34	ot 551	XO9238	22.11.34
403	XO7669	4.1.35	479	XO7631	28.11.33	552	XO9257	18.1.34
404	XO7626	28.5.37	480	XO9203	6.10.34	ot 553	XO9212	20.6.35
ot 405	XO4044	24.9.34	481	XO7650	28.3.34	554	XO9221	2.6.37
406	XO7651	16.5.34	482	XO7663	22.11.33	555	XO9206	15.4.36
ot 407	XO4071	21.8.34	483	XO7603	19.4.34	556	XO9227	s 20.4.36
408	XO4075	12.1.34	484	XO7636	23.2.34	557	XO9239	8.5.34
ot 409	XO7680	19.10.34	485	XO7660	12.2.34	558	XO9216	18.5.37
410	XO7639	10.2.34	486	XO7654	29.1.34	559	XO7697	6.2.37
411	XO4045	30.5.35	487	XO7699	1.9.33	ot 560	XO9252	17.12.34
412	XO4049	6.1.37	488	XO7637	7.9.33	562	XO9284	28.5.35
413	XO4098	27.11.36	489	XO7659	30.1.35	ot 563	XO9256	20.6.35
414	XO4046	7.12.33	490	XO9210	11.6.35	564	XO9261	24.1.35
415	XO4047	13.1.34	491	XO7638	14.11.33	565	XO9247	24.5.37
416	XO4048	27.11.34	492	XO7686	12.5.34	ot 566	XO9264	14.2.35
417	XO4076	6.3.37	493	XO7687	30.5.33	567	XO9258	28.6.37
418	XO4090	22.6.37	494	XO7673	12.5.34	568	XO9201	8.11.33
419	XO4057	1.5.36	495	XO7640	20.2.34	569	XO9240	2.8.35
ot 420	XO4062	2.10.34	496	XO7662	24.5.37	570	XO9253	21.8.34
ot 421	XO4077	3.12.34	497	XO9204	31.3.37	571	XO9262	7.9.35
422	XO4092	6.2.35	ot 498	XO9232	8.1.35	572	XO9228	15.4.37
423	XO7652	11.10.34	ot 499	XO7674	4.2.35	573	XO9300	4.1.35
424	XO7621	20.12.35	500	XO7675	25.8.37	574	XP701	28.6.37
ot 425	XO4084	2.8.34	501	XO7688	28.2.34	575	XO9274	25.9.35
426	XO7665	4.2.37	ot 503	XO7633	2.9.35	576	XO9250	17.7.37
427	XO4065	9.1.34	504	XO7644	17.1.34	577	XP702	s 27.4.37
428	XO4058	31.8.33	505	XO7648	28.10.33	578	XO9267	20.11.34
429	XO4078	s 9.4.37	506	XO7645	12.11.34	579	XO9279	12.7.37
430	XO7681	10.11.33	507	XO7689	8.1.36	580	XO9278	21.6.37
431	XO7666	24.1.35	ot 508	XO7690	19.12.34	581	XO9266	28.6.37
ot 432	XO7682	30.7.34	509	XO7676	16.11.34	582	XP703	c 23.11.37
434	XO4083	8.6.34	510	XO9270	c 23.11.37	583	XO9272	2.6.37
ot 435	XO7608	27.8.34	ot 511	XO7691	28.11.34	585	XO9285	24.5.37
436	XO7653	30.12.36	ot 512	XO7698	4.9.34	586	XP704	22.11.34
437	XO7622	21.9.34	513	XO9222	2.1.34	587	XO9292	16.11.34
438	XO4091	15.11.33	514	XO7646	11.6.35	588	XO9286	5.6.35
439	XO4086	8.9.33	515	XO9218	7.12.33	589	XO9287	13.9.34
440	XO7615	26.2.37	516	XO7641	22.11.33	590	XO9280	9.10.34
ot 441	XO7670	3.1.35	517	XO9223	7.1.36	591	XP705	30.1.37
443	XO7655	16.4.34	ot 518	XO9265	29.5.34	592	XO9293	14.11.34
ot 444	XO4087	20.7.34	519	XO7692	15.3.35	593	XO9281	6.2.35
445	XO4099	6.11.34	ot 520	XO7677	5.10.34	594	XO9288	21.5.37
446	XO7656	21.2.36	521	XO9244	30.4.35	595	XO9277	6.11.34
447	XO4094	14.12.36	ot 522	XO7694	12.7.34	ot 596	XP709	23.11.34
448	XO7624	10.4.34	523	XO7695	6.6.35	597	XO9294	23.1.34
ot 449	XO7664	15.11.34	524	XO7696	25.5.34	598	XO9296	26.3.36
450	XO7607	20.5.35	526	XO9209	12.7.33	599	XO9297	12.7.33
451	XO7643	17.11.33	527	XO9219	17.6.37	600	XO9299	30.8.37
452	XO7661	23.7.36	ot 528	XO9233	18.10.34	601	XP719	31.5.34
453	XO7618	7.9.33	529	XO9282	21.1.35	602	XO9275	23.11.37
454	XO7623	12.1.34	530	XO7647	21.11.33	603	XO9276	15.9.34
455	XO7683	8.2.34	531	XO9234	13.3.34	604	XO9295	25.5.37
456	XO7671	10.3.34	532	XO9207	11.7.34	606	XO9290	27.5.37
457	XO7693	15.11.35	533	XO9220	5.3.36	607	XP710	4.7.34
459	XO7668	17.2.36	534	XO9235	25.11.35	608	XP711	7.2.36
460	XO7625	30.11.37	535	XO7678	4.12.33	609	XO9298	28.4.37
461	XO7617	21.12.33	536	XO9236	13.2.34	610	XO9299	28.4.36
462	XO7700	28.5.35	537	XO9237	15.10.36	611	XP707	6.6.34
463	XO7601	1.5.35	ot 538	XO9215	24.1.35	612	XP712	26.5.37
464	XO7685	7.12.34	539	XO9202	15.9.34	613	XP735	29.7.37
465	XO7628	19.2.36	ot 540	XO9224	18.6.34	614	XP716	23.11.37
466	XO7672	18.12.36	541	XO9251	14.12.34	615	XP708	22.9.36
467	XO7629	3.1.34	542	XO9245	21.6.37	616	XP720	7.6.37
468	XO7649	2.3.35	543	XO9213	2.2.34	617	XP713	8.5.36

NS		Date out of stock	NS		Date out of stock	NS		Date out of stock
618	XP717	c 24.11.37	696	XP763	20.3.34	775	XP4161	9.7.37
619	XP721	19.6.37	697	XP2463	27.10.33	776	XP2517	5.11.35
620	XP724	30.7.37	698	XP2451	24.1.35	778	XP2508	19.3.35
621	XP722	24.1.36	699	XP788	19.6.37	779	XP2545	24.8.37
622	XP736	c 8.11.37	700	XP2466	12.4.34	780	XP4117	26.6.37
623	XP725	3.9.35	701	XP2467	20.8.35	782	XP2518	22.11.35
624	XP714	26.10.34	702	XP798	17.3.34	784	XP4118	30.3.36
625	XP718	13.8.35	703	XP797	28.3.34	785	XP2527	3.7.36
626	XP740	5.10.34	704	XP2501	25.1.35	786	XP2540	9.7.37
627	XP726	24.1.34	706	XP2460	5.11.34	787	XP2528	17.6.37
628	XP741	11.3.35	707	XP2452	23.1.35	788	XP2546	4.6.37
629	XP727	1.12.37	708	XP800	17.12.35	789	XP2509	22.8.34
630	XP715	2.8.35	709	XP2461	7.11.34	790	XP4162	28.8.33
631	XP728	29.9.34	710	XP2453	7.8.37	791	XP2510	7.6.37
632	XP729	18.12.35	711	XP2462	3.8.37	792	XP2519	23.7.34
633	XP733	11.6.37	712	XP2478	c 29.10.37	793	XP2520	26.6.37
634	XP754	23.1.34	713	XP2464	3.6.37	794	XP2511	19.11.35
635	XP755	24.7.37	714	XP2455	29.3.34	795	XP2512	23.3.36
637	XP742	20.9.34	715	XP2479	3.6.37	796	XP2521	24.7.37
638	XP759	20.11.35	716	XP2484	9.4.36	797	XP4119	27.2.36
639	XP743	29.10.34	717	XP2480	29.7.37	799	XP2547	28.7.37
641	XP730	29.7.37	718	XP2456	21.1.35	800	XP2522	6.7.37
642	XP770	5.6.35	719	XP2468	7.2.34	801	XP2531	19.8.37
643	XP731	26.11.34	720	XP2469	17.10.34	802	XP4138	28.12.35
644	XP799	17.6.37	721	XP2470	2.11.34	806	XP2533	6.1.36
645	XP737	9.6.37	722	XP2423	4.12.35	807	XP2549	27.5.37
646	XP744	14.6.37	724	XP2457	31.7.37	808	XP4115	3.5.37
647	XP745	28.5.34	725	XP2465	29.8.34	809	XP4133	2.9.33
648	XP732	13.12.35	726	XP2458	19.6.37	811	XP2534	2.7.37
649	XP733	2.7.34	727	XP2459	7.7.37	812	XP2535	30.7.37
650	XP739	23.6.36	729	XP2473	20.8.37	813	XP2536	20.5.37
651	XP784	7.6.37	730	XP2402	4.6.37	814	XP2537	1.7.37
652	XP789	13.2.36	731	XP2481	9.5.34	816	XP4121	6.12.35
653	XP779	28.5.37	732	XP2474	21.4.37	818	XP2538	25.1.35
654	XP777	21.5.35	733	XP2498	7.10.36	819	XP4108	7.8.35
657	XP771	24.1.35	734	XP2485	4.9.35	820	XP4123	10.6.36
658	XP761	20.11.34	736	XP2475	25.6.37	821	XP4124	c 29.10.37
659	XP747	18.6.37	737	XP2482	11.6.37	822	XP4153	6.12.35
ot 660	XP756	13.9.34	738	XP2483	25.3.36	823	XP4125	28.5.37
661	XP734	14.2.36	739	XP2497	17.9.34	825	XP4139	3.3.34
662	XP748	22.5.37	740	XP2486	18.2.36	827	XP2541	9.11.35
663	XP749	18.8.37	741	XP2492	13.8.34	828	XP4127	25.3.36
664	XP772	12.12.35	742	XP2493	29.7.37	829	XP4128	9.4.37
665	XP783	10.9.35	745	XP2488	9.10.34	830	XP4140	7.6.37
666	XP785	7.3.34	746	XP2489	30.8.34	832	XP4109	6.2.37
667	XP762	1.8.35	747	XP2524	29.6.37	833	XP4130	15.6.37
668	XP750	14.5.35	748	XP2494	30.6.37	834	XP4113	5.7.37
669	XP786	26.4.37	749	XP2477	2.5.34	835	XP4131	19.10.34
670	XP787	1.7.37	750	XP2490	21.6.37	836	XP4147	12.4.34
671	XP751	24.11.33	751	XP2495	9.7.37	837	XP4163	30.6.37
672	XP752	24.9.34	752	XP2499	31.1.36	839	XP4156	28.6.37
673	XP757	7.12.35	753	XP2476	c 8.11.37	840	XP4132	8.11.34
674	XP773	14.6.37	754	XP2503	18.8.37	841	XP4148	15.8.35
675	XP766	17.6.37	755	XP4116	25.11.37	842	XP4141	7.6.37
677	XP758	28.1.35	756	XP2516	26.4.37	843	XP4142	23.3.36
678	XP753	3.10.34	757	XP2500	29.3.34	844	XP4149	23.6.37
679	XP780	29.8.33	758	XP4159	10.11.37	845	XP4150	27.7.37
680	XP768	15.11.35	759	XP2504	5.8.37	846	XP4143	14.12.36
683	XP795	27.8.37	760	XP2525	s 28.1.36	849	XP4157	4.6.37
684	XP778	4.6.37	761	XP2513	24.3.36	850	XP4110	23.8.37
685	XP775	3.8.33	763	XP2543	26.6.37	851	XP4111	17.6.37
686	XP776	24.5.37	764	XP2505	18.1.34	853	XP4145	s c 5.5.36
687	XP781	25.5.37	766	XP2496	1.9.37	855	XP4143	29.1.36
688	XP793	10.7.34	767	XP2544	24.7.33	856	XP4177	20.12.35
689	XP790	30.1.37	768	XP4151	18.4.34	857	XP4189	28.3.34
690	XP782	9.12.35	769	XP4136	30.7.37	859	XP4154	28.9.34
691	XP764	21.6.37	770	XP2526	2.9.37	860	XP4170	23.1.35
692	XP794	19.12.35	771	XP2542	c 29.10.37	861	XP4190	30.8.37
693	XP765	22.7.36	772	XP2506	5.6.37	862	XP4155	11.8.37
694	XP796	12.11.35	773	XP4160	13.12.35	864	XP4191	13.11.33
695	XP791	18.11.35	774	XP2507	20.4.34	865	XP4168	25.6.37

NS	XP	Date out of stock
867	XP4169	23.8.34
868	XP6680	20.9.34
869	XP4193	4.12.35
872	XP4165	15.6.37
874	XP4171	15.6.37
876	XP4172	18.6.35
877	XP4197	1.1.34
878	XP4183	18.10.37
879	XP4177	30.4.37
880	XP4105	14.4.34
882	XP6657	3.7.33
883	XP4173	14.8.35
884	XP4184	22.1.36
885	XP4178	11.2.37
886	XP4185	9.5.36
887	XP4198	24.6.36
888	XP4179	29.1.35
889	XP6681	20.7.33
890	XP4186	14.11.35
891	XP4199	13.6.36
892	XP6601	9.6.36
893	XP4180	8.4.36
894	XP6631	15.1.34
896	XP4200	1.5.36
897	XP6602	2.7.36
898	XP6659	7.2.34
900	XP4194	20.2.37
901	XP6603	13.7.33
903	XP4187	3.3.36
904	XP4196	5.8.37
905	XP4202	4.4.34
906	XP4201	15.6.36
908	XP6604	16.5.35
909	XP4204	c 12.11.37
911	XP6605	5.6.37
912	XP6660	18.8.37
913	XP6623	18.4.34
914	XP6610	14.1.36
915	XP6606	23.4.34
916	XP6607	30.7.35
917	XP6624	5.7.37
918	XP6661	30.4.36
919	XP6625	21.6.37
920	XP6611	31.5.34
921	XP6658	1.3.37
922	XP6608	22.12.36
923	XP6612	25.1.35
924	XP6626	2.8.33
925	XP6621	18.11.37
926	XP6613	25.6.37
929	XP6675	11.5.36
930	XP6642	21.6.37
931	XP6627	s 12.5.37
933	XP6619	26.7.37
934	XP6615	10.10.34
935	XP6633	2.8.35
936	XP6609	29.3.34
939	XP6617	9.3.34
940	XP6650	12.3.37
944	XP6652	21.2.34
946	XP6643	26.5.37
947	XP6676	3.1.34
948	XP6628	4.11.36
949	XP8238	14.7.33
951	XP6662	9.4.34
954	XP6630	12.6.37
955	XP6654	15.3.34
956	XP6677	7.3.34
958	XP6635	17.4.36
959	XP6636	25.5.37
960	XP6645	6.1.34
961	XP6696	12.6.37
962	XP6637	27.8.37
963	XP8279	17.11.36
964	XP6663	25.3.37
965	XP6646	7.1.37
966	XP6684	30.10.36
967	XP8228	14.11.34
968	XP6664	9.8.37
969	XP6640	4.8.33
973	XP8210	29.6.36
974	XP6685	16.1.37
975	XP6672	16.4.34
976	XP6669	10.7.33
978	XP6686	2.3.36
979	XP6691	18.6.36
980	XP6666	16.7.37
981	XP6667	11.8.37
982	XP6687	20.1.34
983	XP8206	8.7.37
984	XP6656	5.11.36
986	XP6225	1.9.33
987	XP6674	5.9.33
988	XP6688	5.6.36
989	XP6678	2.9.37
990	XP6670	c 14.5.36
991	XP8243	19.3.37
992	XP6668	21.4.36
993	XP6649	23.6.37
994	XP6699	2.4.37
995	XP6689	1.5.36
996	XP6690	27.11.33
998	XP6700	26.7.33
1000	XP8207	20.2.37
1001	XP6693	28.5.37
1002	XP8201	18.9.37
1004	XP6697	23.5.34
1005	XP6671	12.7.37
1006	XP8202	22.1.35
1007	XP8274	10.2.37
1009	XP6679	10.12.33
1010	XP8266	7.12.36
1011	XP8204	9.11.34
1013	XP8220	28.3.34
1014	XP6694	22.1.34
1015	XP8218	8.5.36
1017	XR1429	1.4.36
1018	XP8240	20.7.37
1021	XP8219	1.11.34
1022	XP6695	23.12.33
cb 1024	NK6935	not known
1026	XP8221	29.2.36
1027	XP8227	26.10.37
cb 1028	NK7047	9.35
1029	XP8208	5.3.34
1031	XP8213	25.3.37
1032	XP8244	28.2.36
cb ot 1033	NK6919	not known
1034	XP8209	22.5.34
1035	XP8241	19.2.34
cb 1036	NK6918	30.1.36
cb ot 1038	NK6936	10.34
1040	XP8223	5.1.34
1041	XP8215	17.4.34
1042	XP8224	12.6.36
1043	XP8216	29.11.35
1044	XP8275	5.1.34
1045	XR1445	9.4.36
1046	XP8232	14.1.37
cb ot 1047	NK6953	10.34
1048	XP8297	11.3.37
1049	XP8276	6.1.37
1050	XP8234	27.8.37
1051	XR1412	28.12.36
1052	XP8237	21.8.37
cb 1053	NK7048	10.34
1054	XP8235	30.11.37
1055	XP8285	21.5.37
1056	XP8236	19.3.37
1057	XP8277	15.5.36
1058	XP8278	28.8.37
1059	XP8286	16.11.37
1060	XP8250	17.1.34
1061	XR1446	17.8.37
1062	XP8242	2.1.34
1064	XP8245	4.6.36
1065	XP8251	20.7.33
1066	XP8252	3.9.37
1067	XP8246	2.11.36
1068	XP8267	7.2.34
1070	XP8268	21.12.37
1071	XP8254	16.11.33
cb ot 1072	NK6989	10.34
1076	XP8270	27.2.36
1078	XP8255	13.3.37
1079	XP8271	27.12.33
1080	XP8248	27.8.37
1081	XP8261	5.4.37
1082	XP8273	29.8.37
1083	XP8249	1.1.37
1084	XP8256	17.8.37
1085	XP8300	17.7.37
1086	XR1440	19.1.34
1087	XP8288	11.11.33
1088	XR1447	2.11.37
1089	XP8257	15.7.36
1090	XP8269	29.10.36
1091	XP8262	11.8.37
1092	XR1448	2.2.37
cb ot 1093	NK6967	30.1.36
cb ot 1094	NK6990	11.35
1095	XP8289	28.11.36
1096	XP8290	10.1.35
1098	XR1430	17.11.36
1099	XP8264	4.5.37
cb ot 1100	NK7363	15.1.36
1101	XP8291	18.2.36
1102	XP8292	16.12.33
cb ot 1104	NK7049	not known
1106	XR1403	12.7.33
1107	XP8293	3.2.37
1108	XR1404	15.7.33
1109	XP8265	15.1.37
1110	XP8294	18.11.36
1111	XR1450	11.11.36
1112	XR1439	27.2.37
1113	XR1405	17.8.36
1114	XP8298	29.4.37
1115	XP8299	21.7.37
1117	XR1401	19.11.35
1119	XP8233	19.3.37
ot 1120	XR1431	s 17.1.35
1121	XP8295	11.7.33
1122	XR1421	3.11.36
1123	XR1473	21.7.33
1124	XP8280	9.10.36
1125	XR1422	29.1.37
1126	XP8284	23.3.37
1127	XP8281	27.5.37
1128	XR1413	16.1.36
1129	XR4205	s 26.4.37
1130	XP8282	30.8.33
1132	XR1432	1.9.37

NS		Date out of stock
1133	XP8283	28.8.33
1134	XP8296	9.8.37
1136	XR1414	9.9.37
1137	XR1476	19.10.36
1138	XR4206	2.12.38
1139	XR1452	27.10.36
1141	XR1460	13.2.37
1142	XR1443	27.2.34
1144	XR1416	17.6.37
1145	XR1407	3.3.36
1146	XR1477	11.11.36
1147	XR1423	20.4.37
1148	XR1478	29.6.36
cb ot 1149	NK7366	10.34
1150	XR1424	15.11.37
1151	XR1474	5.2.37
1152	XR1461	17.9.36
1153	XR1433	26.6.36
1154	XR1453	16.8.37
1155	XR1454	1.6.37
1156	XR4207	29.11.37
1157	XR1408	17.11.37
1158	XR1489	15.11.37
1159	XR1402	10.11.36
1160	XR1479	25.8.37
1161	XR1409	26.10.37
cb ot 1162	NK7364	11.35
1164	XR1444	18.1.37
1165	XR1411	25.9.37
1166	XR4265	6.7.36
1167	XR1480	3.5.37
1169	XR1463	18.11.37
1171	XR1418	3.3.34
1173	XR1464	23.7.37
1174	XR4208	17.9.36
1175	XR1420	31.5.37
1177	XR1455	30.8.37
1178	XR1490	18.2.37
1179	XR1481	26.8.37
1180	XR1466	3.12.35
1181	XR1435	26.11.36
1182	XR1482	15.1.37
1183	XR1425	6.3.36
1184	XR4209	18.5.37
1185	XR1483	15.10.34
1186	XR1491	7.4.36
1187	XR1492	8.10.37
1188	XR1484	26.4.34
1189	XR1426	28.9.34
ot 1190	XR1485	27.11.34
1191	XR4274	15.1.35
1192	XR4210	16.10.34
1193	XR1462	6.3.37
1194	XR1456	23.7.36
1195	XR1493	9.2.37
1196	XR4227	30.8.37
1197	XR4211	9.11.37
1198	XR1494	13.7.33
1199	XR1427	6.7.37
1200	XR4212	s 22.2.39
1201	XR1428	20.1.34
1202	XR1495	12.8.36
1204	XR4228	28.10.36
1205	XR1457	4.6.36
1206	XU6148	28.7.37
1208	XR1467	13.3.37
1210	XR4219	19.9.36
1211	XR1496	23.10.36
1212	XR4229	21.4.34
1213	XR4220	3.3.37
1214	XR1487	27.8.37

NS		Date out of stock
1215	XR1497	29.11.37
ot 1216	XR1458	20.1.37
1217	XR4266	15.10.34
1218	XR1498	19.5.37
1219	XR1488	17.2.37
1220	XR1468	24.4.36
1221	XR4236	28.12.36
1223	XR1459	27.2.37
1224	XR4247	26.11.37
1225	XR1499	30.7.37
ot 1226	XR1470	10.9.34
1227	XR1471	30.3.37
1228	XR4263	18.9.34
1229	XR1500	16.11.36
1230	XR4230	2.1.37
1231	XR4231	7.5.36
1232	XR4213	20.3.37
1233	XR4201	12.6.36
1234	XR4237	2.3.37
1235	XR1472	20.2.37
1236	XR4214	12.1.37
1237	XR4238	21.4.38
1238	XR4202	15.1.34
1239	XR4215	1.12.36
1240	XR4216	c s 15.5.36
1241	XR4221	19.9.36
1242	XR4239	20.2.34
1243	XR4222	7.11.36
1244	XR4223	19.6.36
1245	XR4224	10.8.37
1246	XR4248	28.5.37
1247	XR4275	5.2.35
1248	XR4246	15.6.37
1249	XR4203	4.2.37
1250	XR4241	21.12.36
1251	XR4267	22.9.37
1252	XR4295	22.6.37
1253	XR4204	13.3.37
1255	XR4232	26.2.36
1256	XR4226	27.3.36
1257	XR4242	18.10.37
1258	XR4233	25.8.37
1260	XR4234	15.10.37
1261	XR4243	9.12.36
1262	XR4235	7.6.37
1263	XR4268	11.6.37
1264	XR4276	17.6.36
ot 1265	XR4250	25.8.34
1266	XR9909	16.8.37
1267	XR4251	24.5.37
1268	XR4217	23.8.37
1269	XR4218	16.2.37
1270	XR4244	19.7.37
1271	XR4296	8.4.36
1272	XR4269	4.11.37
1273	XR4245	14.10.36
1274	XR4252	25.3.37
1275	XR4253	6.10.36
1276	XR4254	6.9.37
1277	XR4246	9.12.35
1278	XR4255	10.7.37
1279	XR4297	14.6.37
1280	XR4277	26.5.37
1281	XR4264	27.2.37
1283	XR4257	27.7.37
1284	XR4278	11.12.34
1285	XR4270	18.3.37
1286	XR4279	24.11.37
1287	XR4271	16.4.37
1288	XR4291	11.4.38
1289	XR9933	22.12.33

NS		Date out of stock
1290	XR4280	17.11.37
1291	XR4298	11.3.36
1292	XR4281	16.6.37
1293	XR4258	29.12.36
1294	XR4283	26.11.36
1295	XR4292	22.10.37
1296	XR4284	22.5.37
1297	XR4282	3.9.37
ot 1298	XR4259	1.1.35
1299	XR9925	11.11.37
1300	XR4299	29.12.36
1301	XR4300	7.1.35
1302	XR4260	2.12.36
1303	XR9900	14.7.37
1304	XR9910	11.11.37
1305	XR9911	13.11.36
1306	XR9944	26.5.37
1307	XR4285	13.2.37
1308	XR4293	13.10.37
1309	XR4261	15.6.37
1310	XR4286	27.2.37
1311	XR4272	30.1.37
1312	XR4294	9.10.36
1313	XR4262	23.2.37
1314	XR9922	29.7.37
1315	XR4273	16.11.37
1316	XR9901	12.1.37
1317	XR9902	26.8.37
1318	XR9903	27.1.34
1319	XR9904	4.11.37
1320	XR9923	6.10.36
1321	XR9928	22.1.35
1322	XR9929	8.12.37
1323	XR9924	25.10.34
1324	XR9905	16.6.37
1325	XR9906	26.5.37
1326	XR9912	c 21.12.37
1327	XR9934	27.5.37
1328	XR9907	c 22.11.37
1329	XR9935	19.12.33
1330	XR9913	4.1.35
1331	XR9945	31.5.37
1332	XR9946	c 24.11.37
1333	XR4287	10.7.36
1334	XR9914	20.5.37
1335	XR9915	21.8.37
1336	XR9930	8.12.36
1337	XR9936	7.7.37
1338	XR9947	21.11.34
1339	XR9948	17.4.34
1340	XR9931	6.10.34
1341	XR9932	11.11.37
1343	XR9956	29.7.37
1344	XR9916	13.2.37
1345	XR9937	23.1.35
1346	XR9938	8.12.33
1347	XR9939	13.2.37
1348	XR9949	22.7.37
1349	XR9950	7.7.37
ot 1350	XR9940	12.11.34
1351	XR9908	4.5.37
ot 1352	XR9951	27.8.34
1353	XR9952	22.7.37
1354	XR9957	16.12.36
1355	XR4288	21.3.34
1356	XR9955	21.9.36
ot 1357	XR9963	6.6.34
1358	XR9958	22.5.35
1359	XR9959	8.2.37
1360	XR9960	28.3.34
1361	XR9964	24.7.37

	NS		Date out of stock		NS		Date out of stock		NS		Date out of stock
	1362	XT6006	26.10.34		1434	XT6050	23.8.35		1505	XU1836	4.6.37
	1363	XT6007	28.8.37	ot	1435	XT6045	23.6.34		1506	XU1833	4.12.35
	1364	XR9965	14.12.34		1436	XT6064	14.1.35		1507	XU1858	23.7.37
	1365	XT6008	9.11.37		1437	XT6051	18.4.34		1508	XU1868	13.5.35
	1366	XR9968	8.3.34	ot	1438	XT6067	4.10.34		1509	XU1837	31.8.35
	1367	XT6016	4.8.37	ot	1439	XT6048	31.8.34		1510	XU1850	19.5.37
	1368	XR9966	6.5.37	ot	1440	XT6052	24.5.34		1511	XU1821	12.12.34
	1369	XT6032	3.11.36		1441	XT6059	5.2.37		1512	XU1851	29.8.34
	1370	XR9969	4.12.34	ot	1442	XT6068	14.8.34		1513	XU1839	18.11.35
	1371	XR9967	16.2.34		1443	XU1835	29.7.35		1514	XU1822	3.4.34
	1372	XT6017	16.6.37		1444	XU1825	2.6.37		1515	XU1823	17.5.34
	1373	XT6033	2.2.34		1445	XT6090	27.4.36		1516	XU1824	27.11.35
	1374	XT6034	11.5.34		1446	XT6061	15.5.35		1517	XU1869	30.4.37
	1375	XT6018	26.8.37	ot	1447	XT6069	11.12.34		1518	XU1842	16.6.37
	1376	XT6035	3.7.34		1448	XU1826	11.5.34		1519	XU1870	31.1.35
	1377	XR9970	6.2.35		1449	XT6062	18.5.34		1520	XU1842	30.6.34
	1378	XR9973	2.5.34		1450	XT6077	26.5.34		1521	XU1843	1.8.35
	1379	XR9971	16.1.37		1451	XT6063	3.9.35	ot	1522	XU1841	4.3.35
	1380	XT6036	25.1.34		1452	XT6070	14.11.35		1523	XU1852	5.3.35
	1381	XT6001	26.1.34		1453	XT6071	19.2.34		1524	XU1834	1.2.35
cb ot	1382	XR9972	12.35		1454	XT6065	2.8.35		1525	XU1871	30.11.35
ot	1383	XT6009	20.2.34		1455	XT6078	22.5.35		1526	XU1840	11.2.35
	1384	XR9974	22.1.35		1456	XU1809	19.11.36		1527	XU1873	22.6.37
	1385	XR9975	21.7.37		1457	XU1846	6.5.37		1528	XU1861	27.4.37
	1386	XT6002	27.2.37		1458	XU1827	14.4.37	to	1529	XU1880	2.4.37
ot	1387	XR9976	11.7.34		1459	XT6072	14.5.37		1530	XU1844	c 29.11 37
	1388	XR9977	10.4.37		1460	XU1801	18.1.37		1531	XU1876	5.11.35
	1389	XT6015	6.10.37		1461	XT6079	3.1.36		1532	XU1881	27.5.37
	1390	XT6010	1.2.35		1462	XU1828	18.4.36		1533	XU1855	28.5.37
	1391	XT6003	24.5.35		1463	XT6066	13.10.33		1534	XU1882	2.1.36
	1392	XT6004	2.11.34	ot	1464	XU1810	3.8.34		1535	XU1853	11.6.37
	1393	XT6005	15.7.37	ot	1465	XT6080	23.8.34		1536	XU1883	14.7.34
	1394	XT6019	23.6.37		1466	XT6073	10.4.34		1537	XU1859	14.6.37
ot	1395	XT6011	23.11.34	ot	1467	XT6074	5.12.34		1538	XU1862	24.5.37
	1396	XT6012	6.3.35		1468	XU1805	2.12.35		1539	XU1856	29.6.34
	1397	XT6020	16.11.33	ot	1469	XU1829	20.6.35		1540	XU1884	4.10.34
	1398	XT6013	4.8.37	ot	1470	XT6086	1.6.34		1541	XU1854	25.2.36
	1399	XT6021	25.5.37	ot	1471	XU1811	26.2.35		1542	XU1885	7.6.37
	1400	XT6022	9.3.36	ot	1472	XT6081	31.12.34	ot	1543	XU1878	25.9.34
	1401	XT6014	24.2.34		1473	XU1830	7.12.36		1544	XU6104	10.2.36
	1402	XT6027	13.7.33		1474	XT6085	24.11.36		1545	XU1877	6.7.37
ot	1403	XT6023	24.10.34		1475	XU1812	4.2.36		1546	XU1872	29.6.34
	1404	XT6024	16.10.33		1476	XT6083	13.3.35		1547	XU1860	14.4.37
	1405	XT6025	10.5.34	ot	1477	XT6087	13.12.34		1548	XU1863	12.3.35
	1407	XT6054	4.6.36		1478	XT6088	22.5.35		1549	XU1890	7.6.37
	1408	XT6076	9.1.35		1479	XT6084	14.4.37		1550	XU1886	28.5.37
ot	1409	XT6030	8.10.34		1480	XU1802	24.8.34		1551	XU1874	13.4.37
	1410	XT6037	28.10.33		1481	XU1819	28.8.35	ot	1552	XU1845	13.7.34
ot	1411	XT6026	19.10.34		1482	XU1864	30.7.37	ot	1553	XU1879	25.5.34
ot	1412	XT6028	2.1.35		1483	XU1816	5.3.35		1554	XU1875	28.1.36
	1413	XT6038	25.1.36	ot	1484	XU1803	11.1.35		1555	XU6124	28.7.34
	1414	XT6029	14.2.34		1485	XU1831	27.5.35		1556	XU1857	9.6.37
	1415	XT6039	5.7.33		1486	XU1804	17.8.37		1557	XU1891	8.7.37
ot	1416	XT6040	14.10.33		1487	XU1832	25.5.37		1558	XU1887	25.5.37
	1417	XT6046	18.6.35		1488	XU1813	26.8.37		1559	XU6101	30.7.37
	1418	XT6031	4.7.36	ot	1489	XU1806	15.11.34		1560	XU6133	6.6.34
	1419	XT6055	17.4.34		1490	XU1865	17.6.36		1561	XU6125	16.7.37
ot	1420	XT6043	15.1.35		1491	XU1866	15.1.36		1562	XU1888	31.1.36
ot	1421	XT6056	3.12.34	ot	1492	XU1817	19.2.35		1563	XU6105	24.5.37
	1422	XT6057	22.3.37		1493	XU1847	31.7.35		1564	XU1889	21.11.35
ot	1423	XT6089	5.9.34	cb ot	1494	NK8405	not known		1565	XU6120	14.4.37
	1424	XT6047	30.7.34	cb ot	1495	NK8406	11.35		1566	XU6126	14.2.36
cb ot	1425	XT6041	12.35		1496	XU1818	31.5.35		1567	XU6102	11.6.37
ot	1426	XT6042	7.9.34		1497	XU1807	5.5.37		1568	XU6108	10.1.36
ot	1427	XT6049	17.9.34		1498	XU1814	5.9.33		1569	XU6103	13.4.37
ot	1428	XT6044	19.12.34		1499	XU1867	14.7.37		1570	XU6106	25.10.35
	1429	XT6058	16.5.35	cb	1500	NK8407	8.35		1571	XU6101	12.6.37
	1430	XT6082	9.2.34		1501	XU1820	9.11.33		1572	XU6107	15.7.36
	1431	XU1808	16.5.34	ot	1502	XU1838	29.11.34		1573	XU6134	14.6.36
cb ot	1432	XT6060	11.35		1503	XU1848	3.11.34		1574	XU6114	20.5.37
	1433	XT6075	15.7.37		1504	XU1849	9.5.34		1575	XU6135	12.8.35

	NS		Date out of stock		NS		Date out of stock		NS		Date out of stock
	1576	XU6122	3.7.36		1657	XW9803	17.12.36		1728	XW9852	19.7.37
	1577	XU6115	16.4.35		1658	XU6197	20.3.37		1729	XW9860	5.12.36
	1578	XU6136	23.6.37		1659	XW9801	15.11.37	ot	1730	XW9863	19.2.34
	1579	XU6137	5.3.37	cb	1660	PE1722	12.35		1731	XW9861	14.5.34
	1580	XU6138	26.8.37		1661	XW9802	28.11.33		1732	XW9845	5.12.34
	1581	XU6139	28.11.34	cb ot	1662	PE1721	12.35	ot	1733	XW9850	25.6.34
	1582	XU6140	9.11.37		1663	XW9807	27.10.36		1734	XW9881	3.8.37
	1583	XU6141	30.7.37		1664	XW9814	15.10.37		1736	XW9883	11.6.37
	1585	XU6142	11.6.37		1665	XW9804	24.6.37		1737	XW9884	7.7.33
	1586	XU6123	27.6.34		1666	XW9808	4.8.37	cb	1739	RO2676	11.35
	1587	XU6109	18.11.33		1667	XW9815	20.2.37	cb	1740	RO3736	7.35
	1588	XU6143	15.5.34		1668	XW9809	5.4.34	cb	1741	RO2677	11.35
	1589	XU6144	7.12.36		1669	XW9810	20.9.37	cb	1742	PE8824	12.35
to	1590	XU6130	2.4.37		1670	XW9811	25.4.36	cb	1743	PE8825	11.35
	1591	XU6145	6.7.37		1671	XW9812	17.2.37		1744	YL8061	19.11.37
	1592	XU6116	13.5.35		1672	XW9816	6.2.36		1745	YL8062	1.11.37
	1593	XU6131	11.12.35		1673	XW9817	31.5.37		1746	YL8063	5.6.37
	1594	XU6127	20.5.37		1674	XW9822	17.11.37	cb	1747	PE8997	11.35
	1595	XU6128	c 29.11.37		1675	XW9818	4.11.36		1748	YL8065	11.10.37
	1596	XU6117	17.6.37		1676	XW9819	25.1.37		1749	YL8066	12.8.37
	1597	XU6132	31.3.37		1677	XW9823	21.4.36	cb ot	1750	PE8998	11.35
	1598	XU6118	8.12.36		1678	XW9813	25.10.37		1751	YL8067	22.10.37
	1599	XU6110	20.11.35		1679	XW9820	12.6.37	cb ot	1752	PE8999	12.35
	1600	XU6111	c 29.11.37		1680	XW9821	10.10.36	cb ot	1753	PE9000	12.35
	1601	XU6112	c 24.11.37	cb ot	1681	PE1726	12.35		1754	YL8068	21.5.37
	1602	XU6146	5.12.35	cb ot	1682	PE1723	10.34		1755	YL8069	28.2.36
	1603	XU6147	26.8.37	ot	1683	XU6190	13.2.35		1756	PE9260	22.6.36
	1604	XU6119	20.11.33	cb ot	1684	PE1724	s .36	cb ot	1757	PE9082	12.35
	1605	XU1815	19.1.37	ot	1685	XW9827	1.2.35	cb ot	1758	PE9180	12.35
cb ot	1606	XU6154	12.35		1686	XW9828	22.3.34		1759	YL8070	c 15.2.38
cb	1607	XU6149	14.1.36	ot	1687	XU6192	31.12.34		1760	YL8071	1.3.37
cb	1608	NK8904	6.1.36		1688	XW9829	5.11.37		1761	PE9672	22.6.36
	1609	XU6150	7.7.36		1689	XW9805	9.7.37		1762	YL8072	12.4.34
cb ot	1610	PD3470	10.35		1690	XW9831	26.6.37		1763	YL8082	19.11.37
cb ot	1612	NK8903	12.35		1691	XW9806	8.12.36		1764	PE9673	5.3.36
cb	1613	XU6151	6.1.36		1692	XW9824	2.11.37		1765	YL8073	30.1.36
	1614	XU6153	30.6.36		1693	XW9832	17.6.37		1766	YL8085	23.8.37
	1615	XU6155	8.3.35		1694	XW9830	27.12.34		1767	YL8074	21.9.37
cb	1616	NK9085	7.35	cb	1695	PE1728	12.35		1768	YL8075	8.7.36
	1620	XU6156	6.7.37	cb ot	1696	PE1727	12.35		1769	YL8086	19.8.37
	1621	XU6157	11.5.34		1697	XW9833	20.11.36		1770	YL8087	21.7.37
	1623	XU6159	14.12.36		1698	XW9834	s 12.5.37		1771	YL8078	1.12.37
	1624	XU6160	11.6.37		1699	XW9825	1.1.36		1772	YL8077	29.11.34
	1625	XU6161	18.11.37		1700	XW9835	9.8.37		1773	YL8076	19.7.37
	1626	XU6168	22.6.37		1701	XW9840	18.3.35		1774	YL8079	18.2.37
	1627	XU6163	30.3.37		1702	XW9836	16.6.37		1775	YL8080	9.2.37
	1629	XU6165	26.5.37	cb	1703	PE1729	3.2.36		1776	YL8091	4.12.36
	1630	XU6169	c 22.11.37		1704	XW9826	1.2.36		1777	YL8081	24.10.34
	1631	XU6172	19.12.36	cb	1705	RO572	9.35		1778	YL8083	9.7.36
	1632	XU6170	5.11.37	cb ot	1706	RO205	not known		1779	YL8088	1.7.36
	1633	XU6171	28.9.34		1707	XW9854	c 8.11.37		1780	YL8084	23.11.37
	1634	XU6174	24.4.36		1708	XW9846	6.8.37		1781	YL8089	1.1.37
	1635	XU6173	25.9.34		1709	XW9855	9.7.37		1782	YL8092	14.8.37
	1636	XU6175	25.10.37	ot	1710	XW9856	10.1.35		1783	YL8090	22.10.37
	1637	XU6176	17.12.35	cb ot	1711	RO571	11.35		1784	YL8093	1.12.37
	1638	XU6177	25.5.37		1712	XW9837	25.6.37		1785	YL8096	20.3.37
	1639	XU6178	c 4.11.37		1713	XW9857	c 23.11.37		1786	YL8097	22.1.37
	1641	XU6180	5.7.37	ot	1714	XW9858	8.9.34		1787	YL8099	8.6.37
	1643	XU182	31.8.33		1715	XW9838	11.1.37		1788	YL8100	29.10.36
	1645	XU6184	21.10.36		1716	XW9839	29.11.37		1789	YN3712	6.7.37
	1646	XU6185	13.3.37	ot	1717	XW9841	14.3.35		1790	YN3713	12.3.35
	1647	XU6186	30.4.37		1718	XW9842	21.12.34	ot	1791	YN3714	16.10.34
	1648	XU6188	17.10.36		1719	XW9843	29.3.34		1792	YN3715	1.1.35
	1649	XU6189	21.12.36		1720	XW9853	7.1.34		1793	YN3716	29.1.35
	1650	XU6187	4.6.37		1721	XW9844	28.7.37		1794	YN3717	2012.33
cb	1651	PE1720	27.2.36		1722	XW9847	s 12.5.37	ot	1795	YN3719	17.6.34
	1652	XU6191	13.7.37	ot	1723	XW9848	18.7.34		1796	YN3718	18.6.35
cb ot	1653	PE1725	s 25.6.38		1724	XW9849	5.5.37		1797	YN3722	21.5.35
	1654	XU6194	10.12.36		1725	XW9862	1.6.34		1798	YN3721	1.4.37
	1655	XU6195	c 4.11.37		1726	XW9859	24.6.37		1799	YN3720	13.7.33
	1656	XU6196	1.12.37		1727	XW9851	23.3.34		1800	YN3723	22.12.36

NS		Date out of stock	NS		Date out of stock	NS		Date out of stock
1801	YN3724	3.4.34	1873	YP6617	16.12.35	1948	YN3707	c 12.11.37
1802	YN3725	19.11.37	1874	YP6618	20.8.34	1949	YN3708	19.6.37
1803	YN3726	18.12.36	1875	YP6619	11.6.37	1950	YN3709	6.10.34
ot 1804	YN3727	28.9.34	1876	YP6620	19.6.37	1951	YN3711	21.10.37
ot 1805	YN3728	4.2.35	1878	YP6626	21.5.37	1952	YN3710	1.2.37
1806	YN3729	11.8.37	1879	YP6627	27.5.37	1953	BT7649	23.5.36
1807	YN3730	16.5.34	1880	YP6628	2.8.35	1954	YP6699	24.11.37
1808	YN3731	26.11.35	1881	YP6629	7.6.37	1955	YP6700	22.11.37
1809	YN3732	22.4.37	1882	YP6630	9.7.37	1956	YR3801	19.8.36
1810	YN3733	27.11.35	1883	YP6631	24.6.37	1957	YR3802	27.7.37
1811	YN3734	12.8.35	1884	YP6635	14.4.37	1958	YR3803	10.8.37
1812	YN3735	10.11.37	1885	YP6636	24.6.37	1959	YR3804	c s 14.5.36
1813	YN3736	5.2.36	1886	YP6637	25.1.35	1960	YR3805	30.11.37
1814	YN3737	6.7.33	1887	YP6638	21.12.35	1961	YR3809	c s 8.5.36
ot 1815	YN3738	28.6.34	1888	YP6639	19.7.37	1962	YR3810	6.10.37
ot 1816	YN3739	21.9.34	1889	YP6640	3.9.37	1963	YR3811	31.8.37
ot 1817	YN3740	1.10.34	1890	YP6641	17.7.37	1964	YR3812	25.8.37
1818	YN3741	27.8.37	1891	YP6642	28.9.37	1965	YR3813	30.8.37
1819	YN3742	20.5.35	1892	YP6644	5.2.36	1966	YR3814	23.7.37
1820	YN3743	20.6.34	1893	YP6643	25.6.37	1967	YR3815	19.3.37
1821	YN3744	19.4.37	1894	YP6645	23.1.34	1968	YR3816	23.1.37
1822	YN3745	6.9.37	1895	YP6646	24.6.36	1969	YR3817	4.11.37
1823	YN3746	18.11.33	1896	YP6662	1.11.37	1970	YR3819	22.3.37
1824	YN3747	c 29.11.37	1897	YP6651	23.7.37	1971	YR3820	21.7.37
1825	YN3748	18.5.37	1898	YP6647	19.4.37	1972	YR3821	13.9.37
1826	YN3749	19.12.33	1899	YP6648	29.7.37	1973	YR3824	6.3.37
1827	YN3750	6.8.37	1900	YP6652	13.1.36	1974	YR3825	6.5.38
ot 1828	YN3751	7.1.35	1901	YP6653	31.12.36	1975	YR3826	18.9.36
1829	YN3752	17.11.37	1902	YP6654	12.10.36	1977	YR3823	28.4.37
1830	YN3753	14.4.37	1903	YP6655	30.6.36	1978	YR3827	10.11.37
1831	YN3754	22.5.35	1904	YP6656	5.7.37	1979	YR3878	5.11.36
ot 1832	YN3755	18.10.34	1907	YP6663	1.9.37	1980	YR3824	11.10.37
1833	YN3756	28.1.35	1908	YP6664	21.10.37	1981	YR3830	22.3.34
1834	YN3757	7.8.37	1909	YP6665	25.8.37	1982	YR3831	27.5.37
1835	YN3758	8.7.37	1910	YP6666	22.1.37	1983	YR3832	24.9.37
1836	YN3759	3.12.35	1911	YP6667	23.8.37	1984	YR3833	27.10.37
1837	YN3760	6.4.34	1912	YP6668	18.8.37	1985	YR3834	18.8.37
1838	YN3761	17.7.37	1913	YP6669	17.2.36	1986	YR3835	6.10.37
1839	YN3762	c s 5.5.36	1914	YP6670	16.1.37	1987	YR3836	19.11.37
1840	YN3763	13.6.35	1915	YP6671	24.7.37	1988	YR3837	11.10.37
1841	YN3764	25.3.37	1916	YP6672	14.4.36	1990	YR3839	18.10.37
1842	YN3765	15.4.37	1917	YP6673	17.3.36	1991	YR3840	8.3.37
ot 1844	YN3767	10.12.34	1918	YP6674	30.7.37	1992	YR3841	9.9.37
1845	YN3768	30.11.34	1919	YP6677	23.8.37	1994	YR3843	16.1.37
1846	YN3769	15.5.35	1920	YP6678	9.3.37	1995	YR3844	m 17.1.38
1847	YN3770	23.5.34	1921	YP6679	13.9.37	1996	YR3845	1.9.37
1848	YN3771	13.6.35	1922	YP6680	18.3.37	1997	YR3846	23.7.37
1849	YN3772	15.4.37	1923	YP6681	20.7.37	1998	YR3847	13.3.37
1850	YN3773	14.6.34	1924	YP6682	17.8.36	1999	YR3848	15.10.37
1851	YN3774	7.11.35	1925	YP6683	11.9.34	2000	YR3849	28.10.36
1852	YN3775	25.11.35	1927	YP6686	c 30.11.37	2001	YR3850	23.8.37
1853	YN3776	29.8.35	1928	YP6687	17.11.37	2002	YR3851	19.2.37
1854	YN3777	19.7.34	1929	YP6688	7.7.37	2003	YR3852	14.4.38
1855	YN3778	3.7.37	1930	YP6689	21.8.37	2004	YR3853	20.9.37
1856	YN3779	2.7.37	1931	YP6690	31.8.37	2006	YR3855	13.10.37
1857	YN3780	2.7.37	1932	YP6691	c 22.11.37	2007	YR3856	c 24.11.37
1858	YN3781	7.6.37	1933	YP6692	3.9.37	2008	YR3857	26.10.37
1859	YN3782	25.6.37	1934	YP6694	18.9.37	2009	YR3858	26.11.37
1860	YN3783	10.7.37	1935	YP6695	30.11.37	2010	YR3859	20.7.37
ot 1861	YN3784	1.12.34	1936	YP6696	28.7.36	2011	YR3860	1.11.37
1862	YP6611	22.5.37	1937	YP6697	8.10.37	2012	YR3861	23.3.37
1863	YP6601	9.6.37	1938	YP6698	27.10.36	2013	YR3862	20.8.37
to 1864	YP6602	1.4.37	1939	YL8094	14.12.37	2014	YR3863	29.4.37
1865	YP6612	4.6.37	1940	YL8095	26.7.37	2015	YR3864	26.8.37
1866	YP6613	1.7.36	1941	YL8098	13.8.37	2016	YR3865	31.5.37
1867	YP6614	30.1.37	1942	YN3703	c 30.11.38	2017	YR3866	27.10.37
1868	YP6615	c 29.10.37	1943	YN3704	2.7.37	2018	YR3868	25.10.37
to 1869	YP6616	10.4.37	1944	YN3701	19.11.37	2019	YR3867	30.8.37
1870	YP6603	25.1.37	1945	YN3702	12.3.36	2020	YR3869	3.6.37
1871	YP6604	19.12.35	1946	YN3706	12.11.36	2021	YR3870	13.2.37
1872	YP6605	21.11.34	1947	YN3705	2.12.36	2022	YR3871	12.12.36

NS		Date out of stock	NS		Date out of stock	NS		Date out of stock
2023	YR3872	14.8.37	2098	YE4360	9.8.37	2169	YT4819	s 15.5.37
2024	YR3873	17.9.34	2099	YH1114	22.6.37	2170	YT4820	9.9.35
2025	YR3874	13.10.37	ot 2100	YH1115	2.10.34	2171	YT4821	c 24.11.37
2026	YR3878	13.10.36	2101	YH1116	4.12.36	2172	YT4822	2.7.37
2027	YR3879	18.12.36	ot 2102	YH1117	11.10.34	2173	YT4823	28.7.37
2028	YR3880	16.7.37	2103	YH1118	c 26.11.37	2174	YT4824	16.7.37
2029	YR3892	8.7.37	2104	YH1119	22.5.37	2175	YT4825	8.7.33
2030	YR3893	27.10.37	2105	YH1120	1.4.37	2176	YT4826	4.8.37
2031	YR3894	3.6.37	2106	YH1121	27.5.37	2177	YT4827	14.6.37
2032	YR3895	7.6.37	2107	YH1122	22.4.36	2178	YT4828	2.6.37
2033	YR3896	3.8.37	2108	YH1123	26.5.37	to 2179	YT4829	2.4.37
2034	YR3897	28.5.37	ot 2109	YH1124	19.6.35	2180	YT4830	15.6.37
2035	YR3898	6.8.37	2110	YH1125	9.4.34	2181	YT4831	14.6.37
2036	YE4301	30.12.36	2111	YH1126	20.3.37	2182	YT4832	27.5.37
2037	YE4303	5.4.38	ot 2112	YH1127	14.12.34	2183	YT4833	27.8.37
2038	YE4302	20.4.36	2113	YH1128	23.5.35	2184	YT4834	24.7.37
2039	YE4304	18.11.36	2114	YH1129	16.6.34	2185	YT4835	16.7.37
2040	YE4305	c 22.11.37	2115	YH1130	12.6.35	2186	YT4836	24.3.36
2041	YE4309	18.8.37	2116	YH1131	2.2.37	2187	YT4837	6.7.37
2042	YE4306	22.11.37	2117	YH1132	6.6.35	2188	YT4838	12.8.37
2043	YE4307	23.11.37	2118	YH1133	13.6.35	2189	YT4839	26.10.37
2044	YE4310	24.7.37	2119	YH1134	23.4.37	2190	YT4840	19.6.35
2045	YE4308	18.9.34	2120	YH1135	22.4.36	2191	YT4841	20.9.37
2046	YE4311	1.12.36	2121	YH1136	11.6.35	2192	YT4842	14.6.37
2047	YE4312	27.4.36	2122	YH1137	19.5.37	2193	YT4843	s 5.1.37
2048	YE4313	9.7.37	2123	YH1138	3.1.34	2194	YT4844	8.7.37
2049	YE4314	3.6.37	2124	YH1139	30.10.33	2195	YT4845	11.2.37
tc 2050	YE4315	7.4.37	2125	YH1140	29.5.37	2196	YT4846	10.6.36
2054	YE4316	1.11.37	2126	YH1141	21.5.37	2197	YT4847	3.9.37
2055	YE4317	19.2.37	2127	YH1142	18.7.34	2198	YT4848	29.7.37
2056	YE4318	31.8.37	2128	YH1143	23.4.36	2199	YT4849	14.1.36
2057	YE4319	2.11.37	2129	YH1144	2.11.35	2200	YT4850	c 26.11.37
2058	YE4320	30.8.37	2130	YH1145	16.1.37	2201	YT4851	26.7.37
2059	YE4321	16.7.37	2131	YH1146	9.12.36	2202	YT4852	15.12.36
2060	YE4322	9.11.36	2132	YH1147	23.4.36	2203	YT4853	17.9.37
2061	YE4323	9.7.37	2133	YH1148	29.5.37	to 2204	YT4854	1.4.37
2062	YE4324	7.8.37	2134	YH1149	24.5.37	2205	YT4855	5.8.37
2063	YE4325	25.10.34	2135	YH1150	25.5.37	2206	YT4856	6.8.37
2064	YE4326	30.8.37	2136	YH1151	1.4.37	2207	YT4857	6.7.37
2065	YE4327	25.6.37	2137	YH1152	7.6.37	2208	YT4858	c 26.11.37
2066	YE4328	26.11.36	2138	YH1153	28.5.37	2209	YT4859	19.5.37
2067	YE4329	18.11.37	2139	YH1154	3.6.37	tc 2210	YT4860	6.4.37
2068	YE4330	13.2.37	2140	YH1155	20.3.37	2211	YT4861	c 25.11.37
2069	YE4331	18.2.37	2141	YH1156	30.1.36	tc 2212	YT4862	3.4.37
2070	YE4332	11.11.37	2142	YH1157	30.6.37	tc 2213	YT4863	10.4.37
2072	YE4334	21.12.33	2143	YH1158	22.2.35	tc 2214	YT4864	7.4.37
2073	YE4335	18.3.37	2144	YH1159	8.4.36	2215	YT4865	31.8.37
2074	YE4336	22.12.33	2145	YH1160	26.5.37	tc 2216	YT4866	3.4.37
ot 2075	YE4337	1.2.35	2146	YH1161	24.5.37	tc 2217	YT4867	8.4.37
2076	YE4338	22.2.37	2147	YH1162	22.5.37	tc 2218	YT4868	1.4.37
2077	YE4339	6.2.37	2148	YH1163	5.6.34	2219	YT4869	8.10.37
2078	YE4340	18.11.37	2149	YH1164	29.6.37	tc 2220	YT4870	9.4.37
2079	YE4341	20.8.37	2150	YH1165	c 26.11.37	tc 2221	YT4871	6.4.37
2080	YE4342	c 25.11.37	2151	YT4801	17.12.36	tc 2222	YT4872	1.4.37
2081	YE4343	18.8.36	2152	YT4802	31.8.37	tc 2223	YT4873	5.4.37
2082	YE4344	8.3.35	2153	YT4803	6.9.35	tc 2224	YT4874	6.4.37
2083	YE4345	22.9.37	2154	YT4804	31.5.37	tc 2225	YT4875	9.4.37
2084	YE4346	22.12.33	2155	YT4805	1.6.37	tc 2226	YT4876	2.4.37
2085	YE4347	30.3.37	2156	YT4806	5.7.37	tc 2227	YT4877	2.4.37
ot 2086	YE4348	21.6.34	2157	YT4807	28.7.37	tc 2228	YT4878	9.4.37
2087	YE4349	11.12.33	2158	YT4808	22.7.37	2229	YR3875	24.6.37
2088	YE4350	31.7.37	2159	YT4809	5.6.37	2230	YW7983	26.8.37
ot 2089	YE4351	30.5.34	2160	YT4810	22.6.34	2231	WU6715	21.10.37
2090	YE4352	22.5.34	2161	YT4811	4.6.37	to 2232	YT4880	2.4.37
ot 2091	YE4353	14.3.35	2162	YT4812	15.6.37	tc 2233	YT4881	1.4.37
ot 2092	YE4354	24.1.35	2163	YT4813	c 30.11.37	tc 2234	YT4882	7.4.37
2093	YE4355	12.7.37	2164	YT4814	11.6.37	tc 2235	YT4883	8.4.37
2094	YE4356	4.1.37	2165	YT4815	15.6.37	tc 2236	YT4884	3.4.37
2095	YE4357	3.5.34	2166	YT4816	26.7.37	tc 2237	YT4885	5.4.37
2096	YE4358	13.4.37	2167	YT4817	c 12.11.37	tc 2238	YT4886	8.4.37
2097	YE4359	21.4.37	2168	YT4818	28.7.37	tc 2239	YT4887	5.4.37

NS		Date out of stock	NS		Date out of stock	NS		Date out of stock
	2240	YT4888	6.4.36	2292	UC2278	25.2.35	2341	YW7964	29.5.37
	2241	YU6225	16.11.37	2293	UC2279	19.5.36	2342	YW7984	14.6.37
	2242	YT4890	6.2.37	2294	UC2280	7.2.36	2343	YW7965	3.6.37
	2245	YT4879	14.8.36	2295	UC2281	s 25.3.37	2344	YW7982	4.6.37
	2246	YT4889	c 30.11.38	2296	UC2282	4.5.34	2345	YW7979	31.5.37
	2247	YT4893	24.11.36	2297	UC2284	15.12.36	2346	YW7967	23.11.36
	2248	YT4894	12.7.37	2298	YW7951	11.2.36	2347	PE2427	24.8.37
	2249	YU6202	18.6.36	2299	UC2283	31.3.37	2348	PE2421	27.8.37
	2250	YU6203	24.11.37	2300	UC2285	2.3.36	2349	PE2424	20.3.36
	2252	YU6205	22.10.36	2301	UC2296	20.5.37	2372	YW8042	4.11.35
	2253	YU6206	26.8.37	2302	YW7952	24.5.37	2373	YW8033	23.3.37
	2254	YU6210	23.11.37	2303	YW7953	21.1.37	2374	YW8040	30.1.37
	2255	YU6211	8.7.37	2304	UC2297	29.4.36	2375	YW8041	8.4.37
	2256	YU6212	15.10.36	2305	UC2286	4.2.36	2376	YW8034	13.3.37
	2257	YT4895	2.11.37	2306	YW7966	20.2.36	2377	YW8043	4.11.35
	2258	YT4896	2.11.37	2307	UC2287	26.5.37	cb ot 2378	MP1460	12.35
	2259	YT4897	21.10.37	2308	YW7954	12.4.37	2379	YH1197	22.6.34
	2260	YU6201	12.7.33	2309	YW7968	7.4.37	2380	YH1190	27.6.34
	2261	YU6207	22.10.37	2310	YW7955	25.5.37	2381	YH1198	20.7.34
	2262	YU6208	1.11.37	2311	UC2288	26.11.35	2382	YH1180	17.7.34
	2263	YU6209	20.2.37	2312	YW7980	23.6.37	2383	YH1181	1.8.34
	2264	YU6213	5.11.37	2313	YW7981	11.6.37	2384	YH1193	2.8.34
	2265	YU6214	19.11.36	2314	YW7974	25.5.37	2385	YH1178	15.9.34
	2266	YU6215	6.2.34	2315	UC2298	14.4.37	2386	YH1187	27.6.34
	2267	YU6216	8.6.36	2316	UC2289	1.12.37	2387	YH1195	3.8.34
	2268	YU6217	26.11.37	2317	UC2290	22.5.37	2388	YH1179	22.5.34
	2269	YU6218	28.9.37	2318	UC2291	22.5.37	2389	YH1199	30.7.34
	2270	YU6219	20.9.37	2319	YU6226	16.4.37	2390	YH1191	26.7.34
	2271	YU6220	16.11.37	2320	UC2292	30.3.37	2391	YH1188	27.7.34
	2272	YU6221	6.4.37	2321	UC2293	c 29.11.37	2392	YH1185	12.10.34
	2273	YU6222	20.2.37	2322	UC2294	s 24.3.37	2393	YH1194	30.7.34
	2274	YU6223	6.11.36	2323	YW7956	27.2.37	2394	YH1192	24.7.34
	2275	YU6224	16.1.37	2324	YW7975	26.7.37	2395	YH1183	27.7.34
	2276	YU6227	19.7.37	2325	YW7957	21.5.37	2396	YH1186	28.7.34
	2277	YU6228	26.1.37	2326	UC2295	10.2.36	2397	YH1196	26.6.34
	2278	UC2202	28.7.37	2327	YW7969	26.5.37	2398	YH1182	19.6.34
	2279	UC2257	16.8.37	2328	YW7958	31.5.37	2399	YH1189	11.10.34
	2280	UC2258	7.1.37	2329	YW7959	2.4.36	2400	YH1184	16.5.34
	2281	UC2259	22.3.37	2330	YW7976	4.6.37	2401	YH1176	1.8.34
	2282	UC2260	29.1.37	2331	YW7977	c 26.11.37	2402	YH1174	26.9.34
	2283	UC2262	1.2.37	2332	YW7970	19.12.36	2403	YH1175	25.6.34
cb	2284	UC2263	by 12.35	2333	YW7960	30.1.37	2404	YH1172	13.7.34
cb	2285	UC2264	by 12.35	2334	YW7961	30.11.37	2405	YH1173	19.6.34
	2286	UC2273	6.3.37	2335	YW7962	c 30.11.37	2406	YH1177	26.7.34
	2287	UC2274	16.12.36	2336	YW7978	3.6.37	2407	YH1169	1.10.34
	2288	UC2275	20.3.37	2337	YW7963	10.6.37	2408	YH1168	2.8.34
	2289	UC2276	20.12.34	2338	YW7971	23.4.37	2409	YH1179	11.7.34
	2290	GC3953	15.11.37	2339	YW7972	23.1.36	2410	YH1171	13.9.34
	2291	UC2277	28.11.35	2340	YW7973	31.5.37	2411	YH1167	2.8.340

c   Chassis only – body scrapped earlier
cb   Country bus
m   Transferred to museum collection
ot   Open top body
tc   Original type tunnel body with closed staircase and clerestory
to   Later type open staircase tunnel body
s   Converted to service vehicles as follows:
    NS 13, 43, 853, 990, 1240, 1839, 1959, 1961 to Tramways Dept as tower wagons
    NS 173, 250, 289, 429, 577, 931, 1120, 1698, 1722, 2169, 2295, 2322 as mobile staff canteens
    NS 556, 1653, 1684, 2193 as tree loppers
    NS 760 to Tram & Trolleybus Dept as trolley wire lubricator
    NS 1200 to towing lorry at Chiswick Works

L

The L classification was used by Chiswick for all acquired Leyland vehicles until January 1934, including LBs, the series reaching L 127 by the end of 1933. In January 1934, the Titans, Tigers and Lions were given their own classifications, the code then referring only to LB-type Leylands. The LBs which had been taken into stock before January 1934, with numbers scattered between 47 and 91, were renumbered at that time into the gaps left by the other models, including the original L 47.

The LB was a chassis designed specifically for the London market and was a popular choice among Independent operators in the 1920s. The LB2 was a lighter version of Leyland's G7 model with three independent brakes and a quiet four-speed gearbox to satisfy the requirements of the Metropolitan Police. It was powered by a four-cylinder 40 hp petrol engine. The first of the line was bought by the famous first Independent to break the LGOC monopoly in 1922, Chocolate Express, who remained loyal to the LB until the Titan was available. In 1923 an improved version was introduced, the LB4, closely followed by the LB5 which remained in production until 1927. All originally had solid tyres but in most cases these were replaced by pneumatics after 1927.

The LPTB acquired 21 of the type from 13 Independents, the largest number coming from City, which was noted for its conservative approach to design. However, L 65 was a 1925 vintage LB5 which had been rebuilt extensively by City in 1928 as a forward control vehicle with many mechanical refinements and pneumatic tyres.

Chassis:	Leyland LB4 (L 52, 61, 62); LB5 (L 45–51, 54–60, 63–65, 67)
Engine:	Leyland 4-cylinder 40 hp petrol
Transmission:	Leyland 4-speed crash
Bodywork:	Birch (L 54–55); Dodson (L 45–51, 56–61, 63–65, 67);
	Strachan & Brown (L 52); Wilton (L 62)
Capacity:	O29/26RO (L 65); O26/22RO (remainder)
L.T. codes:	not allocated
Built:	1923 (L 46, 62); 1924 (L 48, 52, 54, 56, 58, 61); 1925 (L 49, 51, 63); 1926 (L45, 67); 1927 (L 47, 50, 55, 57, 59, 60); 1928 (L 65 – rebuild); 1929 (L 64)

Number acquired: 21   Number in stock: 1.7.33: Nil;   31.12.39: Nil   Last in stock: 3.9.35

		First LT No	Acquired from	Date into stock	Date out of stock
45	YR2258	L 47	Glen Omnibus Company (London) Ltd, New Cross	30.10.33	15.5.34
46	XX9059	L 66	United Omnibus Company Ltd, Camberwell	30.10.33	16.5.34
47	HM7440	L 67	Renown Traction Company Ltd, East Ham	9.11.33	18.5.34
48	XU9118	L 79	C.H. Pickup, Camberwell	8.11.33	16.5.34
49	HM4662	L 83	Essex Omnibus Company Ltd, East Ham	9.11.33	15.5.34
50	ML1800	L 86	Earl Motor Omnibus Company Ltd, Tottenham	22.11.33	15.5.34
51	YL417	L 90	Triumph O. Co. Ltd (A. Tagg & S. Pauling), Battersea	22.11.33	16.5.34
52	XR2120	L 91	F.G. Woolvett & W.R. Carswell (Carswool), Peckham	23.11.33	18.5.34
54	XW6188		Birch Bros. Ltd, Kentish Town	21.2.34	s c 2.8.35
55	YH6292		Birch Bros. Ltd, Kentish Town	21.2.34	s c 2.8.35
56	XU7498		Chocolate Express Omnibus Co. Ltd, Battersea	9.8.34	17.9.35
57	HM7254		Miller Traction Company Ltd, Ilford	28.8.34	s c 20.2.36
58	PU5052		City Motor Omnibus Co. Ltd Peckham and Kentish Town	5.11.34	s c 17.5.34
59	YT7380		City Motor Omnibus Co. Ltd Peckham and Kentish Town	5.11.34	s c 20.6.35
60	XW9346		City Motor Omnibus Co. Ltd Peckham and Kentish Town	5.11.34	s c 23.7.35
61	XR6498		City Motor Omnibus Co. Ltd Peckham and Kentish Town	5.11.34	* 11.2.38
62	XP8535		City Motor Omnibus Co. Ltd Peckham and Kentish Town	5.11.34	s c 23.7.35
63	MH2484		City Motor Omnibus Co. Ltd Peckham and Kentish Town	5.11.34	s c 19.6.35
64	GU6062		City Motor Omnibus Co. Ltd Peckham and Kentish Town	5.11.34	s 7.11.34
65	XX6193		City Motor Omnibus Co. Ltd Peckham and Kentish Town	5.11.34	26.7.35
67	TW3167		Victory Omnibus Company Ltd, Romford	6.11.34	3.9.35

* Lorry at this time   c Chassis only   s Became service vehicles

D

The classification D was used by London Transport to cover several types of Dennis vehicles, continuing a series previously used by the LGOC for vehicles acquired from the London Public Omnibus Company. The numbers D 184–186, 188 and 190 were allocated at first to five of the Dennis H type, which became DH 4–8 in January 1934, while D 193 was allocated to a Dennis E which became DE 28 in January 1934. In consequence the 4-ton models which were originally numbered D 187, 189, 191, 192, 195, were renumbered into the gaps and those numbers allocated to vehicles acquired subsequently. It is not clear why this was considered necessary.

The Dennis 4-ton was a popular model with London Independents during the 1920s. Many of these passed into the hands of the LGOC as the companies were acquired but none remained in stock when the LPTB took over. A total of 26 were acquired by the Board between October 1933 and November 1934 but as they were all open-toppers they were earmarked for early withdrawal and all had been sold out of stock by the end of July 1935.

Chassis:	Dennis 4-ton
Engine:	Dennis 4-cylinder 36 bhp petrol
Transmission:	4-speed crash
Bodywork:	Birch (D 184); Dodson (D 175, 177–183, 185–189, 194, 197); Hickman (D 195); Strachan (D 190–193); Strachan & Brown (D 176)
Capacity:	O26/22RO
L.T. codes:	Not allocated
Built:	1924 (D 175–177); 1925 (D 178, 179, 181, 185–187, 189, 197, 200); 1926 (D 188, 198, 201); 1927 (D 180, 182, 184, 190–194, 199); 1928 (D 183, 195)

Number acquired: 26
Number in stock 1.7.33: Nil;   31.12.39: Nil   Last in stock: 25.7.35

Note: D196 was a lorry acquired from the Westminster Omnibus Co.

	First LT No	Acquired from	Date into stock	Date out of stock
175	XW3890	Cardinal Omnibus Co. Ltd (Claremont), Islington	30.10.33	14.5.34
176	MH1595	Chariot Omnibus Services Ltd (E. Davidson)	31.10.33	16.5.34
177	XW2210	F.W. Hayes (Adelaide O. Co. Ltd), Thornton Heath	30.10.33	17.5.34
178	MH5040	Supreme Motor Omnibus Co. Ltd, Edmonton	31.10.33	15.5.34
179	MK403	J. Ryan (Ryan Omnibus Company), Cricklewood	30.10.33	22.5.34
180	HM8065	Renown Traction Co. Ltd, East Ham	9.11.33	16.5.34
181	MH3380	B. Convey & C.W. Clayton (C.C.), Stockwell	9.11.33	15.5.34
182	YE6281	A.G. Summerskill Ltd (A.G.S.), Twickenham	22.11.33	17.5.34
183	YW4483	A.G. Summerskill Ltd (A.G.S.), Twickenham	22.11.33	s 30.6.34
184	YU4689 D 187	W.C. Holliday & P.R. Bangs (H.B.)	1.12.33	14.5.34
185	PU6034 D 189	R.R. Powell & L.G. Whybrow, Romford	13.12.33	22.5.34
186	XX7690 D 191	Gordon Omnibus Co. Ltd, Leyton	13.12.33	17.5.34
187	XX2572 D 192	Gordon Omnibus Co. Ltd, Leyton	13.12.33	14.5.34
188	YR2358 D 195	The Premier Omnibus Co. Ltd, Shepherd's Bush	19.12.33	s 27.8.34
189	PU6034	R.R. Powell & L.G. Whybrow (Chadwell), Romford	13.12.33	s 13.2.34
190	HM7507	Paterson Omnibus Co. Ltd (A.H. Martin)	12.6.34	s 15.4.35
191	HM7999	Paterson Omnibus Co. Ltd (A.H. Martin)	12.6.34	25.7.35
192	HM8139	Paterson Omnibus Co. Ltd (A.H. Martin)	12.6.34	25.7.35
193	HM8092	Paterson Omnibus Co. Ltd (A.H. Martin)	12.6.34	25.7.35
194	HM7855	Paterson Omnibus Co. Ltd (A.H. Martin)	12.6.34	26.7.35
195	HM9043	Paterson Omnibus Co. Ltd (A.H. Martin)	12.6.34	24.7.35
197	XX9806	The St George Omnibus Co. Ltd, Peckham	16.7.34	25.7.35
198	YR3672	Sphere Omnibus Co. Ltd, Holloway	28.8.34	25.7.35
199	YF6913	Reliance Omnibus Co. Ltd, Chingford	6.11.34	2.7.35
200	XX5800	Reliance Omnibus Co. Ltd, Chingford	6.11.34	24.7.35
201	YM2955	Reliance Omnibus Co. Ltd, Chingford	6.11.34	25.7.35

s   Transferred to Miscellaneous Vehicle fleet as stores lorries (numbered 156D, 155D, 152D, 153D in 1939 numbering)

LS

The LS was the first three-axle bus purchased by the London General Omnibus Company and the first to have pneumatic tyres from the outset. LS 1 and 2 also had enclosed staircase bodywork but they were later converted to open staircase in common with the remaining double-deckers. With a potential capacity of between 66 and 72 passengers, the LS was also the largest bus yet built but the number of seats eventually settled at 60. It was manufactured by Associated Daimler at great speed in 1927 to get the first into service before the London Public Omnibus Company could introduce its six-wheeled Guys. Eleven double-deckers and one single-decker (LS 6) were bought and all except LS 2, 3 and 12 were fitted with a Daimler CV35 5.7 litre petrol engine. The three exceptions had the AEC A121 four-cylinder 7.6 litre engine which had been designed for the type but had not been ready for the others. The Daimler engines were replaced by the new Rackham-designed A130 or A135 engines The AEC A121 engines may also have been replaced by the new type but this cannot be confirmed. The model was not an outstanding success and no more were built.

When taken over by London Transport the LS class was allocated entirely to Cricklewood garage, the double-deckers running on route 16A. They were withdrawn in 1937 at the time when the last NSs were also being withdrawn. The only significant change made to them by London Transport was to cut their seating capacity to 56, ostensibly to reduce their laden weight when a weight limit was placed on the bridge over the railway in Kilburn High Road. This was done between July 1934 and September 1935, which casts some doubt on the urgency of the change.

Chassis:	Associated Daimler 802, three-axle
Engine:	AEC A130 or A135 6-cylinder ohc 6.1 litre 95 bhp petrol (LS 1, 4, 5, 7–11);
	AEC A121 6-cylinder 7.6 litre petrol (LS 2, 3 12)
Transmission:	AEC 4-speed crash
Bodywork:	LGOC
Capacity:	H60RO* (except LS 6: B34R)
L.T. codes:	Not allocated
Built:	1927
Number built:	12
Number in stock	1.7.33: 12 31.12.39: Nil Last in stock: 9.3.39

* Reduced to 56 in 1934/1935.
All into stock 1.7.33

LS		Date out of stock	LS		Date out of stock	LS		Date out of stock
1	YH 1200	17.9.37	5	UC 2246	1.10.37	10	YW 7986	s 20.3.38
2	YU 1166	17.9.37	7	UC 2266	21.9.37	11	YW 7988	9.3.39
3	UC 2201	s 4.3.38	8	YW 7989	s 20.1.38	12	YW 8003	17.9.37
4	UC 2255	30.9.37	9	YW 7985	20.9.37			

s Chassis used for breakdown tender (221U, 219U, 220U, 222U respectively)

Facing page **The bodywork fitted to the LS class was an enlarged version of the NS but their bonnet and radiator design was an ADC product specially produced for these buses. The style also appeared on some single-deck ADC coaches. Despite their great size by contemporary standards, with a potential capacity of at least 66 in normal service, during the last three or four years of operation they had only 56 seats, purportedly because of a weight restriction on the railway bridge in Kilburn High Road. D.W.K. Jones**

TD

When the Titan was introduced by Leyland Motors Ltd in 1927 its design was a big advance on what was then available and has been claimed as the first of the modern generation. It incorporated the dropped frame pioneered on the NS, with an underslung worm-drive rear axle and an offset, inclined transmission line which allowed the saloon gangway to be set at a lower level than on the Leviathan which had preceded it. An important element in the success of the TD1 was a new Rackham-designed 6.8 litre 6-cylinder overhead camshaft engine which was claimed to develop 98 bhp at 2,200 rpm. The TD2 was a heavier duty version introduced in 1931 to take advantage of the new national length and weight regulations under the 1930 Road Traffic Act, which allowed double-deckers to be built to an overall length of 26ft. The engine was increased in size to 7.6 litres and fully floating rear axles were adopted. Braking power was also increased by the use of the triple servo type.

No TDs were purchased new by London Transport or the LGOC and its associates but the Titan was a popular model among London Independents, and no fewer than 129 double-deckers came into LPTB stock from that source during 1933 and 1934. Forty-one more formed part of the fleet on vesting day, 34 from Maidstone & District whose operations in the Gravesend and Dartford area were acquired, two from Thames Valley with the Staines–Windsor service and five from London General Country Services who had acquired them when taking over other companies. Both TD1 and TD2 models were represented with bodywork by six different manufacturers, both covered and open top and with both enclosed and open staircases. There were also 21 single-deckers and coaches. Four more double-deckers were added in 1935 when Maidstone & District took over Redcar Services of Tunbridge Wells and handed over the Sevenoaks–Tonbridge bus service and the London coach operation to the Board.

Nine of these Short Bros bodied TD1s dating from 1928/1929 were part of the LPTB's starting stock, acquired from Maidstone & District Motor Services Ltd. Unnumbered in this spring 1934 view, this 51-seater became TD 151B in 1935 and received a covered top in December that year. The fleet name GENERAL** was used for a time on all London Transport buses.** J.F. Higham collection; Omnibus Society

The 41 in stock on 1st July 1933 were all allocated to the Country Bus department and therefore did not receive fleet numbers until 1935, when they became TD 133B–173B. The four added to the fleet in 1935 became TD 192B–195B, the gap in numbers being occupied by single-deckers. The first Titans to join Central Bus stock were 14 from the five operators formally acquired on 30th October 1933. At this time Chiswick was allocating numbers in the L series to all acquired Leylands and this continued until January 1934 when the TD class was created, while the LB-type Leylands remained as the L class. The first 71 Titans received L numbers, as shown in the list below and the first to be numbered directly into the class was TD 72, one of two taken over from Empress on 31st January 1934.

Until January 1934, acquired buses were kept at the former Independents' garages but in that month they were absorbed into the LPTB fleet and the petrol-engined TDs all went to Upton Park, where they were joined by subsequent acquisitions. Oil-engined Titans were allocated to Hanwell (HW) garage. Only one open-top Titan was acquired, TD 31 from Charles H. Pickup who was famous for favouring open-toppers and this did not operate in service, although remaining intact in the fleet until June 1935 when its body was scrapped; its chassis was retained for another two years. In contrast the open-toppers in the Country Area (TD 143B–151B) were all fitted with top covers during 1935. Seven of the Central Bus TDs (2, 17, 19, 47, 52, 53, 57) were repainted in January 1934 and transferred to Country Buses which was in need of additional double-deckers in the turbulent early days of the Board. They went initially to Northfleet but were later dispersed and remained with Country Buses until withdrawn.

The Central Bus Titans arrived with a considerable variety of route and destination indicators, ranging from standard London-style board displays to various types of roller blind display. Although some parts of some of these displays were not used by London Transport, no fundamental changes were made to them during their operational life. Most of the Country Bus examples, not constrained by the requirements of the Metropolitan Public Carriage Office, had the single-aperture display of the standard models. These were enlarged by the Board to take a display incorporating route number, destination and two lines of intermediate points.

Only two Titans had oil engines when they were acquired, TD 85 from Birch and TD 121 from City, but between November 1934 and December 1935 London Transport replaced the petrol units in five more with new oil engines (TD 94–6, 98, 105). All seven went to Southall garage and are believed to have been part of a study of the Leyland engine by Chiswick, which eventually culminated in the purchase of the STDs in 1937.

This offside view of TD 144B, taken at Slough station shows it still in original condition but in the new London Transport Country Bus livery. TD 143 to TD 145 had 48-seat bodies and were new in 1928.
J.F. Higham collection; Omnibus Society

In the normal way withdrawal of the TDs would have started no earlier than 1938 but the process began rather prematurely at the end of 1937 because of the reduction in vehicle requirements caused by cuts following the strike earlier that year. Their lifetime in London was further curtailed, with the abrupt withdrawal of the remaining 30 vehicles in September 1939 at the outbreak of war. In the Country Area, the former open-toppers and those with lowbridge bodywork were withdrawn in October and November 1936 following delivery of the new STLs but the remainder stayed in service until the summer of 1939. The lowbridge buses were disposed of in July 1938 but no others went until early in 1939 and at the end of that year there were still 113 in stock awaiting disposal.

TD 148B in service from Slough Langley Road garage after being fitted with an NS type covered top in September 1935. For some reason the route number is being carried on the destination board, rather than on a separate stencil at the top of the front window. J. Higham

The standard Birch body had strong similarities to the more common Dodson type but had subtle distinctions, most notably in the downward slope of the driver's cab canopy and the curved fairing between the cab and the lower saloon windows. TD 82, formerly owned by Birch Bros Ltd, is at Gonville Street in Westbourne Grove. J. Higham

This rear view of TD 8 shows the typical standard London open staircase which varied little between all types of bus conforming to the requirements of the Metropolitan Police. The plate above the standard London Transport Used Ticket box is the Metropolitan Stage Carriage licence plate, which had to be carried on buses until the late 1930s. London's Transport Museum

Dodson bodied TD 17B, formerly owned by the United Omnibus Co., had its route boards replaced by a standard Country Bus size indicator box after its transfer from Central Buses in January 1934. It is seen at Windsor Castle after being repainted into the later two-tone green colour scheme of Country Buses. D.W.K. Jones

Still in the colours of the Premier Omnibus Co but operating for LPTB from its new base at Upton Park, TD 66 carries the company's favoured Duple bodywork. Another design almost identical to Dodson products, the Duple had five-bay bodywork and three 'hopper' type vents above the lower deck windows, as had earlier Dodson bodies on Titans. D.W.K. Jones

This unusual design of Dodson enclosed staircase five-bay bodywork was carried by TD 171B, acquired from LGCS but originally from Aston of Watford. D.W.K. Jones

The covered top Titans acquired from Maidstone & District in 1933 had Short Bros 48-seat bodywork, of a style based on the standard Leyland design. TD 141B has had a larger indicator box fitted than the inherited fixture and is in service from Godstone garage on route 409. A.N. Porter

The rear of TD 161B somewhere in North Kent, shows the curved rear end of the Short Bros body with its single large upper deck window, looking very modern for a bus built in 1930. The cut-away at the rear of the platform was narrower than imminent new regulations would allow on future buses.
Ken Glazier collection

TD 110 was one of the TD1s 'specials' built for the City Motor Omnibus Company in 1931 which were actually based on the Tiger TS3 chassis. Their Dodson 56-seat bodies were anachronistic in having open staircases and a high skirt line more typical of the previous generation of buses. Nevertheless they had been built with enclosed drivers' cabs and the front of the upper deck had a slightly more modern appearance than many of its contemporaries, being curved with two half-drop opening windows. It is in Bishops (Bridge) Road at 'The Royal Oak'. J. F. Higham

TD 27 was one of seventeen Titans which had the heavier duty, more powerful, TD2 chassis introduced by Leyland in 1931. When built for the Renown Traction Company in 1933 it became the last new bus delivered to any London Independent and also almost certainly the last open staircase bus to be built anywhere in the country. The reason for the open staircase on such a late bus was that Dodson had decided to wind up his business as its main source of orders, the Independents, was about to disappear. This body was therefore probably built using redundant materials still in stock. D.W.K. Jones

Dodson introduced this new style of body at the 1931 Commercial Motor Show, adapting the contemporary fashion for 'piano fronts' in their own distinctive way but retaining the six-bay formation. TD 73 was a TD2 which had been built for Empress Motors of Bethnal Green in 1932. D.W.K. Jones

TD 85 was the only oil-engined TD2 acquired by London Transport, the other oiler being a TD1 'special' TD 121. TD 85 came from Birch and carried that company's latest style of body built in 1932, with a full length upper deck and a neatly styled front which compared favourably with its Dodson contemporary on TD 73. Being an oiler it was allocated to Hanwell garage and is on route 18C at Wembley on Rugby Cup Final Day 4th May 1935. D.W.K. Jones

Chassis:	Leyland Titan TD1 (TD 1–3, 5–10, 13–26, 28, 31–36, 38–71, 74–83, 87–97, 99–107, 109, 122, 126–129, 133–195 Leyland Titan TD1spl (TD 110–121) Leyland Titan TD2 (TD 4, 11, 12, 27, 29, 30, 37, 72, 73, 84, 85, 98, 108, 123–125, 130)
Engine:	Leyland 6-cylinder 6.8 litre ohc 98 bhp petrol (TD1s); Leyland 6-cylinder 7.6 litre ohc 98 bhp petrol (TD2s); Leyland 6-cylinder 8.1 litre direct injection 87 bhp oil (TD 85, 121) NOTE: the following had their petrol engines replaced by new oil engines: TD 94, 96 (October 1934), TD 95 (December 1935), TD 98 (October 1934), TD 105 (October 1934)
Transmission:	Leyland 4-speed crash
Bodywork:	Birch (TD 36, 37, 39, 40, 74–87) Dodson (TD 1–35, 38, 41–57, 65, 72, 73, 88–130, 170, 171) Duple (TD 58–64, 66–71, 131, 132, 174–191) Leyland (TD 167–169, 172, 173, 194, 195) Short Bros. (TD 133–166) Weymann (TD 192, 193)
Capacity:	O30/26RO (TD 31); O27/24RO (TD 146–151[1]); O24/24RO (TD 143–145[1]); H30/26RO (TD 8, 16–20[5,7], 26–28[6], 32, 33[6], 36[9], 37, 39, 40, 43–46[6], 74–83[11], 96–98[11,15,22], 106, 107, 110–120[16,17]); H30/26R H30/24RO (TD 121); H28/26RO (TD 4, 87[13]); H28/26R (TD 72[10], 73[10], 123[18], 124[19]); H28/24RO (TD 1–3[4], 5–7, 9, 10, 12–15, 21–25, 34[8], 35, 38, 42, 47–71[4,5,21], 88–95[14], 99–105, 109, 122, 126–129); H28/24R; (TD 84, 85[12]); H27/26R (TD 11, 29, 125[20] 130); H27/24R (TD 192–195); H26/26R (TD 30, 108); H26/24R (TD 41, 170); H24/24R (TD 133–142, 154–166[2], 171, 173); L27/24RO (TD 167–169[3]); L24/24R (TD 152, 153, 172 173)

[1] TD 143–151 fitted with covered tops, becoming H26/24RO (except TD 146 H24/24RO) in April (TD 144), August (TD 150), September (TD 148), October (TD 145, 146), November (TD 143, 149) or December (TD 147, 151) 1935.

[2] TD 154, 155, 165, 166 reseated to H30/24 in April 1937

[3] TD 168, 169 reseated to L24/24RO in December 1933

[4] TD 2, 47 reseated to H24/24RO when transferred to Country Buses

[5] TD 17, 19 reseated to H26/22RO and TD 52, 53, 57 reseated to H24/24RO when transferred to Country Buses. TD 52 was again reseated to H30/24RO in July 1936

[6] TD 28, 33, 46 reseated to H28/26R in April 1934 (or March 1934 (TD 46))

[7] TD 18 reseated to H28/26RO in April 1934 and back to H30/26RO in June 1936

[8] TD 34 reseated to H26/24RO in January 1935 and back to H28/24RO in March 1936

[9] TD 36 reseated to H28/26RO in January 1934

[10] TD 72, 73 reseated to H28/24R in April 1934; TD 73 again reseated to H28/26R in September 1936

[11] TD 83, 98 reseated to H28/26RO in March and October 1934 respectively, TD 83 reverting to H30/26R in October 1936

[12] TD 85 reseated to H25/25RO in March 1934

[13] TD 87 seating reduced to H28/24RO in August 1934 and to 50 in December 1936

[14] TD 95 reseated to H30/26RO in October 1934

[15] TD 97 reseated to H30/24RO November 1935, H30/26RO January 1937

[16] TD 113 reseated to H28/26RO in December 1934 and back to H30/26RO May 1937

[17] TD 114, 116, 118–120 reseated to H28/26RO in December 1934 (TD 114, 118,119) or January 1935; TD 114, 116, 120 reverted to H30/26RO in February 1936 (TD 114) or June 1937.

[18] TD 123 reseated to H24/26R in December 1934

[19] TD 124 reseated to H30/26R in January 1935 and to H26/26R in June 1937

[20] TD 125 reseated to H25/26R in December 1934

[21] TD 52 and 57 reseated to H30/24RO in July 1936 and February 1937 respectively

[22] TD 98 was reseated to 54 at an unknown date.

		First LT number	Acquired from	Date into stock	Date out of stock
1	UW6734	L 45	Cardinal Omnibus Co. (Claremont)	30.10.33	6.2.39
2	GJ8489	L 46	Glen Omnibus Co. (London) Ltd	30.10.33	
3	GC3354	L 48	F.W. Hayes (Adelaide Bus Co)	30.10.33	
4	GX1914	L 49	Nelson Omnibus Co. Ltd	30.10.33	2.2.39
5	GC7493	L 50	Nelson Omnibus Co. Ltd	30.10.33	
6	GC1804	L 51	Nelson Omnibus Co. Ltd	30.10.33	
7	MY2742	L 52	Supreme Motor Omnibus Co. Ltd	31.10.33	
8	HX2643	L 53	Supreme Motor Omnibus Co. Ltd	31.10.33	
9	UW6777	L 54	A.H. Raper (Standard Omnibus Co)	31.10.33	
10	GN4832	L 55	A.H. Raper (Standard Omnibus Co)	31.10.33	
11	GW550	L 56	A.H. Raper (Standard Omnibus Co)	31.10.33	
12	GY2042	L 57	A.H. Raper (Standard Omnibus Co)	31.10.33	
13	MY4650	L 58	J. Ryan (Ryan Omnibus Co)	30.10.33	9.1.39
14	GC4321	L 59	United Omnibus Co. Ltd	30.10.33	2.2.39
15	GC1679	L 60	United Omnibus Co. Ltd	30.10.33	14.2.39
16	GK607	L 61	United Omnibus Co. Ltd	30.10.33	10.2.39
17	GK608	L 62	United Omnibus Co. Ltd	30.10.33	
18	GP168	L 63	United Omnibus Co. Ltd	30.10.33	
19	GP2512	L 64	United Omnibus Co. Ltd	30.10.33	
20	GW738	L 65	United Omnibus Co. Ltd	30.10.33	
21	HV93	L 68	Renown Traction Co. Ltd	9.11.33	18.1.39
22	HV453	L 69	Renown Traction Co. Ltd	9.11.33	
23	HV702	L 70	Renown Traction Co. Ltd	9.11.33	28.1.39
24	HV898	L 71	Renown Traction Co. Ltd	9.11.33	
25	HV1188	L 72	Renown Traction Co. Ltd	9.11.33	
26	HV1540	L 73	Renown Traction Co. Ltd	9.11.33	6.1.39
27	HV2822	L 74	Renown Traction Co. Ltd	9.11.33	
28	GP3379	L 76	A. Mills (Omega Bus)	7.11.33	
29	EV5860	L 77	Pro Bono Publico	8.11.33	
30	MV6306	L 78	Eagle Omnibus Co. Ltd	9.11.33	20.1.39
31	UW1478	L 80	Charles H. Pickup	8.11.33	c 9.7.37
32	GO4367	L 81	Charles H. Pickup	8.11.33	
33	GO5424	L 82	Charles H. Pickup	8.11.33	27.1.39
34	HV190	L 84	Essex Omnibus Co. Ltd	9.11.33	
35	MY2806	L 85	Earl Motor Omnibus Co	22.11.33	14.2.39
36	GC5781	L 87	A.G. Summerskill Ltd (A.G.S.)	22.11.33	27.1.39
37	GW1285	L 88	A.G. Summerskill Ltd (A.G.S.)	22.11.33	
38	UV5764	L 89	A.Tegg & E. Pauling (Triumph Omnibus Co.)	22.11.33	
39	GK6337	L 92	G.H. Allitt & Sons Ltd	1.12.33	13.1.39
40	GN3185	L 93	G.H. Allitt & Sons Ltd	1.12.33	25.1.39
41	UV7395	L 96	Peraeque Transport Co. Ltd	1.12.33	13.1.39
42	UW8539	L 97	Peraeque Transport Co. Ltd	1.12.33	20.5.38
43	GK8779	L 98	Peraeque Transport Co. Ltd	1.12.33	
44	GK8780	L 99	Peraeque Transport Co. Ltd	1.12.33	3.3.39
45	GK9834	L 100	Peraeque Transport Co. Ltd	1.12.33	
46	GT1083	L 101	Peraeque Transport Co. Ltd	1.12.33	
47	GJ3435	L 102	Enterprise Transport Co. Ltd	1.12.33	
48	GH1100	L 103	Enterprise Transport Co. Ltd	1.12.33	1.2.39
49	GH1101	L 104	Enterprise Transport Co. Ltd	1.12.33	17.1.39
50	GK8925	L 105	Enterprise Transport Co. Ltd	1.12.33	
51	GO8472	L 106	Enterprise Transport Co. Ltd	1.12.33	31.1.39
52	MY1315	L 107	J.F & F.G. Stevens (Pioneer Omnibus Co.)	1.12.33	
53	MY1140	L 108	J.F & F.G. Stevens (Pioneer Omnibus Co.)	1.12.33	
54	HX2492	L 109	J.F & F.G. Stevens (Pioneer Omnibus Co.)	1.12.33	
55	GC6664	L 110	Cleveland Omnibus Co. Ltd	29.11.33	
56	VX2198	L 112	Gordon Omnibus Co. Ltd	13.12.33	18.1.39
57	VX5169	L 113	Gordon Omnibus Co. Ltd	13.12.33	
58	GJ7536	L 114	The Premier Omnibus Co. Ltd	19.12.33	9.2.39
59	GJ7537	L 115	The Premier Omnibus Co. Ltd	19.12.33	
60	GC1214	L 116	The Premier Omnibus Co. Ltd	19.12.33	16.1.39
61	GH889	L 117	The Premier Omnibus Co. Ltd	19.12.33	
62	GJ7538	L 118	The Premier Omnibus Co. Ltd	19.12.33	2.2.39
63	GH890	L 119	The Premier Omnibus Co. Ltd	19.12.33	
64	GH2491	L 120	The Premier Omnibus Co. Ltd	19.12.33	20.1.39
65	UV5906	L 121	The Premier Omnibus Co. Ltd	19.12.33	

		First LT number	Acquired from	Date into stock	Date out of stock
66	GK893	L 122	The Premier Omnibus Co. Ltd	19.12.33	
67	GK891	L 123	The Premier Omnibus Co. Ltd	19.12.33	24.1.39
68	GK892	L 124	The Premier Omnibus Co. Ltd	19.12.33	17.1.39
69	GK896	L 125	The Premier Omnibus Co. Ltd	19.12.33	
70	GK895	L 126	The Premier Omnibus Co. Ltd	19.12.33	3.2.39
71	GK894	L 127	The Premier Omnibus Co. Ltd	19.12.33	11.1.39
72	GX2692	—	Empress Motors Ltd	30.1.34	20.1.39
73	GX2693	—	Empress Motors Ltd	30.1.34	18.1.39
74	GK6431	—	Birch Bros. Ltd	21.2.34	3.2.39
75	GK8660	—	Birch Bros. Ltd	21.2.34	9.2.39
76	GK9718	—	Birch Bros. Ltd	21.2.34	30.1.39
77	GN4380	—	Birch Bros. Ltd	21.2.34	1.2.39
78	GN4381	—	Birch Bros. Ltd	21.2.34	23.1.39
79	GN5880	—	Birch Bros. Ltd	21.2.34	
80	GN5881	—	Birch Bros. Ltd	21.2.34	
81	GO1525	—	Birch Bros. Ltd	21.2.34	
82	GO1526	—	Birch Bros. Ltd	21.2.34	
83	GP7289	—	Birch Bros. Ltd	21.2.34	11.1.39
84	GX132	—	Birch Bros. Ltd	21.2.34	9.1.39
85	GX131	—	Birch Bros. Ltd	21.2.34	1.8.39
87	GX1955	—	Hawkins & Co. Ltd (Nil Desperandum)	12.6.34	31.1.39
88	UW2308	—	Westminster Omnibus Co. Ltd	10.7.34	20.1.39
89	UW2309	—	Westminster Omnibus Co. Ltd	10.7.34	
90	UW2310	—	Westminster Omnibus Co. Ltd	10.7.34	24.1.39
91	UW2311	—	Westminster Omnibus Co. Ltd	10.7.34	
92	GC3170	—	Westminster Omnibus Co. Ltd	10.7.34	3.3.39
93	GC3171	—	Westminster Omnibus Co. Ltd	10.7.34	16.1.39
94	GC3172	—	Westminster Omnibus Co. Ltd	10.7.34	
95	GN184	—	Westminster Omnibus Co. Ltd	10.7.34	4.8.39
96	GX2602	—	Westminster Omnibus Co. Ltd	10.7.34	
97	GO5448	—	The St George Omnibus Co. Ltd	16.7.34	23.1.39
98	JJ1269	—	The St George Omnibus Co. Ltd	16.7.34	
99	UV9097	—	The Chocolate Express Omnibus Co. Ltd	9.8.34	30.1.39
100	UW6154	—	The Chocolate Express Omnibus Co. Ltd	9.8.34	25.1.39
101	UW6987	—	The Chocolate Express Omnibus Co. Ltd	9.8.34	18.1.39
102	GC6087	—	The Chocolate Express Omnibus Co. Ltd	9.8.34	11.1.39
103	GO1636	—	The Chocolate Express Omnibus Co. Ltd	9.8.34	
104	VX4269	—	Miller Traction Co. Ltd	28.8.34	
105	VX5859	—	Miller Traction Co. Ltd	28.8.34	
106	VX8831	—	Miller Traction Co. Ltd	28.8.34	
107	VX8835	—	Miller Traction Co. Ltd	28.8.34	
108	EV7308	—	Miller Traction Co. Ltd	28.8.34	
109	MY2177	—	Perkins Omnibus Co. Ltd	28.8.34	10.1.39
110	GN7571	—	The City Motor Omnibus Co. Ltd	5.11.34	20.1.39
111	GO1348	—	The City Motor Omnibus Co. Ltd	5.11.34	cb 30.11.38
112	GO1933	—	The City Motor Omnibus Co. Ltd	5.11.34	
113	GO1932	—	The City Motor Omnibus Co. Ltd	5.11.34	
114	GO1346	—	The City Motor Omnibus Co. Ltd	5.11.34	
115	GO1930	—	The City Motor Omnibus Co. Ltd	5.11.34	
116	GW2758	—	The City Motor Omnibus Co. Ltd	5.11.34	
117	GW2759	—	The City Motor Omnibus Co. Ltd	5.11.34	
118	GW2760	—	The City Motor Omnibus Co. Ltd	5.11.34	
119	GW2761	—	The City Motor Omnibus Co. Ltd	5.11.34	
120	GW2762	—	The City Motor Omnibus Co. Ltd	5.11.34	
121	GX1839	—	The City Motor Omnibus Co. Ltd	5.11.34	
122	UW4198	—	Reliance Omnibus Co. Ltd	6.11.34	
123	EV6510	—	Reliance Omnibus Co. Ltd	6.11.34	
124	EV6692	—	Reliance Omnibus Co. Ltd	6.11.34	
125	EV8335	—	Reliance Omnibus Co. Ltd	6.11.34	
126	VX4261	—	Victory Omnibus Co. Ltd	6.11.34	
127	MY2643	—	Prince Omnibus Co. Ltd	4.12.34	
128	MY2917	—	Prince Omnibus Co. Ltd	4.12.34	
129	MY4043	—	Prince Omnibus Co. Ltd	4.12.34	
130	MV1376	—	Prince Omnibus Co. Ltd	4.12.34	
133	KJ1906	—	Maidstone & Dist Motor Services Ltd	1.7.33	

		First LT number	Acquired from	Date into stock	Date out of stock
134	KJ1910	—	Maidstone & Dist Motor Services Ltd	1.7.33	
135	KJ1911	—	Maidstone & Dist Motor Services Ltd	1.7.33	
136	KJ1912	—	Maidstone & Dist Motor Services Ltd	1.7.33	
137	KJ1914	—	Maidstone & Dist Motor Services Ltd	1.7.33	
138	KJ1915	—	Maidstone & Dist Motor Services Ltd	1.7.33	
139	KJ1919	—	Maidstone & Dist Motor Services Ltd	1.7.33	
140	KJ1920	—	Maidstone & Dist Motor Services Ltd	1.7.33	
141	KJ1934	—	Maidstone & Dist Motor Services Ltd	1.7.33	
142	KJ1935	—	Maidstone & Dist Motor Services Ltd	1.7.33	
143	KO7338	—	Maidstone & Dist Motor Services Ltd	1.7.33	
144	KO7344	—	Maidstone & Dist Motor Services Ltd	1.7.33	
145	KO7343	—	Maidstone & Dist Motor Services Ltd	1.7.33	
146	KP3055	—	Maidstone & Dist Motor Services Ltd	1.7.33	
147	KP3056	—	Maidstone & Dist Motor Services Ltd	1.7.33	
148	KP3057	—	Maidstone & Dist Motor Services Ltd	1.7.33	
149	KP3061	—	Maidstone & Dist Motor Services Ltd	1.7.33	
150	KP3065	—	Maidstone & Dist Motor Services Ltd	1.7.33	
151	KP3067	—	Maidstone & Dist Motor Services Ltd	1.7.33	
152	KP3393	—	Maidstone & Dist Motor Services Ltd	1.7.33	22.7.38
153	KP3404	—	Maidstone & Dist Motor Services Ltd	1.7.33	22.7.38
154	KR1721	—	Maidstone & Dist Motor Services Ltd	1.7.33	
155	KR1722	—	Maidstone & Dist Motor Services Ltd	1.7.33	
156	KR1723	—	Maidstone & Dist Motor Services Ltd	1.7.33	
157	KR1724	—	Maidstone & Dist Motor Services Ltd	1.7.33	
158	KR1725	—	Maidstone & Dist Motor Services Ltd	1.7.33	
159	KR1726	—	Maidstone & Dist Motor Services Ltd	1.7.33	
160	KR1727	—	Maidstone & Dist Motor Services Ltd	1.7.33	
161	KR1728	—	Maidstone & Dist Motor Services Ltd	1.7.33	
162	KR1730	—	Maidstone & Dist Motor Services Ltd	1.7.33	
163	KR1732	—	Maidstone & Dist Motor Services Ltd	1.7.33	
164	KR1734	—	Maidstone & Dist Motor Services Ltd	1.7.33	
165	KR6535	—	Maidstone & Dist Motor Services Ltd	1.7.33	
166	KR8396	—	Maidstone & Dist Motor Services Ltd	1.7.33	
167	CW9243	—	London General Country Services Ltd [2]	1.7.33	26.7.38
168	RX4350	—	Thames Valley Traction Co. Ltd	1.7.33	22.7.38
169	RX4351	—	Thames Valley Traction Co. Ltd	1.7.33	26.7.38
170	UR6729	—	London General Country Services Ltd [1]	1.7.33	
171	UR6730	—	London General Country Services Ltd [1]	1.7.33	
172	UR7035	—	London General Country Services Ltd [2]	1.7.33	12.8.38
173	UR9240	—	London General Country Services Ltd [2]	1.7.33	
192	KJ2577	—	Maidstone & Dist Motor Services Ltd [3]	31.7.35	
193	KJ2578	—	Maidstone & Dist Motor Services Ltd [3]	31.7.35	
194	KJ2579	—	Maidstone & Dist Motor Services Ltd [3]	31.7.35	
195	KJ2580	—	Maidstone & Dist Motor Services Ltd [3]	31.7.35	

c Chassis only; body scrapped earlier
cb Chassis only; body transferred to ST 1140 (see RT 1)
[1] Formerly C. Aston Watford
[2] Formerly E & F Prentice (Chiltern Omnibus Co.), Tring
[3] Formerly Redcar Services, Tunbridge Wells

DH

The H was the first purpose-built double-deck chassis from Dennis and went into production in 1927. It was a forward control model, powered by a 4-cylinder 70bhp engine. Two more powerful 6-cylinder versions were introduced in 1930, first the HS which had improved engine mountings and servo-assisted brakes, then the HV which had vacuum brakes. In 1929 the LGOC bought three of the H type with Hall Lewis open top bodywork, a somewhat anachronistic specification at such a late date when the company was on the verge of a major fleet renewal programme and when the H itself was soon to be replaced by the more powerful models. They were said to be experimental. Originally numbered D 146–148 in the main LGOC Dennis series, they were transferred to Overground Ltd at Potters Bar garage in October 1932 but returned to General in December 1932, which is when they were renumbered DH 1–3. These passed to London Transport and were later joined by another 15 acquired from various Independent operators, a mixture of all three models with open top, closed top, open staircase and closed staircase designs. DH 4–8 were numbered in the old LGOC D series until January 1934, when they were renumbered into the DH class. The former Aldershot & District bus, OU1108, was never numbered.

DH 4, 5, 8–16 were transferred to the Country Bus department on various dates between 22nd February and 6th July 1934. The five open-toppers and one of the open staircase covered top vehicles were sold in 1935 but the Country buses remained in stock until 1936.

DH 3 was one of three Dennis H type bought by the LGOC in 1929. The Hall Lewis 50-seat bodywork was in the standard London style and originally had an open driver's cab. Note the nearside headlamp, a requirement for working over the country roads out to Potters Bar, where this type was based in LT days. J. Higham

This unusually styled 55-seat body with its distinctive inward rake on the upper deck and generally smooth lines, was supplied by Hickman to the Paterson Omnibus Co in 1929, an early example of an enclosed staircase vehicle. DH 12 was transferred to Country Buses in 1934 when it lost its number temporarily. It was still without a driver's windscreen when photographed at Slough soon after receiving its new colours. J. Higham

Chassis:	Dennis H (DH 1–3, 7, 10, 11, 18; HV (DH 4, 8, 16); or HS (DH 5, 6, 9, 12–15, 17, OU1108)
Engine:	Dennis 4-cylinder 6.24 litre 70 bhp petrol (H type); 6-cylinder 6.1 litre 70 bhp petrol (HS and HV types)
Transmission:	4-speed crash
Bodywork:	Birch (DH 5, 6, 8, 10, 11, 15, 16; Dodson (DH 4, 7, 9, 17, 18); Hall Lewis (DH 1–3); Hickman (DH 12–14); Strachan OU1108
Capacity:	L22/26R (OU1108); O30/26RO (DH 6, 18); O26/24RO (DH1–3); H30/26RO (DH 7); H30/26R (DH 4, 8–11, 15, 16); H29/26R (DH 12, 14); H28/26RO (DH 5, 17); H28/26R (DH 13)
L.T. codes:	Not allocated
Built:	1927 (DH 6); 1928 (DH 17, 18); 1929 (DH 1–3, 5, 7, 9–14); 1930 (DH 8, 15, 16); 1931 (DH 4)
Number acquired: 18	
Number in stock 1.7.33: 18 31.12.39: Nil Last in stock: 18.5.36	

DH 4,5,7,8–16 were reseated to 26/22 during 1934 or 1935.

	First LT No.		Acquired from	Date into stock	Date out of stock
1	YW8004		London General Omnibus Co. Ltd	1.7.33	19.3.35
2	YW8005		London General Omnibus Co. Ltd	1.7.33	19.3.35
3	YW8006		London General Omnibus Co. Ltd	1.7.33	19.3.35
4	GN5896	D 184	E. Puttergill (Golden Arrow), Stockwell	22.11.33	8.4.36
5	MY1689	D 185	F.A. Rasey (F.A.R.)	22.11.33	14.4.36
6	GJ5506	D 186	W.C. Holliday & P.R. Bangs (H.B), Tulse Hill	1.12.33	8.4.36
7	UU4830	D 188	E. Brickwood Ltd (Redline), North Kensington	1.12.33	18.5.36
8	VX7702	D 190	B.B.P. Omnibus Co. Ltd, Romford	13.12.33	14.4.36
9	UU1506		Empress Motors Ltd, Bethnal Green	30.1.34	18.5.36
10	GU977		Birch Bros. Ltd	21.2.34	14.4.36
11	GU6436		Birch Bros. Ltd	21.2.34	18.5.36
12	VX9014		A.H. Martin (Paterson Omnibus Co. Ltd), Ilford	12.6.34	18.5.36
13	VW1361		A.H. Martin (Paterson Omnibus Co. Ltd), Ilford	12.6.34	18.5.36
14	VX97		A.H. Martin (Paterson Omnibus Co. Ltd), Ilford	12.6.34	16.5.36
15	VX5533		A.H. Martin (Paterson Omnibus Co. Ltd), Ilford	12.6.34	16.5.36
16	GH5342		A.H. Martin (Paterson Omnibus Co. Ltd), Ilford	12.6.34	14.4.36
17	VX3453		Ambassador Bus Co. Ltd, Holloway	28.8.34	29.7.35
18	VX6848		Reliance Omnibus Co. Ltd, Chingford	6.11.34	25.7.35
	OU1108		Aldershot & District Traction Co. Ltd	1.8.33	10.34

Although very similar to the LT2 and LT2/1 open staircase Renowns, LT 1 had a different design of body, originally intended as an improved model for the LS class. As it was intended to carry route and destination boards, rather than a blind, the front between-decks panel was flat with a curved panel connecting it to the sides. The skirt panel had a concave rather than convex curvature. It is in Whitehall on route 53, running from Plumstead garage where it spent most of the period covered by this book. J. Bonell

LT

The LT class was the first of three new models introduced by the LGOC in 1929 and became the company's standard bus for a time between 1930 and 1932. The prototype, LT 1, carried a fifty-four seat covered top open staircase body originally intended as an improved design for the LS. It therefore differed in many details from the production run, notably in having a flat upper deck front panel, curved at the corners, designed to accommodate board indicators (coded 1LT1). Its internal appointments were a considerable improvement on earlier designs, including deeply cushioned seats and concealed lighting. LT 2–50 (1/2LT2), new in January/February 1930, were sixty-seaters. The bodywork was broadly similar to LT 1, with square cab but with a rearward slope to the front panel between the indicator box and the side pillars. LT 51–150 (1/2LT2/1), new in the autumn of 1930, had rounded cabs but were otherwise similar to the LT2s. The LT2s and 2/1s were the last LGOC buses to be built with open staircases and the first standard type to go into production from the outset with covered tops. The next 350 (nominally LT 151–500; 2LT3 but with variations as described later) were to the same basic design but with enclosed straight staircases and full width rear platforms which reduced their seating capacity to fifty-six. The upper deck seating was all forward-facing, arranged in pairs of doubles ahead of the staircase, two triples and one double alongside the stairwell and a bench for five across the back. Downstairs, there were longitudinal seats over the wheel arches for five on the nearside and two on the offside, with the rest in forward facing pairs of doubles. Ninety of the LT3 bodies were built by Park Royal, eighty each by Strachan and Short Bros. and the rest by the LGOC at Chiswick. One of the Chiswick-built bodies, fitted originally to LT 345, was an improved design with a pronounced inward slope to the upper deck and a domed rear roof. It was coded LT4. The LT3s and LT4 were built during the first half of 1931.

The LT2 type body fitted to the first 49 production chassis retained the square cab of LT 1 but now had angled panels at the front between decks, following the line of the upper deck windows, and convex skirt panels. LT 147 was photographed at the West Hampstead (West End Green) terminus of route 153 and is carrying a notice announcing the introduction of fixed bus stops in Woolwich from 13th October 1937. D.A. Ruddom collection

Below left **The rear of LT 29, preparing to make a garage run from Dulwich to Nunhead, shows how the time-honoured London style of open staircase had been adapted to suit the crisp neat design of the LT2 and LT2/1 bodies. The white square above the registration plate was where the route number stencil would have been carried normally.** Alan Cross

Below right **The LT2 open staircase body was identical in almost all respects to the LT1 type but had the rounded cab introduced in 1930. Although LT 43 is partially obscured by a tree in Dulwich, this feature is clear and the curve of the open staircase can be seen through the lower saloon.** G.J. Robbins collection

Apart from the enclosed platform and staircase, the LT3 body illustrated was identical to the LT2/1 design. On these vehicles the original small indicator box at the front had been replaced by the larger box shown, on which the destination, three lines of intermediate points and the route number could be displayed. LT 769 was one of the early conversions to oil engine, in February 1934. G.J. Robbins collection

The next 350, delivered in the second half of 1931, had a modified version of the LT4 body, with a less pronounced tumblehome and a destination indicator set into the cab roof (nominally LT 501–850; 2LT5 but with variations). The next 150 were given substantially improved indicators incorporating at the front a separate box for the route number on the roof and a destination strip in the driver's cab roof, leaving the large box for the intermediate point displays (nominally LT 851–950; 2LT5/1 with variations). A large box for intermediate displays was also added at the back but no separate route number box was carried.

One of this batch (LT 741) was fitted with the prototype of the new 'Bluebird' body which was the first LGOC bus to have the upper deck extended over the driver's cab. By adopting a very upright design, in combination with a curved staircase and half-width platform, a seating capacity of sixty was achieved, three being added to the longitudinal bench on the offside of the lower deck and one to the upper deck. The upstairs seating was re-arranged in forward-facing pairs, except that there were two single seats on the nearside next to the head of the stairs, a feature which was to be continued on subsequent double-deckers until 1939. The weight of the body was contained within legal limits by the use of lightweight construction methods, including plywood-backed seats upholstered in foam rubber. The seats were of a new more austere looking design but were the first to have toprails. The 'Bluebird' established the basic layout which was to endure for the next thirty years. The last 272 LTs (nominally LT 951–999 and 1204–1426; LT6, 7, 8 and variants) were built to this design but with the improved destination blinds as fitted to the LT5/1s. They were new during the first half of 1932.

LT 1137 was an experimental Green Line coach with a fifty-seat forward-entrance body finished internally to coach standards of seating and trim, with a forward entrance and rear staircase. The design was basically an LT5 but with a concave-curved panel linking the upper deck to the front of the cab roof. A single destination blind box was carried in the canopy and there was a roof-mounted box displaying 'GREEN LINE' in an illuminated panel. It had one bay fewer than the buses which lengthened the windows. These were of the half-drop type and protected by glass louvres. Another unique feature was its 'sunsaloon' roof in which the central section could be opened and folded back. It was relegated to bus use early in 1935, renumbered LT 1137B and its fleet name altered to LONDON TRANSPORT, but no other alterations were made at that time. At some later date its staircase was moved to the front, its seating capacity increased to fifty-six and a full size standard destination blind box fitted. This is likely to have happened when it went through Chiswick for overhaul in March 1937.

An improved display was possible on the LT5 body, allowing an extra line of intermediate points on a board between decks and a larger route number on the blind shared with the destination, set in the driver's cab canopy. LT 594 still had a petrol engine when photographed at Trafalgar Square in 1935 and remained so equipped until October 1939 when an A180 8.8 litre oil was installed.
London's Transport Museum

A full display of information at the front was restored with the LT5/1 body, in the interesting arrangement shown. The route number was changed by the conductor leaning out of the front window to reach the handle which hung down from the box. The overall styling was also improved by a slight inward slope to the upper deck side panels, which had been pioneered on the experimental LT4 body originally mounted on LT 345. LT 628 was fitted with an oil engine in January 1934, changing its classification from 2LT5/1 to 12LT5/5. The extra length of the engine compartment caused by this conversion can be seen in the slight extension behind the radiator. W.J. Haynes

The ultimate design of LT-type bodywork was the Bluebird, which set the basic layout for double-deckers that was to prevail for over 30 years. LT 1228 had just had its petrol engine replaced by an 8.8 litre oil unit when photographed at the National Gallery on Sunday only route 92, which became part of route 9 soon afterwards. G.H.F. Atkins

All but one of the AECs had the short-wheelbase Renown 663 chassis and were twenty-seven feet long but LT 1137 was mounted on one of the long wheelbase 664 version originally intended for a single-decker but was only six inches longer than the buses because its rear overhang was shorter (coded 1/1LTL2). The standard specification comprised the AEC A145 petrol engine, D124 4-speed crash gearbox, triple-servo brakes and semi-floating rear axles but the LT class was used as a test bed for developing oil engines, preselective transmission and hydraulic brakes and there were therefore many variations. Together with the development of the body design these established the basis of the standard specification for the rest of the 1930s. Experiments with oil engines started in March 1931 when LT 191–199 were fitted with AEC Acro A155 engines, but these were not successful and were later modified to the improved Ricardo A161 version. A further twenty-three were fitted with the A161 engine, including three transferred from STs (originally LT 590, 643, 750–768, 948, 949; coded 4LT3/1) and one, the experimental 'Bluebird' LT 741, had a Gardner, originally a 5LW but replaced by a 6LW in August 1932 (9LT7). LT 590 was one of twenty-two which had been delivered new in July and August 1931 with preselective gearboxes and fluid transmission (LT 439, 448, 549–552, 566–571 and 583–592; 3LT3/2 or 5/2) and was therefore the first London bus to have the combination of oil engine and Wilson gearbox which was to become standard. Lockheed hydraulic brakes were first tried on LT 673, which also had a Wilson gearbox, in February 1932 and then on LT 1325–1354, also with Wilson gearbox (6LT6/1). The Lockheed brakes had been removed from LT 673 before it was acquired by the LPTB.

The last seventy-two LTs all had oil engines. Sixty-two had the new AEC A165 8.8 litre Ricardo engine, of which twenty (LT 1355–1374; 8LT6/3) had D128 preselective gearboxes and hydraulic brakes, the specifications which became London Transport's standard from 1934, while the remainder had crash boxes but were in two distinct batches (LT 1375–1404; 7LT6/2 and LT 1405–1416; 10LT8). The 10LTs differed from all other LTs in having a single 35-gallon fuel tank and repositioned batteries but were otherwise standard. The last ten were powered by Gardner 6LW engines whose greater length required a shortened body and caused the bonnet to extend forwards in a snout (LT 1417–1426; 9LT7).

There were four other vehicles which were not AEC Renowns but were included in the class by the LGOC for convenience (LT 1000, 1051, 1202, 1203; coded CC). These had experimental chassis built by the LGOC in 1930/1931, part of an aborted project which was intended to total twelve and to include vehicles similar to the ST and T classes but, apart from the LTs, extended only to three Ts. As built, they had six-cylinder Meadows petrol engines but these were replaced with AEC engines between September 1932 and July 1933.

Between October 1933 and October 1934 all the petrol engined crash gearbox 'Bluebirds' (170 buses, recoded 11LT) and 168 of the LT 151–949 batch (recoded 12LT) were given new A165 oil engines and their petrol engines were transferred to new STL chassis. A similar exchange, involving twenty-four buses, was made with new LTC coaches in 1937. Body codes were also altered, as shown in the summary. A further 550 LTs were fitted with 8.8 litre oil engines in 1939 and 1940 (1/12LT) but this time their petrol engines were scrapped, the new A180 engine being so economical that there was strong financial justification for the outlay. One other Renown, LT 21, was fitted with an oil engine, in 1935, but this was a 7.7 litre A171 engine (the type used in STLs: 2/12LT2/2). Two additional LTs were also equipped with the Wilson gearboxes removed from T 307 and 308 in 1934, bringing the total to seventy-four.

Apart from seven which were about to be converted to oil in January 1940, the only remaining petrol-engined double-deck LTs at the end of 1939 were the open staircase buses (LT 1–150, allocated to Leyton, Loughton and Potters Bar garages), LT 1137 (St Albans) and the fifty-four fitted with preselective gearboxes, which were all at Plumstead (3LT and 6LT – see summary).

The LT5/1s and the Bluebirds were the only types in the class to have a separate intermediate point display at the back. Even these did not have a route number box, as can be seen on Bluebird LT 1245 at the Bank of England. These LTs were the first London buses to have the Y-shaped centre bar in the rear upper deck window which became such a characteristic of the 1930s, and the design was a clear ancestor of the STL.
Alan Cross

Chassis:	AEC Renown 663 (LT 1–999, 1204–1426; AEC Renown 664 (LT 1137); LGOC CC (LT 1000, 1051, 1202, 1203)
Engine:	AEC A145 6-cylinder 7.4 litre 130 bhp petrol (all except oil-engined vehicles listed); AEC A161 6-cylinder 8.8 litre 130 bhp oil (LT 191–199, 590, 643, 750–768, 948, 949); AEC A165 6-cylinder 8.8 litre 130 bhp oil (LT 1355–1416). Gardner 6LW 6-cylinder oil (LT 741, 1417–1426)
Transmission:	AEC D124 4 speed crash; or Daimler D128 4-speed direct selection pre-selective with fluid flywheel (originally LT 439, 448, 549–552, 566–571, 583–592, 1355–1374).
Bodywork:	LGOC (Chiswick), Park Royal, Strachan or Short Bros.
Capacity:	H30/24RO (LT 1); H32/28RO (LT 2–150); H33/23R (nominally LT 151–740, 742–950); H34/26R (LT 741 and nominally LT 951–999, 1204–1426); H31/23R (LT 1000, 1051, 1202, 1203).
L.T. chassis code: (1933)	1LT (LT 1); 1/2LT (2–150); 2LT (LT 151–947, except 3LT or 4LT examples); 3LT (originally LT 439, 448, 549–552, 566–571, 583–592); 4LT (LT 191–199, 590, 643, 750–768, 948, 949); 5LT (LT nominally 950–999, 1204–1324); 6LT (LT 1325–1354); 7LT (LT 1375–1404); 8LT (LT 1355–1374); 9LT (LT 741, 1417–1426); 10LT (LT 1405–1416): 1/1LTL (LT 1137)
L.T. body codes (1933):	LT1 (LT 1); LT2 or 2/1 (LT 2–150); LT3 or 3/1 or 3/2 (nominally LT 151–500); ; LT4 (LT 329 – originally LT 345); LT5, 5/2 or 5/3 (nominally LT 501–850); LT5/1 or 5/4 nominally LT 851–949); LT6 (LT 950–999, 1204–1324); LT6/1 (LT 1325–1354); LT6/2 (LT 1375–1404); LT6/3 (LT 1355–1374; LT7 (LT 741, 1417–1426); LT8 (LT 1405–1416) LTL2 (LT 1137). There is no record of any codes being allocated to the CC-type (LT 1000, 1051, 1202, 1203)
Built:	1929–1932
Number built:	1227
Number in stock:	1.7.33: 1227 31.12.39: 1223

The following changes to chassis codes were made when oil engines replaced petrol:
2LT to 12LT (1933–1937 conversions);
2LT to 1/12LT (1938/1939)
2LT to 2/12LT (LT 21 only)
5LT to 11LT

The following changes were made to body codes when oil engines replaced petrol:
LT3 to LT3/1 (1934–1937); to LT3/3 (1938–1939)
LT5 to LT5/6 (1934–1937); to LT5/8 (1938–1939)
LT5/1 to LT5/5 (1934–1937); to 5/7 (1938–1939)
LT6 on 2LT chassis to LT6/4 (1938–1939)

At 31.12.39 the 3LT chassis were LT 271, 401, 451, 469, 470, 571, 573, 580, 582, 588, 591–593, 649, 651, 652, 658, 659, 662, 786, 798, 827, 909, 914.

At 31.12.39 the 6LT chassis were on LT 964, 1235–1238 and 1330–1354

All double-deck LTs were taken into stock on 1.7.33 from the LGOC.

Facing page, top **LT 1418 was one of ten Bluebirds which had been fitted with Gardner engines when new, the extra length of that robust unit causing the bonnet to be extended in a pronounced snout and the body to be shortened in compensation.** J.F. Higham

Facing page, bottom **The unique LT 1137B had started life as an experimental Green Line coach but was relegated to bus work in 1935. It originally had a rear staircase allied to its forward entrance but this had been moved forward, the sliding platform door removed and other changes made to the interior by the time this photograph was taken on route 340. In this condition it had no seats in front of the staircase upstairs. The larger destination blind box was fitted when it became a bus.** Ken Glazier collection

LT

#	Code	#	Code	#	Code
1	UU6611	70	GH3834	139	GH8031
2	UU6666	71	GH3793	140	GH8035
3	UU6667	72	GH3841	141	GH8040
4	GC3917	73	GH 606	142	GH8029
5	UU6685	74	GH3795	143	GH8032
6	UU6668	75	GH 638	144	GH8042
7	UU6669	76	GH3836	145	GH8037
8	GC3904	77	GH3796	146	GH8038
9	UU6670	78	GH3866	147	GH8036
10	UU6671	79	GH3837	148	GH8045
11	GC3905	80	GH3850	149	GH8043
12	UU6678	81	GH3838	150	GH8044
13	GC3902	82	GH 605	151	GK3161
14	GC3920	83	GH3846	152	GK3162
15	UU6686	84	GH3843	153	GK3167
16	UU6680	85	GF7275	154	GK3165
17	UU6688	86	GH 608	155	GK3168
18	GC3906	87	GH3840	156	GK3170
19	UU6676	88	GH8013	157	GK3163
20	GC3914	89	GH3871	158	GK3159
21	GC3922	90	GH3877	159	GK3160
22	GC3923	91	GH3835	160	GK3169
23	GC3915	92	GH3869	161	GK3164
24	GC3924	93	GH3875	162	GK5314
25	GC3925	94	GH3870	163	GK5317
26	UU6681	95	GH3842	164	GK5322
27	GC3927	96	GH3867	165	GK5323
28	UU6682	97	GH3868	166	GK5313
29	UU6672	98	GH3847	167	GK5320
30	UU6673	99	GH3498	168	GK5326
31	UU6679	100	GH3844	169	GK5327
32	UU6677	101	GH3845	170	GK5316
33	UU6675	102	GH8021	171	GK5325
34	UU6674	103	GH8007	172	GK5319
35	UU6683	104	GH3874	173	GK5318
36	GC3921	105	GH8019	174	GK5315
37	UU6687	106	GH3851	175	GK5321
38	GC3901	107	GH3848	176	GK5324
39	GC3903	108	GH8008	177	GK5353
40	GC3907	109	GH3858	178	GK5355
41	UU6684	110	GH 610	179	GK5352
42	GC3916	111	GH8018	180	GK5371
43	GC3919	112	GH3876	181	GK5354
44	GC3908	113	GH3852	182	GK5366
45	GC3913	114	GH8011	183	GK5341
46	GC3910	115	GH3859	184	GK5367
47	GC3909	116	GH3872	185	GK5331
48	GC3911	117	GH3863	186	GK5351
49	GC3912	118	GH3860	187	GK5340
50	GC3918	119	GH8041	188	GK5339
51	GF7271	120	GH3873	189	GK5356
52	GH 609	121	GH8009	190	GK5365
53	GF7272	122	GH8010	191	GK5466
54	GH3799	123	GH8030	192	GN2067
55	GH 640	124	GH8028	193	GN2172
56	GH3839	125	GH8016	194	GN2054
57	GH 607	126	GH8033	195	GN2042
58	GH 604	127	GH8017	196	GN2066
59	GH3797	128	GH8014	197	GN2119
60	GH3832	129	GH8027	198	GN2125
61	GF7273	130	GH8012	199	GK5465
62	GF7274	131	GH8039	200	GK5428
63	GH3833	132	GH8015	201	GK5431
64	GH3831	133	GH8022	202	GK5416
65	GH 639	134	GH8023	203	GK5417
66	GH3784	135	GH8024	204	GK5409
67	GH3830	136	GH8025	205	GK5459
68	GH 637	137	GH8034	206	GK5457
69	GH3798	138	GH8026	207	GK5427

LT

208	GK5458
209	GK5437
210	GK5462
211	GK5432
212	GK5429
213	GK5436
214	GK5446
215	GK5430
216	GN2139
217	GK5480
218	GK5463
219	GK5464
220	GK5445
221	GK5478
222	GK5454
223	GK5433
224	GN2083
225	GN2043
226	GK5484
227	GN2049
228	GN2012
229	GN2117
230	GK5485
231	GN2047
232	GN2045
233	GN2013
234	GN2014
235	GN2050
236	GN2040
237	GN2046
238	GN2051
239	GN2038
240	GN2044
241	GN2041
242	GN2052
243	GN2048
244	GN2055
245	GN2062
246	GN2057
247	GN2053
248	GN2074
249	GN2061
250	GN2073
251	GN2058
252	GN2022
253	GN2065
254	GN2056
255	GN2060
256	GN2059
257	GN2071
258	GN2070
259	GN2072
260	GN2063
261	GN2082
262	GN2064
263	GN2077
264	GN2078
265	GN2092
266	GN2088
267	GN2085
268	GN2076
269	GN2081
270	GN2123
271	GN2101
272	GN2087
273	GN2084
274	GN2100
275	GN2091
276	GN2124

LT

277	GN2129
278	GN2102
279	GN2118
280	GN2122
281	GN2121
282	GN2099
283	GN2120
284	GN2137
285	GN2126
286	GN2133
287	GN2134
288	GN2132
289	GN2127
290	GN2141
291	GN2140
292	GN2131
293	GN2151
294	GN2135
295	GN2130
296	GN2138
297	GN2152
298	GN2144
299	GN2143
300	GN2136
301	GN2142
302	GN2148
303	GN2158
304	GN2186
305	GN2164
306	GN2150
307	GN2159
308	GN2147
309	GN2192
310	GN2149
311	GN2185
312	GN2165
313	GN2195
314	GN2171
315	GN2166
316	GN2169
317	GN2157
318	GN2167
319	GN2170
320	GN2184
321	GN2168
322	GN2196
323	GN2193
324	GN2194
325	GN2190
326	GN4662
327	GN4616
328	GN4685
329	GN4615
330	GN4667
331	GN4629
332	GN4656
333	GN4655
334	GN2197
335	GN4654
336	GN4677
337	GN4653
338	GN4618
339	GN4659
340	GN4626
341	GN4627
342	GN4652
343	GN4663
344	GN4658
345	GN4657

LT

346	GN4630
347	GN4617
348	GN4628
349	GN4660
350	GN4665
351	GN4687
352	GK3198
353	GN4676
354	GN4686
355	GN4691
356	GH8084
357	GN4664
358	GN4661
359	GN4678
360	GK3197
361	GO 619
362	GN4690
363	GN4666
364	GK3200
365	GN4706
366	GN4688
367	GK5500
368	GK3199
369	GH8085
370	GN4679
371	GN4680
372	GN4681
373	GN4689
374	GN4710
375	GN4711
376	GN4735
377	GO 675
378	GN4703
379	GN4716
380	GN4705
381	GN4712
382	GN4717
383	GN4718
384	GN4702
385	GN4704
386	GN4719
387	GN4720
388	GN4787
389	GO 604
390	GN4713
391	GN4709
392	GN4729
393	GN4708
394	GN4714
395	GN4747
396	GN4724
397	GO 633
398	GN4721
399	GN4727
400	GN4743
401	GN4736
402	GN4753
403	GO 679
404	GN4723
405	GN4744
406	GN4722
407	GN4728
408	GO 632
409	GN4799
410	GN4748
411	GN4764
412	GN4752
413	GN4781
414	GN4749

LT

415	GO 620
416	GN4745
417	GN4737
418	GO 621
419	GO 622
420	GN4750
421	GO 623
422	GN4751
423	GN4778
424	GN4779
425	GN4746
426	GO 608
427	GN4774
428	GO 609
429	GO 612
430	GO 611
431	GN4782
432	GN4800
433	GO 624
434	GO 613
435	GO 674
436	GO 683
437	GO 694
438	GO 676
439	GO7124
440	GO 691
441	GO 690
442	GO 682
443	GO 677
444	GO 681
445	GO 680
446	GO 693
447	GO 692
448	GO7193
449	GO5117
450	GO5154
451	GO5119
452	GO5118
453	GO5120
454	GO5126
455	GO5115
456	GO5135
457	GO5116
458	GO5155
459	GO5147
460	GO5157
461	GO5153
462	GO5168
463	GO5156
464	GO5158
465	GO5179
466	GO5184
467	GO5183
468	GO7127
469	GO7123
470	GO7134
471	GO7111
472	GO7112
473	GO7126
474	GO7132
475	GO7131
476	GO7113
477	GO7122
478	GO7140
479	GO7130
480	GO7133
481	GO7137
482	GO7138
483	GO7139

LT

484	GO7143
485	GO7168
486	GO5194
487	GO7101
488	GO7170
489	GO7176
490	GO7198
491	GO7174
492	GO7169
493	GO7175
494	GO7187
495	GO7199
496	GO7190
497	GO7196
498	GO7195
499	GO7194
500	GO7188
501	GO7197
502	GO7189
503	GP3411
504	GO7191
505	GP3416
506	GP3419
507	GP3444
508	GP3413
509	GP3417
510	GP3412
511	GP3418
512	GP3446
513	GP3447
514	GP3452
515	GP3453
516	GP3445
517	GP3442
518	GP3450
519	GP3441
520	GP3451
521	GP3440
522	GP3459
523	GP3467
524	GP3471
525	GP3460
526	GP3477
527	GP3472
528	GP3478
529	GP3458
530	GP3474
531	GP3461
532	GP3462
533	GP3468
534	GP3469
535	GP3473
536	GP3466
537	GP3479
538	GP3470
539	GP3493
540	GP3496
541	GP3487
542	GP3489
543	GP3503
544	GP3492
545	GP3502
546	GP3501
547	GP3504
548	GP3488
549	GP3520
550	GP3530
551	GP3519
552	GP3505

LT

553	GP3495
554	GP3494
555	GP3486
556	GP3506
557	GP3510
558	GP3508
559	GP3509
560	GP3522
561	GP3516
562	GP3511
563	GP3518
564	GP3517
565	GP3531
566	GP3507
567	GP3532
568	GP3529
569	GP3524
570	GP3523
571	GP3515
572	GP3521
573	GP3535
574	GP3534
575	GP3536
576	GP3539
577	GP3540
578	GP3537
579	GP3538
580	GP3550
581	GP3556
582	GP3547
583	GP3533
584	GP3544
585	GP3541
586	GP3542
587	GP3545
588	GP3543
589	GP3554
590	GP3576
591	GP3560
592	GT5036
593	GP3546
594	GT7419
595	GP3553
596	GP3552
597	GP3549
598	GP3551
599	GP3548
600	GP3558
601	GP3555
602	GP3567
603	GP3559
604	GP3557
605	GP3564
606	GP3561
607	GP3566
608	GP3562
609	GP3563
610	GP3577
611	GP3565
612	GP3568
613	GP3570
614	GP3572
615	GP3573
616	GP3589
617	GP3571
618	GP3569
619	GP3574
620	GP3584
621	GP3588

LT

622	GP3575
623	GP3583
624	GP3582
625	GP3578
626	GP3579
627	GP3586
628	GP3581
629	GP3580
630	GP3585
631	GP3594
632	GP3587
633	GP3590
634	GP3592
635	GP3597
636	GP3591
637	GP3593
638	GP3596
639	GP3595
640	GP3598
641	GP3599
642	GT5009
643	GT5012
644	GT5010
645	GT5011
646	GT5017
647	GT5024
648	GT5025
649	GT5018
650	GT5021
651	GT5019
652	GT5020
653	GT5037
654	GT5026
655	GT5023
656	GT5035
657	GT5038
658	GT5041
659	GT5039
660	GT5049
661	GT5050
662	GT5042
663	GT5040
664	GT5043
665	GT5051
666	GT5048
667	GT5063
668	GT5055
669	GT5056
670	GT5058
671	GT5065
672	GT5057
673	GT7586
674	GT5066
675	GT5064
676	GT5073
677	GT5089
678	GT5081
679	GT5082
680	GT5091
681	GT5093
682	GT5096
683	GT5097
684	GT5092
685	GT5105
686	GT5103
687	GT5104
688	GT5106
689	GT5114
690	GT5164

LT

691	GT5119
692	GT5126
693	GT5116
694	GT5115
695	GT5117
696	GT5146
697	GT5121
698	GT5122
699	GT5118
700	GT5123
701	GT5124
702	GT5125
703	GT5134
704	GT5127
705	GT5129
706	GT5128
707	GT5131
708	GT5132
709	GT5130
710	GT5133
711	GT5138
712	GT5168
713	GT5140
714	GT5141
715	GT5137
716	GT5139
717	GT5143
718	GT5142
719	GT5147
720	GT5163
721	GT5158
722	GT5194
723	GT5148
724	GT5149
725	GT5150
726	GT5151
727	GT5160
728	GT5156
729	GT5155
730	GT5152
731	GT5154
732	GT5159
733	GT5162
734	GT5174
735	GT5157
736	GT5161
737	GT5196
738	GT5170
739	GT5180
740	GT5165
741	GT5167
742	GT5166
743	GT5173
744	GT5174
745	GT5177
746	GT5182
747	GT5175
748	GT5176
749	GT5181
750	GT5144
751	GT5169
752	GT7467
753	GT7462
754	GT7466
755	GT7478
756	GT7479
757	GT7480
758	GT7481
759	GT7497

LT

760	GT7536
761	GT7562
762	GT7537
763	GT7522
764	GT7563
765	GT7582
766	GT7590
767	GT7585
768	GW5837
769	GT5172
770	GT5187
771	GT5179
772	GT5178
773	GT5185
774	GT7404
775	GT5186
776	GT5184
777	GT7420
778	GT5193
779	GT5192
780	GT5190
781	GT5191
782	GT7424
783	GT7402
784	GT7425
785	GT7451
786	GT5195
787	GT5199
788	GT7410
789	GT5200
790	GT7489
791	GT5198
792	GT5197
793	GT7408
794	GT7403
795	GT7407
796	GT7405
797	GT7401
798	GT7412
799	GT7406
800	GT7411
801	GT7415
802	GT7416
803	GT7445
804	GT7409
805	GT7517
806	GT7414
807	GT7416
808	GT7413
809	GT7417
810	GT7465
811	GT7434
812	GT7447
813	GT7427
814	GT7450
815	GT7448
816	GT7449
817	GT7433
818	GT7428
819	GT7471
820	GT7430
821	GT7463
822	GT7426
823	GT7459
824	GT7429
825	GT7485
826	GT7461
827	GT7432
828	GT7435

LT

829	GT7460	898	GT7504	967	GT7594		
830	GT7564	899	GT7510	968	GT7598		
831	GT7472	900	GT7553	969	GT7600		
832	GT7436	901	GT7508	970	GW5831		
833	GT7453	902	GT7521	971	GW5821		
834	GT7458	903	GT7527	972	GW5845		
835	GT7437	904	GT7523	973	GW5857		
836	GT7431	905	GT7524	974	GW5860		
837	GT7452	906	GT7531	975	GW5841		
838	GT7438	907	GT7558	976	GW5856		
839	GT7548	908	GT7526	977	GW5844		
840	GT7444	909	GT7529	978	GW5843		
841	GT7500	910	GW5824	979	GW5848		
842	GT7442	911	GT7533	980	GT7596		
843	GT7483	912	GT7540	981	GW5830		
844	GT7547	913	GT7525	982	GW5826		
845	GT7496	914	GT7550	983	GW5838		
846	GT7468	915	GT7520	984	GW5847		
847	GT7443	916	GT7532	985	GW5854		
848	GT7454	917	GT7543	986	GW5827		
849	GT7484	918	GT7539	987	GW5823		
850	GT7457	919	GT7530	988	GW5855		
851	GT7455	920	GT7528	989	GW5851		
852	GT7456	921	GT7560	990	GW5834		
853	GT7514	922	GT7538	991	GW5833		
854	GT7476	923	GT7551	992	GW5842		
855	GT7469	924	GT7544	993	GW5836		
856	GT7482	925	GT7546	994	GW5861		
857	GT7473	926	GT7565	995	GW5897		
858	GT7464	927	GT7561	996	GW5876		
859	GT7470	928	GT7554	997	GW5835		
860	GT7488	929	GT7549	998	GW5888		
861	GT7499	930	GT7555	999	GW5859		
862	GT7474	931	GT7579	1000	GF7254	4.8.39	
863	GT7475	932	GT7583	1051	GK3003	9.8.39	
864	GT7492	933	GT7569	1137	GP3456		
865	GT7518	934	GT7573	1202	GT5099	10.8.39	
866	GT7487	935	GT7584	1203	GT5153	9.8.39	
867	GT7552	936	GT7576	1204	GW5870		
868	GT7495	937	GT7567	1205	GW5853		
869	GT7589	938	GT7568	1206	GW5849		
870	GT7486	939	GT7571	1207	GW5892		
871	GT7519	940	GT7572	1208	GW5867		
872	GT7493	941	GT7570	1209	GW5894		
873	GT7516	942	GT7575	1210	GW5865		
874	GT7557	943	GT7577	1211	GX5212		
875	GT7545	944	GT7581	1212	GW5850		
876	GT7494	945	GT7574	1213	GW5866		
877	GT7513	946	GT7580	1214	GW5877		
878	GT7491	947	GT7578	1215	GW5864		
879	GT7541	948	GW5829	1216	GW5863		
880	GT7490	949	GW5900	1217	GW5880		
881	GT7509	950	GW5846	1218	GW5887		
882	GT7498	951	GW5828	1219	GW5873		
883	GT7566	952	GW5858	1220	GW5872		
884	GT7534	953	GW5825	1221	GW5885		
885	GT7535	954	GT7593	1222	GW5886		
886	GT7501	955	GT7587	1223	GW5884		
887	GT7559	956	GT7597	1224	GW5906		
888	GT7542	957	GW5839	1225	GW5915		
889	GT7556	958	GT7591	1226	GW5903		
890	GT7511	959	GT7595	1227	GW5911		
891	GT7512	960	GT7599	1228	GW5913		
892	GT7515	961	GW5852	1229	GW5910		
893	GT7503	962	GW5840	1230	GW5898		
894	GT7502	963	GW5832	1231	GW5893		
895	GT7507	964	GT7588	1232	GW5862		
896	GT7505	965	GW5822	1233	GW5869		
897	GT7506	966	GT7592	1234	GW5883		

LT

1235	GW5879	1299	GX5233	1363	GX5361
1236	GW5874	1300	GX5231	1364	GX5362
1237	GW5868	1301	GX5242	1365	GX5363
1238	GW5871	1302	GX5240	1366	GX5364
1239	GW5896	1303	GX5235	1367	GX5365
1240	GW5908	1304	GX5262	1368	GX5366
1241	GW5875	1305	GX5255	1369	GX5367
1242	GW5912	1306	GX5243	1370	GX5368
1243	GW5878	1307	GX5253	1371	GX5369
1244	GW5881	1308	GX5248	1372	GX5370
1245	GW5895	1309	GX5239	1373	GX5371
1246	GW5907	1310	GX5247	1374	GX5372
1247	GW5889	1311	GX5257	1375	GX5294
1248	GW5882	1312	GX5250	1376	GX5284
1249	GX5202	1313	GX5261	1377	GX5283
1250	GW5904	1314	GX5251	1378	GX5280
1251	GW5909	1315	GX5246	1379	GX5289
1252	GX5220	1316	GX5252	1380	GX5312
1253	GW5920	1317	GX5254	1381	GX5296
1254	GW5901	1318	GX5249	1382	GX5295
1255	GW5899	1319	GX5256	1383	GX5341
1256	GX5201	1320	GX5260	1384	GX5298
1257	GW5917	1321	GX5263	1385	GX5300
1258	GW5919	1322	GX5264	1386	GX5297
1259	GW5905	1323	GX5265	1387	GX5306
1260	GX5203	1324	GX5258	1388	GX5307
1261	GW5902	1325	GX5266	1389	GX5309
1262	GX5216	1326	GX5268	1390	GX5313
1263	GX5206	1327	GX5272	1391	GX5339
1264	GX5221	1328	GX5269	1392	GX5308
1265	GW5918	1329	GX5267	1393	GX5340
1266	GW5914	1330	GX5299	1394	GX5342
1267	GX5244	1331	GX5270	1395	GX5343
1268	GW5916	1332	GX5293	1396	GX5344
1269	GX5241	1333	GX5275	1397	GX5345
1270	GX5226	1334	GX5274	1398	GX5346
1271	GX5204	1335	GX5292	1399	GX5347
1272	GX5236	1336	GX5271	1400	GX5348
1273	GX5211	1337	GX5276	1401	GX5349
1274	GX5237	1338	GX5281	1402	GX5350
1275	GX5217	1339	GX5273	1403	GX5351
1276	GX5219	1340	GX5278	1404	GX5352
1277	GX5213	1341	GX5279	1405	GX5373
1278	GX5230	1342	GX5286	1406	GX5374
1279	GX5210	1343	GX5303	1407	GX5375
1280	GX5205	1344	GX5277	1408	GX5376
1281	GX5225	1345	GX5285	1409	GX5377
1282	GX5207	1346	GX5282	1410	GX5378
1283	GX5227	1347	GX5287	1411	GX5379
1284	GX5208	1348	GX5288	1412	GX5380
1285	GX5245	1349	GX5301	1413	GX5381
1286	GX5214	1350	GX5311	1414	GX5382
1287	GX5209	1351	GX5310	1415	GX5383
1288	GX5238	1352	GX5305	1416	GX5384
1289	GX5218	1353	GX5302	1417	GX5385
1290	GX5223	1354	GX5304	1418	GX5386
1291	GX5215	1355	GX5353	1419	GX5387
1292	GX5222	1356	GX5354	1420	GX5388
1293	GX5259	1357	GX5355	1421	GX5389
1294	GX5224	1358	GX5356	1422	GX5390
1295	GX5232	1359	GX5357	1423	GX5391
1296	GX5228	1360	GX5358	1424	GX5392
1297	GX5229	1361	GX5359	1425	GX5393
1298	GX5234	1362	GX5360	1426	GX5394

ST

The ST class, based on the AEC Regent 661 chassis, was introduced by the LGOC at the end of 1929, following trial operation of a Short Bros-bodied prototype (which later became ST 1139) by its subsidiaries East Surrey Traction Co. Ltd and Autocar Ltd. This was the only General-owned ST with an open staircase. The standard STs, which entered service in 1930/31, were the first LGOC production buses to have an enclosed staircase and platform and a total of 906 more or less identical buses was built, including those supplied to East Surrey and the National Omnibus & Transport Co. to operate on behalf of General. ST 1 was built with a square cab of the type used on the T1s and LT 1–50, and this was repeated on forty-six bodies by Ransomes Sims and Jefferies of Ipswich supplied to East Surrey, which became ST 1085–1088/1091–1132 when the Country Bus fleet was numbered in 1935 (coded ST9). Except for the six lowbridge buses supplied to National, ST 2–836 (coded ST 1/1, 2 or 2/1) and thirty built by Short Bros. for East Surrey, which became ST 1040–1069 in 1935 (coded ST9), had rounded cabs but otherwise the same standard body as ST 1, a forty-nine seat, shortened version of the LT3. Although the number ST 1051 was allocated, the bus which would have carried that number was destroyed by fire in May 1933 and never joined the London Transport fleet. One body in this series, mounted on ST 211, was built by Metro-Cammell using their patented metal framework and could be distinguished from the rest by its smoother side panels (coded ST3). This body was mounted on ST 589 when it came into London Transport's ownership, moved onto ST 478 in October 1933, ST 539 in October 1934 and ST 150 in November 1935, which is the number it was carrying at the end of 1939. Two other bodies had curved staircases, increasing their capacity to fifty-one seats, although this was later reduced to fifty. On acquisition by

ST 785 illustrates how most STs looked when they entered the London Transport fleet in 1933, resembling a shortened version of the LT3 with a large single composite blind box and rounded cab. C. Martin

The standard STs inherited by Country Buses from London General Country Services were given the all-embracing classification ST9, rather than ST2. They still had the original small indicator box at the front and were fitted with a similar display over the platform but did not have a rear display. They remained in this condition throughout their lives with London Transport. ST 116 had been one of the type allocated to National for operation on behalf of the LGOC but had migrated to Windsor by the time this photograph was taken. J.F. Higham collection

the LPTB, these were mounted on ST 741 and ST 539 respectively and by the end of 1939 were mounted on ST 195 (ST6/1) and ST 294 (ST6). The last ten ST bodies built by LGOC had their front destination indicators mounted in the cab roof, like the LT5/1s, and were classified ST2/1. The six randomly numbered lowbridge buses supplied to National for operation on route 336 had forty-eight seat bodywork by Short Bros. Two similar vehicles were purchased by Amersham & District (ST 1089, 1090; coded ST9/1 and 9/3) and these joined the LPTB fleet when that company was acquired in October 1933. The last twenty-three LGOC STs supplied to London General Country Services Ltd in 1932 (ST 1032–1039 and 1070–1084; coded ST4) had a new style of bodywork based on the LT 'Bluebird' design but their capacity was held at forty-eight.

The 46 bodies supplied to East Surrey by Ransomes Sims and Jefferies were of the same design as prototype ST 1 with square cab, although for country service they were fitted with wicket type driver's cab doors. At first, the side lamps on these buses were carried on each side of the canopy but were later moved to the more normal positions at lower deck waistrail level. ST 1088B, seen operating from Hatfield garage on route 303, had originally been allocated to Autocar of Tunbridge Wells, hence its Kent registration. D.W.K. Jones

This nearside view of ST 1097B shows the profile of the standard ST body and illustrates the capacious full width platform, a feature shared with the LT class but which must have been of little or no value on even the busiest Country services. The side number indicator was either removed altogether in later years or replaced by a box of the same type as fitted at the front. Snook & Son; Ken Glazier collection

In addition to the Amersham & District pair, London Transport acquired another 201 STs from other independent operators acquired in 1933. The largest contingent comprised 191 short wheelbase Regents which had been purchased by Thomas Tilling Ltd in 1930/31 to replace Tilling Stevens petrol-electrics (ST 837–1027; coded ST7). These had distinctive rather old-fashioned looking Tilling-built bodywork with open staircases. Four London Independents contributed one each. Two of these had open staircase bodywork, Dodson-bodied ST 1029 from F.J.C. Kirk and Birch-bodied ST 1031 from Pembroke. The two enclosed staircase vehicles came from Chariot (ST 1028, Birch body) and Pro Bono Publico (ST 1030, Dodson). The open staircase with which ST 1028 had been built had been enclosed by the time it was acquired but London Transport converted it back to its original condition in June 1934. The remaining six STs were acquired from the Lewis Omnibus Co. Ltd of Watford in October 1933 and originally had Short Bros enclosed staircase bodywork (ST 1133–1138), but by 1939 ST 1135 had been rebodied with a standard ST2 body and ST 1136 and 1137 with ST1/1 bodies.

ST 1–817 and 822–1031 joined the Central Bus fleet, painted red, and the remainder went into the Country Bus department and were painted green. Two Country STs were transferred to Central and painted red in 1937, ST 819 and 820. The STs continued in uneventful service until the summer of 1939 when a start was made on their withdrawal. ST 1028, 1030, 1031 and 42 Tillings were taken out of service and put into store, where they were at the end of 1939.

There were six STs with lowbridge Short Bros bodywork, bought by the LGOC specifically for operation on route N6 (later renumbered 336) by the National Omnibus and Transport Company. They were standard models from that manufacturer and were based on the design patented by Leyland for their Titan, but with two sunken gangways on each side of the upper deck. The Short Bros personality was stamped on the design by the oval window on the rear panel of the lower saloon. ST 141B is at Watford Junction at the outset of its journey to Berkhamsted, a destination served by the route until May 1936. D.A. Ruddom collection

There is some uncertainty about the provenance of the body on ST 1090B, one of the two lowbridge Regents acquired from Amersham & District, but most probably it was built by Strachan to a design very similar to the Short Bros product. In London Transport ownership these two buses were used alongside the former LGOC vehicles on route 336. D.W.K. Jones

The legal lettering shows that ST 898 is now owned by the LPTB, it has received an LPTB style fleet number and has been fitted with standard garage and running number plates but it still carries the Thomas Tilling fleet name. The Tilling version of the ST had an old-fashioned appearance although contemporary with the LGOC type, notably in its adherence to the three-window arrangement at the front of the upper deck, the open staircase and the high skirt line. The Omnibus Society

In 1939, when the Tilling STs were becoming due for withdrawal, ST 839 had its lower deck altered with STL-type panels, a lower skirt and an STL driver's cab. The purpose of the alterations is not known. It is at Thornton Heath Pond, the northern extremity of route 59 on Monday–Saturday. D.W.K. Jones

ST 1028 was one of four broadly similar vehicles acquired from London Independents, in this case from Chariot Omnibus Services Ltd of Shepherd's Bush. Its Birch body had come to London Transport with an enclosed back but had reverted to its original open staircase condition in June 1934. It was unusual in having half-drop windows in the nearside and offside sections of the upper deck front and an oval window in the staircase panel. It has also had its original cab replaced by one of the standard LGOC rounded type. D.W.K. Jones

ST 1029 had a Dodson six-bay body and had been the sole bus in the fleet of F.J. Kirk of Leyton. Like the other former Independent STs it was allocated by London Transport to Croydon garage and is seen on route 75 at Caterham. D.W.K. Jones

The five-bay Birch body mounted on ST 1031, which came from E.G. Hope of Brixton, was of a more familiar style than ST 1028, the downward slope of the driver's cab canopy being a characteristic of Birch's designs of the period. The staircase panel is also set at a lower, more normal, level. D.W.K. Jones

The Country Bus 'Bluebird' STs were identical in all respects other than being shorter, to the equivalent LTs in the Central Area but their potential capacity was not exploited and they had only 48 seats. APC163, which became ST 1033B in 1935, is at Rickmansworth. J.F. Higham

The six STs acquired from the Lewis Omnibus Co. of Watford had standard Short Bros highbridge bodies of the same basic six-bay design as the LGOC's lowbridge examples. That originally on ST 1138 had been built later than the others and was of a slightly different design. ST 1133B has been transferred south to Reigate garage, probably in exchange for Bluebird STs, and is on route 405 at Crawley. The angle of view well illustrates the heavily V-shaped front upper deck windows and the projection of the between decks section forward of the upper deck saloon windows. G.J. Robbins

UU6610 was the oldest Regent in the fleet but took the highest number, ST 1139, in 1935 because of the position in the alphabet of its registration letters. Its Short Bros body was of the same basic design as the LGOC lowbridge and former Lewis highbridge buses. It was one of the many double-deck buses drafted into Grays for the busy Purfleet road, on which route it was working when photographed in Grays Town Centre. Ken Glazier collection

Chassis:	AEC Regent 661
Engine:	AEC A140 6-cylinder 6.1 litre 95bhp petrol
Transmission:	AEC D124 4-speed crash
Bodywork:	LGOC (Chiswick), Short Bros. or Strachan (ST 1–836); Thos. Tilling or Dodson (ST 837–1027); LGOC (ST 1032–1039, 1070–1084); Short Bros. (ST 1040–1069, 1089, 1133–1139[1]); Ransomes Sims and Jefferies (ST 1085–1088, 1091–1132); Strachan (ST 1090); Birch (ST 1028, 1031); Dodson (ST 1029, 1030)
Capacity:	L24/24R (ST 136, 140, 141, 157, 162, 163, 1089, 1090); H30/26R (ST 1028)[2]; H30/26RO (ST 1031)[3]; H30/24R (ST 1030)[4]; H30/24RO (ST 1029)[5]; H27/25RO (837–1027); H26/22R (1032–1039, 1070–1084); H27/24RO (1139); H29/20R (remainder).[6]
L.T. chassis code:	1 or 2/1ST (1–836, 1040–1069, 1085–1139, except lowbridge: 3/1ST); 2ST (837–1027, 1031); 1/2ST (ST 1028–1030); 3ST (1032–1039, 1070–84).
L.T. Body codes:	ST3 (see text); ST4 (1032–1039, 1070–1084); ST6 (see text); ST6/1 (see text); ST7 (838–1027); ST8 (ST 1028–1031); ST9 (107, 111, 116, 129, 132, 135, 143, 152, 159, 818–821, 1040–1069, 1085–1088, 1091–1139); ST9/1 (lowbridge except ST 1090); ST9/3 (ST 1090); ST1/1, ST2 or ST2/1 (remainder).
Built:	1929–1932
Number built:	1138 (plus one instructional chassis)
Number in stock:	1.7.33: 935 31.12.39: 1137 (plus ST 169 – instruction chassis)

[1] ST 1135–1137 rebodied with standard ST bodies in March, June and May 1939 respectively
[2] Reseated as H28/26R in 5.34; converted to open staircase as H28/24RO in 6.34; and reseated to H28/26RO in 11.38
[3] Reseated to 52 in 5.34 and to 54 in 9.36
[4] Reseated to H30/23R in 12.34
[5] Later reseated to H30/26RO
[6] Reclassified as H28/20R during 1939 (by making the rear upper deck seat for four instead of five)

ST

No.	Reg.	No.	Reg.	No.	Reg.
1	UU6614	36	GC3952	71	GC3990
2	GO7154	37	GC3950	72	GC3987
3	GC3927	38	GC3972	73	GC3989
4	GC3928	39	GC3961	74	GC3995
5	GC3930	40	GC3971	75	GF423
6	GC3931	41	GC3959	76	GF409
7	GC3939	42	GC3981	77	GF416
8	GC3937	43	GC3975	78	GF467
9	GC3932	44	GC3976	79	GC3998
10	GC3942	45	GC3962	80	GF401
11	GC3935	46	GC3954	81	GC3994
12	GC3938	47	GC3963	82	GF405
13	GC3933	48	GC3964	83	GF406
14	GC3936	49	GC3967	84	GC3999
15	GC3944	50	GC3965	85	GF431
16	GC3946	51	GC3980	86	GF403
17	GC3941	52	GC3985	87	GF7203
18	GC3934	53	GC3982	88	GF410
19	GC3940	54	GC3977	89	GF418
20	GC3951	55	GC3978	90	GF417
21	GC3955	56	GC3979	91	GF469
22	GC3945	57	GC3986	92	GF414
23	GC3943	58	GF486	93	GF422
24	GC3947	59	GC3983	94	GF487
25	GC3970	60	GC3974	95	GF462
26	GC3968	61	GC3997	96	GF443
27	GC3958	62	GF404	97	GF484
28	GC3969	63	GC3991	98	GF407
29	GC3949	64	GC3992	99	GF411
30	GC3966	65	GC3993	100	GF413
31	GC3973	66	GC3984	101	GF412
32	GC3960	67	GC3988	102	GF415
33	GC3956	68	GF408	103	GF442
34	GC3948	69	GC3996	104	GF436
35	GC3957	70	GF402	105	GF424

ST

106	GF437	174	GN2075	242	GH554
107	GF425	175	GF7206	243	GH569
108	GF426	176	GF7219	244	GH567
109	GF421	177	GF7223	245	GH558
110	GF429	178	GF7224	246	GH559
111	GF427	179	GF7225	247	GH561
112	GF430	180	GF7220	248	GH562
113	GF432	181	GF7221	249	GH563
114	GF419	182	GF7226	250	GH574
115	GF420	183	GF7227	251	GH580
116	GF428	184	GF7229	252	GH565
117	GF439	185	GF7222	253	GH566
118	GF433	186	GF7230	254	GH568
119	GF472	187	GF7231	255	GH564
120	GF434	188	GF7242	256	GH572
121	GF435	189	GF7235	257	GH573
122	GF444	190	GF7232	258	GH587
123	GF478	191	GF7234	259	GH571
124	GF448	192	GF7236	260	GH570
125	GF451	193	GF7240	261	GJ7966
126	GF473	194	GF7241	262	GH577
127	GF7211	195	GF7233	263	GH578
128	GF7209	196	GF7238	264	GJ7967
129	GF438	197	GF7239	265	GH579
130	GF454	198	GF7237	266	GH588
131	GF447	199	GF7248	267	GH581
132	GF440	200	GF7243	268	GH582
133	GF445	201	GF7249	269	GJ7968
134	GF466	202	GF7244	270	GH591
135	GF441	203	GF7245	271	GH592
# 136	GF7213	204	GF7247	272	GH593
137	GF7210	205	GF7246	273	GH594
138	GF452	206	GF7250	274	GH596
139	GF7202	207	GF7252	275	GH597
# 140	GF7214	208	GJ7954	276	GH595
# 141	GF7217	209	GJ7955	277	GH598
142	GF450	210	GJ7953	278	GH599
143	GF457	211	GK3002	279	GH583
144	GF477	212	GF7253	280	GF552
145	GF453	213	GJ7956	281	GF553
146	GF463	214	GJ7951	282	GF554
147	GF461	215	GJ7958	283	GF556
148	GF458	216	GJ7952	284	GJ7969
149	GF446	217	GH544	285	GF7260
150	GF465	218	GH547	286	GJ7970
151	GF7204	219	GH545	287	GF489
152	GF474	220	GJ7964	288	GH600
153	GF459	221	GH541	289	GH601
154	GH3863	222	GH555	290	GH584
155	GF455	223	GH556	291	GH602
156	GF449	224	GH546	292	GH585
# 157	GF7201	225	GH548	293	GH589
158	GF7205	226	GH549	294	GH603
159	GF475	227	GH550	295	GF7255
160	GF464	228	GJ7957	296	GF7256
161	GF460	229	GJ7962	297	GF7257
# 162	GF7218	230	GJ7960	298	GH590
# 163	GF7215	231	GJ7959	299	GF7258
164	GF456	232	GH543	300	GH586
165	GF470	233	GJ7963	301	GF7259
166	GF7212	234	GJ7961	302	GH3878
167	GF471	235	GH560	303	GH3879
168	GF468	236	GJ7965	304	GH3880
a 169		237	GH542	305	GH3891
170	GF490	238	GH551	306	GH8006
171	GF476	239	GH552	307	GH8020
172	GF7228	240	GH553	308	GH8050
173	GF485	241	GH557	309	GH8052

a Instruction chassis at Chiswick Works; never bodied.
lowbridge body

ST

ST		ST		ST	
310	GH8046	381	GK3043	452	GK3099
311	GH8053	382	GK3045	453	GK3133
312	GH8055	383	GK3123	454	GK3080
313	GH8048	384	GK3038	455	GK3114
314	GH8056	385	GK3057	456	GK3135
315	GH8047	386	GK3028	457	GK3130
316	GH8054	387	GK3120	458	GK3139
317	GH8057	388	GK3059	459	GK3117
318	GH8064	389	GK3040	460	GK3151
319	GH8060	390	GK3083	461	GK3149
320	GH8051	391	GK3048	462	GK3054
321	GH8059	392	GK3119	463	GK3079
322	GH8058	393	GK3036	464	GK3056
323	GH8063	394	GK3029	465	GK5305
324	GH8062	395	GK3047	466	GK3055
325	GH8069	396	GK3134	467	GK3091
326	GH8067	397	GK3063	468	GK5311
327	GH8066	398	GK3118	469	GK3086
328	GH8061	399	GK3044	470	GK3141
329	GH8070	400	GK3030	471	GK5308
330	GH8065	401	GK3062	472	GK3142
331	GH8068	402	GK3116	473	GK3126
332	GH8071	403	GK3065	474	GK3088
333	GH8075	404	GK3052	475	GK3103
334	GK3005	405	GK3129	476	GK3085
335	GH8072	406	GK3115	477	GK3087
336	GH533	407	GK3053	478	GK5302
337	GH8074	408	GK3064	479	GK5303
338	GH535	409	GK3145	480	GK3093
339	GH8076	410	GK3081	481	GK5312
340	GK3006	411	GK3061	482	GK5309
341	GH536	412	GK3068	483	GK3106
342	GK3008	413	GK3089	484	GK3136
343	GK3037	414	GK3071	485	GK3121
344	GH534	415	GK3122	486	GK3104
345	GK3009	416	GK3096	487	GK3102
346	GK3012	417	GK3066	488	GK3125
347	GK3042	418	GK5301	489	GK3153
348	GK3014	419	GK3137	490	GK3124
349	GK3001	420	GK3072	491	GK3109
350	GK3004	421	GK3095	492	GK3143
351	GK3017	422	GK3074	493	GK5307
352	GK3018	423	GK3138	494	GK5310
353	GK3016	424	GK3094	495	GK3146
354	GK3007	425	GK3097	496	GK3152
355	GK3031	426	GK3084	497	GK5304
356	GK3013	427	GK3069	498	GK3131
357	GK3010	428	GK3107	499	GK3148
358	GK3021	429	GK3157	500	GK3140
359	GK3022	430	GK3073	501	GK5306
360	GK3041	431	GK3158	502	GF7261
361	GK3015	432	GK3110	503	GF7262
362	GK3023	433	GK3098	504	GF7263
363	GH8077	434	GK3105	505	GF7264
364	GH8078	435	GK3039	506	GF7265
365	GK3027	436	GK3156	507	GF7266
366	GK3019	437	GK3111	508	GF7267
367	GK3020	438	GK3128	509	GF7268
368	GK3024	439	GK3154	510	GH3861
369	GK3033	440	GK3060	511	GH3853
370	GH8073	441	GK3144	512	GH3854
371	GK3011	442	GK3113	513	GH3862
372	GK3032	443	GK3051	514	GH3856
373	GK3025	444	GK3058	515	GH3855
374	GK3046	445	GK3112	516	GH3857
375	GK3155	446	GK3147	517	GH3865
376	GK3082	447	GK3150	518	GK5330
377	GK3067	448	GK3127	519	GK5334
378	GK3035	449	GK3092	520	GK5332
379	GK3034	450	GK3078	521	GK5329
380	GK3026	451	GK3077	522	GK5328

ST

523	GK5344
524	GK5335
525	GK5346
526	GK5337
527	GK5336
528	GK5345
529	GK5350
530	GK5343
531	GK5357
532	GK5349
533	GK5362
534	GK5348
535	GK5338
536	GK5347
537	GK5376
538	GK5370
539	GK5364
540	GK5363
541	GK5359
542	GK5369
543	GK5360
544	GK5361
545	GK5377
546	GK5358
547	GK5375
548	GK5373
549	GK5368
550	GK5374
551	GK5372
552	GK5380
553	GK5393
554	GK5378
555	GK5379
556	GK5395
557	GK5384
558	GK5381
559	GK5391
560	GK5385
561	GK5389
562	GK5382
563	GK5383
564	GK5388
565	GK5392
566	GK5390
567	GK5396
568	GK5394
569	GK5386
570	GK5387
571	GK5398
572	GK5397
573	GK5402
574	GK5399
575	GK5406
576	GK5401
577	GK5414
578	GK5412
579	GK5418
580	GK5404
581	GK5424
582	GK5419
583	GK5423
584	GK5403
585	GK5407
586	GK5434
587	GK5413
588	GK5405
589	GK5422
590	GK5410
591	GK5453
592	GK5420
593	GK5426

ST

594	GK3194
595	GK5435
596	GK5425
597	GN4697
598	GK5421
599	GK5411
600	GK5438
601	GN4797
602	GK5440
603	GK5439
604	GK5456
605	GK5444
606	GK5448
607	GK5452
608	GK5451
609	GK5455
610	GK5449
611	GN4695
612	GK5443
613	GK5447
614	GK5450
615	GK5461
616	GK5479
617	GK5481
618	GK5460
619	GK5471
620	GK5469
621	GK5477
622	GK5470
623	GK5476
624	GN2028
625	GN2025
626	GN2009
627	GN2011
628	GK5473
629	GK5472
630	GK5483
631	GN2030
632	GK5468
633	GN2026
634	GK5467
635	GN2032
636	GN2010
637	GN2037
638	GK5475
639	GN2031
640	GK5474
641	GN2033
642	GK5482
643	GN2029
644	GN2027
645	GN4798
646	GN2036
647	GN2035
648	GK3196
649	GN2039
650	GN4693
651	GN4768
652	GN2096
653	GN2034
654	GN4769
655	GN2114
656	GN4631
657	GN2115
658	GN4765
659	GN4754
660	GN4636
661	GN4604
662	GN2160
663	GK3193
664	GN4640

ST

665	GN4632
666	GN4694
667	GN4755
668	GN4606
669	GN2111
670	GN2095
671	GN4675
672	GN4772
673	GN4773
674	GO603
675	GN4639
676	GN4633
677	GN4605
678	GN2113
679	GN4674
680	GN4760
681	GN2182
682	GN4641
683	GN4767
684	GN4766
685	GN4651
686	GK3195
687	GH3808
688	GN2116
689	GN4757
690	GN4786
691	GN4759
692	GN4770
693	GN2183
694	GN4692
695	GN2110
696	GN2181
697	GN2098
698	GN2112
699	GN2162
700	GN2097
701	GN4698
702	GN4696
703	GN4650
704	GN4613
705	GN4644
706	GN2175
707	GN4622
708	GN4619
709	GN4638
710	GN4611
711	GN2189
712	GN4610
713	GN4607
714	GN2173
715	GH8086
716	GH8087
717	GN4758
718	GN4771
719	GN4634
720	GN2155
721	GN4646
722	GN4645
723	GN4642
724	GH8088
725	GN2174
726	GN2154
727	GN4608
728	GN4620
729	GO7183
730	GN4788
731	GN2156
732	GN4609
733	GN2153
734	GN4635
735	GN4621

ST		ST		Date into stock	ST		Date into stock
736	GN4756	807	GO5151		878	GJ2054	1.10.33
737	GN4668	808	GO5142		879	GJ2055	1.10.33
738	GN2161	809	GO5140		880	GJ2056	1.10.33
739	GN2180	810	GO5148		881	GJ2057	1.10.33
740	GN4643	811	GO5150		882	GJ2058	1.10.33
741	GN4612	812	GO5189		883	GJ2059	1.10.33
742	GN4637	813	GO5190		884	GJ2060	1.10.33
743	GN4669	814	GO5195		885	GJ2061	1.10.33
744	GN2187	815	GO7105		886	GJ2062	1.10.33
745	GN2188	816	GO7106		887	GJ2063	1.10.33
746	GO7110	817	GO7114		888	GJ2064	1.10.33
747	GO615	818	GN4614		889	GJ2065	1.10.33
748	GO616	819	GH3809		890	GJ2066	1.10.33
749	GO602	820	GN2163		891	GJ2067	1.10.33
750	GO610	821	GK3192		892	GJ2068	1.10.33
751	GO634	822	GN2128		893	GJ2069	1.10.33
752	GO657	823	GN2093		894	GJ2070	1.10.33
753	GO652	824	GN2089		895	GJ2071	1.10.33
754	GO653	825	GN2090		896	GJ2072	1.10.33
755	GO645	826	GN2094		897	GJ2073	1.10.33
756	GO5106	827	GN4649		898	GJ2074	1.10.33
757	GO658	828	GN4623		899	GJ2075	1.10.33
758	GO663	829	GN4624		900	GJ2076	1.10.33
759	GO678	830	GN4625		901	GJ2077	1.10.33
760	GO659	831	GN4670		902	GJ2078	1.10.33
761	GO5108	832	GN4733		903	GJ2079	1.10.33
762	GO697	833	GN4731		904	GJ2080	1.10.33
763	GO5130	834	GN4732		905	GJ2081	1.10.33
764	GO662	835	GN4730		906	GJ2082	1.10.33
765	GO5109	836	GN4734		907	GJ2083	1.10.33
766	GO5145	837	GJ2013	1.10.33	908	GJ2084	1.10.33
767	GO664	838	GJ2014	1.10.33	909	GJ2085	1.10.33
768	GO660	839	GJ2015	1.10.33	910	GJ2086	1.10.33
769	GO686	840	GJ2016	1.10.33	911	GJ2087	1.10.33
770	GO687	841	GJ2017	1.10.33	912	GJ2088	1.10.33
771	GO5172	842	GJ2018	1.10.33	913	GJ2089	1.10.33
772	GO5163	843	GJ2019	1.10.33	914	GJ2090	1.10.33
773	GO696	844	GJ2020	1.10.33	915	GJ2091	1.10.33
774	GO5110	845	GJ2021	1.10.33	916	GJ2092	1.10.33
775	GO695	846	GJ2022	1.10.33	917	GJ2093	1.10.33
776	GO5149	847	GJ2023	1.10.33	918	GJ2094	1.10.33
777	GO5101	848	GJ2024	1.10.33	919	GJ2095	1.10.33
778	GO5136	849	GJ2025	1.10.33	920	GJ2096	1.10.33
779	GO5121	850	GJ2026	1.10.33	921	GJ2097	1.10.33
780	GO5105	851	GJ2027	1.10.33	922	GJ2098	1.10.33
781	GO5103	852	GJ2028	1.10.33	923	GJ2099	1.10.33
782	GO5102	853	GJ2029	1.10.33	924	GJ2100	1.10.33
783	GO5122	854	GJ2030	1.10.33	925	GK1001	1.10.33
784	GO5111	855	GJ2031	1.10.33	926	GK1002	1.10.33
785	GO5104	856	GJ2032	1.10.33	927	GK1003	1.10.33
786	GO5112	857	GJ2033	1.10.33	928	GK1004	1.10.33
787	GO5128	858	GJ2034	1.10.33	929	GK1005	1.10.33
788	GO5107	859	GJ2035	1.10.33	930	GK1006	1.10.33
789	GO5123	860	GJ2036	1.10.33	931	GK1007	1.10.33
790	GO5133	861	GJ2037	1.10.33	932	GK1008	1.10.33
791	GO5124	862	GJ2038	1.10.33	933	GK1009	1.10.33
792	GO5144	863	GJ2039	1.10.33	934	GK1010	1.10.33
793	GO5131	864	GJ2040	1.10.33	935	GK1011	1.10.33
794	GO5143	865	GJ2041	1.10.33	936	GK1012	1.10.33
795	GO5139	866	GJ2042	1.10.33	937	GK1013	1.10.33
796	GO7107	867	GJ2043	1.10.33	938	GK1014	1.10.33
797	GO5141	868	GJ2044	1.10.33	939	GK1015	1.10.33
798	GO5164	869	GJ2045	1.10.33	940	GK1016	1.10.33
799	GO5125	870	GJ2046	1.10.33	941	GK1017	1.10.33
800	GO5138	871	GJ2047	1.10.33	942	GK1018	1.10.33
801	GO5134	872	GJ2048	1.10.33	943	GK1019	1.10.33
802	GO5191	873	GJ2049	1.10.33	944	GK1020	1.10.33
803	GO5127	874	GJ2050	1.10.33	945	GK1021	1.10.33
804	GO5180	875	GJ2051	1.10.33	946	GK1022	1.10.33
805	GO5129	876	GJ2052	1.10.33	947	GK1023	1.10.33
806	GO5137	877	GJ2053	1.10.33	948	GK1024	1.10.33

ST		Date into stock	ST		Date into stock	ST		Date into stock
949	GK1025	1.10.33	1013	GK6289	1.10.33	1077	GX5321	
950	GK1026	1.10.33	1014	GK6290	1.10.33	1078	GX5322	
951	GK1027	1.10.33	1015	GK6291	1.10.33	1079	GX5323	
952	GK1028	1.10.33	1016	GK6292	1.10.33	1080	JH4646	
953	GK1029	1.10.33	1017	GK6293	1.10.33	1081	JH4647	
954	GK1030	1.10.33	1018	GK6294	1.10.33	1082	JH4648	
955	GK1031	1.10.33	1019	GK6295	1.10.33	1083	JH4649	
956	GK1032	1.10.33	1020	GK6296	1.10.33	1084	JH4650	
957	GK1033	1.10.33	1021	GK6297	1.10.33	1085	KR3886	
958	GK1034	1.10.33	1022	GK6298	1.10.33	1086	KR3892	
959	GK1035	1.10.33	1023	GN6225	1.10.33	1087	KR3893	
960	GK1036	1.10.33	1024	GP6227	1.10.33	1088	KR3894	
961	GK6237	1.10.33	1025	GP6228	1.10.33	* 1089	KX4656	1.10.33
962	GK6238	1.10.33	1026	GP6230	1.10.33	* 1090	KX5055	1.10.33
963	GK6239	1.10.33	1027	GP6236	1.10.33	1091	PG7593	
964	GK6240	1.10.33	1028	GJ8501	31.10.33	1092	PG7724	
965	GK6241	1.10.33	1029	VX7487	31.10.33	1093	PG7725	
966	GK6242	1.10.33	1030	VX7553	8.11.33	1094	PG7726	
967	GK6243	1.10.33	1031	GJ3020	9.11.33	1095	PG7727	
968	GK6244	1.10.33	1032	APC162		1096	PG7728	
969	GK6245	1.10.33	1033	APC163		1097	PG7836	
970	GK6246	1.10.33	1034	APC164		1098	PG7963	
971	GK6247	1.10.33	1035	APC165		1099	PG7964	
972	GK6248	1.10.33	1036	APC166		1100	PG7965	
973	GK6249	1.10.33	1037	APC168		1101	PG7966	
974	GK6250	1.10.33	1038	APC169		1102	PG7967	
975	GK6251	1.10.33	1039	APC170		1103	PG7968	
976	GK6252	1.10.33	1040	GN4699		1104	PG7969	
977	GK6253	1.10.33	1041	GN4707		1105	PG7970	
978	GK6254	1.10.33	1042	GN4715		1106	PG7971	
979	GK6255	1.10.33	1043	GN4725		1107	PG7972	
980	GK6256	1.10.33	1044	GN4726		1108	PG7973	
981	GK6257	1.10.33	1045	GN4761		1109	PG7974	
982	GK6258	1.10.33	1046	GN4762		1110	PG7975	
983	GK6259	1.10.33	1047	GN4780		1111	PG7976	
984	GK6260	1.10.33	1048	GN4789		1112	PG7977	
985	GK6261	1.10.33	1049	GN4796		1113	PG7978	
986	GK6262	1.10.33	1050	GO635		1114	PG7979	
987	GK6263	1.10.33	1051	GO636		1115	PG7980	
988	GK6264	1.10.33	1052	GO646		1116	PG7981	
989	GK6265	1.10.33	1053	GO647		1117	PG7982	
990	GK6266	1.10.33	1054	GO654		1118	PG7983	
991	GK6267	1.10.33	1055	GO698		1119	PG7984	
992	GK6268	1.10.33	1056	GO700		1120	PG7985	
993	GK6269	1.10.33	1057	GO5132		1121	PG7986	
994	GK6270	1.10.33	1058	GO5146		1122	PG7987	
995	GK6271	1.10.33	1059	GO5152		1123	PG7988	
996	GK6272	1.10.33	1060	GO5181		1124	PG7989	
997	GK6273	1.10.33	1061	GO5182		1125	PG7990	
998	GK6274	1.10.33	1062	GO5188		1126	PG7991	
999	GK6275	1.10.33	1063	GO5193		1127	PG7992	
1000	GK6276	1.10.33	1064	GO7108		1128	PG7993	
1001	GK6277	1.10.33	1065	GO7109		1129	PG7994	
1002	GK6278	1.10.33	1066	GO7115		1130	PG7995	
1003	GK6279	1.10.33	1067	GO7136		1131	PG7996	
1004	GK6280	1.10.33	1068	GO7156		1132	PG7997	
1005	GK6281	1.10.33	1069	GO7157		1133	UR5506	1.10.33
1006	GK6282	1.10.33	1070	GX5314		1134	UR5507	1.10.33
1007	GK6283	1.10.33	1071	GX5315		1135	UR5508	1.10.33
1008	GK6284	1.10.33	1072	GX5316		1136	UR5509	1.10.33
1009	GK6285	1.10.33	1073	GX5317		1137	UR5510	1.10.33
1010	GK6286	1.10.33	1074	GX5318		1138	UR7879	1.10.33
1011	GK6287	1.10.33	1075	GX5319		1139	UU6610	
1012	GK6288	1.10.33	1076	GX5320				

All STs were taken into stock from LGOC and LGCS on 1.7.33 unless otherwise shown.
* Lowbridge body

Although the MCCW metal-framed bodies of the DLs were virtually identical to the standard ST, they had a cleaner finish without the deep moulding below the lower deck windows and a modified design of dash panel to suit the Dennis radiator. DL 12 is at the Hadley Highstone terminus of route 284A, which became part of the 134 in October 1934.
J.F. Higham

DL

The LGOC bought a batch of 25 of the newly introduced Dennis Lance in 1931 for its Overground subsidiary at Potters Bar. They had Metro-Cammell metal-framed bodywork of the same basic design as the standard ST and similar to one fitted to ST 211. There were detail differences from the ST design, notably the absence of the deep moulding below the lower saloon windows and the ventilator grille on the driver's dash. The wheelbase of the Lance was longer than on the ST which meant that the rear bay had to be shorter and the doorway narrower. They were numbered D 1–25 in the Overground fleet and these were the numbers carried when they were taken over by London Transport. They were always classified DL by the LGOC and this classification was adopted by the LPTB. They were not taken into stock officially by London Transport until 7th July 1933.

Eight more Lances were acquired from Independent operators between October 1933 and November 1934 and these were eventually sent to Potters Bar to join the main batch. All the double-deck DLs remained there until November/December 1936 when they were transferred to Sutton, where they were presumably expected to spend several more years in service. However, the big reduction in the number of buses required following service cuts after the Busmen's strike in May 1937 led to their premature withdrawal and the last ran on 29th November 1937, one day before the last NS.

There were also six single-deckers and coaches included in the DL class.

Although its Overground fleet name has been replaced by 'GENERAL' and it is bearing LPTB legal lettering and colours, this Metro-Cammell bodied Dennis Lance in Buckingham Palace Road still carries the fleet number D 9, which was later changed to DL 9.
D.W.K. Jones

The first type of enclosed staircase Birch body was otherwise the same as the latest open staircase design although in the case of this former Ambassador bus the roof route number box alters its appearance significantly. The windscreen of DL 29 was fitted by London Transport as Ambassador was one of a small band of hardy operators who preferred not to have them. The familiar background of The Two Brewers at Hadley Highstone is now served by route 134, the new number for the former 284 group.
D.W.K. Jones

The final Birch design, although somewhat severe in appearance, was much the most modern looking bus produced for the Independent market, with its uncluttered upper deck front and generally clean lines. This photograph was taken at New Barnet on 1st April 1934, six weeks after DL 28 joined the London Transport fleet from Red Rover who had bought it in 1932. D.W.K. Jones

DL 27 came from Convey and Clayton of Edmonton and was in every way a typical Independent bus with Dodson six-bay open-staircase bodywork. The photograph was taken sometime in 1934 when the GENERAL fleet name was in use and the route was still numbered 284. D.W.K. Jones

Chassis:	Dennis Lance
Engine:	Dennis 6-cylinder 6.1 litre 100 bhp petrol
Transmission:	Dennis 4-speed crash
Bodywork:	Birch (DL 28,29); Dodson (DL 26, 27, 30–33); Metro-Cammell (DL 1–25)
Capacity:	H30/26R (DL 29[4]); H30/24RO (DL 27[2]); H29/25R (DL 28[3]);
	H29/20R (DL 1–25); H28/26R (DL 30[4,5]); H28/24RO (DL 26[1]);
	H28/24R (DL 31[4]); H27/24R (DL 32[6], 33[4])
L.T. codes:	Not allocated
Built:	1930 (DL 26, 27, 29, 31–33); 1931 (DL 1–24); 1932 (DL 25, 28, 30)
Number built:	33
Number in stock	1.7.33: Nil 31.12.39: Nil Last in stock: 12.4.38

[1] DL 26 reseated to H26/24RO in 1.34
[2] DL 27 reseated to H28/24RO in 2.34 and to H30/24RO in 5.37
[3] DL 28 reseated to H28/25R in 5.34
[4] DL 29–33 reseated to H24/24R in 10.34 or 12.34 (DL 32, 33)
[5] DL 30 further reseated to H24/26R in 11.35
[6] DL 32 further reseated to H26/24R in 3.36

		Acquired from	Date into stock	Date out of stock
1	GP3414	Overground Ltd, Potters Bar (owned by LGOC)	7.7.33	12.4.38
2	GO7182	Overground Ltd, Potters Bar (owned by LGOC)	7.7.33	8.4.38
3	GP3410	Overground Ltd, Potters Bar (owned by LGOC)	7.7.33	12.4.38
4	GP3424	Overground Ltd, Potters Bar (owned by LGOC)	7.7.33	9.4.38
5	GP3408	Overground Ltd, Potters Bar (owned by LGOC)	7.7.33	12.4.38
6	GP3428	Overground Ltd, Potters Bar (owned by LGOC)	7.7.33	11.4.38
7	GP3426	Overground Ltd, Potters Bar (owned by LGOC)	7.7.33	11.4.38
8	GP3423	Overground Ltd, Potters Bar (owned by LGOC)	7.7.33	11.4.38
9	GP3443	Overground Ltd, Potters Bar (owned by LGOC)	7.7.33	12.4.38
10	GP3482	Overground Ltd, Potters Bar (owned by LGOC)	7.7.33	11.4.38
11	GP3463	Overground Ltd, Potters Bar (owned by LGOC)	7.7.33	12.4.38
12	GP3427	Overground Ltd, Potters Bar (owned by LGOC)	7.7.33	12.4.38
13	GP3465	Overground Ltd, Potters Bar (owned by LGOC)	7.7.33	12.4.38
14	GP3449	Overground Ltd, Potters Bar (owned by LGOC)	7.7.33	7.4.38
15	GP3475	Overground Ltd, Potters Bar (owned by LGOC)	7.7.33	8.4.38
16	GP3464	Overground Ltd, Potters Bar (owned by LGOC)	7.7.33	9.4.38
17	GP3483	Overground Ltd, Potters Bar (owned by LGOC)	7.7.33	11.4.38
18	GP3425	Overground Ltd, Potters Bar (owned by LGOC)	7.7.33	12.4.38
19	GP3476	Overground Ltd, Potters Bar (owned by LGOC)	7.7.33	12.4.38
20	GP3484	Overground Ltd, Potters Bar (owned by LGOC)	7.7.33	9.4.38
21	GP3600	Overground Ltd, Potters Bar (owned by LGOC)	7.7.33	8.4.38
22	GP3409	Overground Ltd, Potters Bar (owned by LGOC)	7.7.33	6.4.38
23	GP3497	Overground Ltd, Potters Bar (owned by LGOC)	7.7.33	8.4.38
24	GP3526	Overground Ltd, Potters Bar (owned by LGOC)	7.7.33	12.4.38
25	GT5001	Overground Ltd, Potters Bar (owned by LGOC)	7.7.33	6.4.38
26	GK8667	Cardinal Omnibus Co. Ltd (Claremont), Islington	30.10.33	12.4.38
27	HX2171	B. Convey & C.W. Clayton (C.C.), Edmonton	9.11.33	12.4.38
28	GY1961	Red Rover Omnibus Co. Ltd, Fulham	14.2.34	9.4.38
* 29	GK7167	Ambassador Bus Company Ltd, Upper Holloway	25.8.34	8.4.38
* 30	GX143	Ambassador Bus Company Ltd, Upper Holloway	25.8.34	8.4.38
31	GK7166	Sphere Omnibus Co. Ltd, Upper Holloway	28.8.34	11.4.38
32	VX8363	Reliance Omnibus Company Ltd, Chingford	6.11.34	7.4.38
33	VX8364	Reliance Omnibus Company Ltd, Chingford	6.11.34	8.4.38

* Two Dennis Lancet coaches and two buses were at first given the numbers DL 29 , 30, 34, 35 but were later renumbered DT 4 –7 (see volume on single-deckers).

The three DST class Daimler CH6s acquired from the LGOC had standard ST-type 49-seat bodywork built at Chiswick, the only significant difference being the treatment of the driver's cab dash panel. The frame of the driver's windscreen on DST 2 appears to have been painted black at some time. G. Robbins Collection

DST

The original three DSTs were a landmark in the development of the standard London bus as they were the first to be bought by the LGOC with epicyclic gearboxes and fluid transmission and their success in this respect soon led to further experiments on ST and LT-type buses. They were Daimler CH6s with the same 5.7 litre sleeve valve petrol engine as used in the LS-type, which had not proved very successful. DST 3 was fitted with a new poppet valve engine in 1931, when this became available from Daimler but the others were not altered. DST 1–3 were fitted with Chiswick-built 49-seat bodies of the ST type.

Two more double-deck Daimlers were acquired, one each from the Eagle Omnibus Company (DST 4) and E. Brickwood (DST 5). DST 4 was a CF6 and was an early casualty, being withdrawn in 1934 but the others continued in service until February 1935 when they were withdrawn. Their chassis were sold but their bodies were retained and mounted on four special short-wheelbase AEC Regents numbered STL 1260–1263. One other vehicle was numbered in the class, DST 6, a coach which will be found in the single-deck volume.

Chassis:	Daimler CF6 (DST 4); CH6 (DST 1–3, 5)
Engine:	Daimler CV35 6-cylinder sleeve-valve 5.76 85 bhp petrol (DST 1, 2, 4, 5); or 6-cylinder poppet-valve 6.56 litre 90 bhp petrol (DST 3)
Transmission:	Daimler/Wilson preselective with fluid flywheel
Bodywork:	Birch (DST 4, 5); LGOC (DST 1–3);
Capacity:	H30/26RO (DST 4); H28/24R (DST 5); H29/20R (DST 1–3)
L.T. codes:	not allocated
Built:	1930 (DST 4); 1931 (DST 1–3, 5)
Number built or acquired:	5
Number in stock	1.7.33: 3 31.12.39: Nil Last in stock: 28.8.35

DST		Date into stock	Date out of stock
1	GK5333	1.7.33	c 28.8.35
2	GK5415	1.7.33	c 6.3.35
3	GK5408	1.7.33	c 1.3.35
4	GC7388	9.11.33	4.7.35
5	GO5538	1.12.33	c 4.3.35

c – Chassis only; bodies used for STL 1260–1263

The style of the enclosed staircase Birch body on DST 5 appears to have been unique to this bus. Notable features include the two opening windows at the front of the upper deck and the mixture of board and roller blind indicators. The combination of the roof box route number indicator with the front window layout gave the bus the look of an LGOC design. J.F. Higham

STL

New Regulations which increased the maximum permitted length of double-deckers from 25ft to 26ft and the maximum gross weight for two-axle vehicles from 9½ to 10 tons, prompted AEC to launch a longer, 16ft 3in wheelbase version of the Regent chassis at the end of 1931. This was ordered by both Thomas Tilling Ltd, who put the first into service in October 1932, and the London General Omnibus Company. There were eighty of the Thomas Tilling version (STL 51–130), built to a six-bay design based on the company's STs but with enclosed staircases, the upper deck brought forward over the driver's cab and a deeper skirt panel. Internally they had polished mahogany window finishers and lightweight tubular framed seats. Tilling's specification called for a downrated version of the A140 engine (A140E) which had a swept volume of only 5.5 litres, with a view to economy of operation, and excluded self-starters. Self-starters were fitted by London Transport during 1934 and most buses received more powerful engines of the A140 type when their originals became due for replacement. They were given the code 8STL4 when the new system was introduced by LPTB. There were to have been another twenty-two to complete the replacement of the General owned Tilling Stevens O type but these were never ordered and London Transport standardised instead on the LGOC design. For reasons unknown, the missing numbers were never used. Other changes made by London Transport included the replacement during 1934–1935 of driver's windscreens by a more robust type with a larger opening section and the removal at first overhaul of the nearside route number blind, which was replaced by a standard stencil plate holder at the bottom of the rear lower deck saloon window. Following the experimental reduction of the seating capacity of STL 79 and 62 to fifty-five and fifty-four respectively, the remainder were altered to 55-seaters between September 1934 and August 1935. They reverted to fifty-six seats between March 1936 and June 1937.

The Bluebird design was adapted for use on a third chassis type to provide the bodies for the first 100 STLs ordered by the LGOC. The upper deck was carried well forward to be in line with the radiator, enabling 60 seats to be fitted into a 26ft long bus. These were also the first enclosed staircase buses to have a full display of route number, intermediate point and destination indicators at the back. STL 184, here ready to set off from Elmers End garage on route 54, was delivered after the formation of the LPTB. The Omnibus Society

This offside view of STL 173 at Victoria in May 1937 makes an interesting comparison with Q 3 behind it.
G.H.F. Atkins

There were two batches of the original LGOC type (STL 1–50 and 153–202). Their body design was based on the Bluebird LT and the same seating capacity of sixty was achieved by carrying the upper deck as far forward as possible, in line with the radiator. To keep within the gross weight limit the bodywork was austerely finished with lightweight seats, single panelling throughout and without the deep side mouldings which had been characteristic of the T, ST and LT types. Another difference from the Bluebird LTs was the arrangement of route and destination indicators which were brought together in a group between the decks. For the first time, a similar three-piece display was carried at the back as well. All but one had the A140 petrol engine and D124 crash gearbox, the exception being STL 50 which was fitted with a Daimler preselective gearbox, without fluid flywheel. It was coded 3STL1, although its chassis differed from the later 3STLs and the body was not identical to the other STL1s. It was later reclassified 3STL1/1. Twenty of the first batch were fitted with fully floating rear axles and the second (2STL1) had a coil ignition and differences in the exhaust system. The 2STL1s, which were part of an order for one hundred, were still being delivered when the LPTB was formed and the remainder of the type were the first new buses put into service by the Board.

The Tilling STL was a lengthened, closed staircase version of the ST design with the upper deck extended over the driver's cab and a deeper skirt panel. Their six-bay construction and three-window arrangement at the front gave them an outdated and cramped look but their interior finish of polished mahogany panels and tubular steel framed seats was superior to that of the LGOC type. They later had their sidelamps moved down from the canopy to waistrail level. Like the STs they remained loyal to former Tilling garages throughout the 1930s. STL 124 is a Croydon bus at Rennell Street, Lewisham soon after the Tilling business was acquired. Ken Glazier collection

In 1933, the LGOC had decided to standardise on a capacity of fifty-six for double-deckers and this cleared the way for an improved design with a sloping front and more rounded back, which was applied to the last fifty of the second batch, delivered between August and October 1933 (STL 203–252; 3STL2). These had petrol engines and Daimler D128 preselective gearboxes, without fluid flywheels. The last LGOC order was for one hundred, fifty with preselective gearboxes (STL 253–291, 4STL3/2; 342–352, 5STL3/1), of which the last eleven were to have the new experimental A171 oil engine and fluid flywheels, and fifty with crash (STL 292–341; 6STL3). These were completed between November 1933 and April 1934. The petrol engines for STL 253–341 were reconditioned units removed from LTs and were therefore of the A145 type. The LTs received new 8.8 litre oil engines.

A number of experiments were carried out during the early days of these vehicles. An alternative to the fluid flywheel, the Sinclair Traction Coupling was tried on STL 252 in March 1934. Although not adopted it was tried out on a larger number of later STLs. STL 221 was fitted with a Leyland hydraulic torque convertor which used the Lysholm Smith system and retained this transmission until August 1937. Seven of the oil-engined batch were fitted with crash gearboxes for a time (STL 343–344, 347–350) and two ran with synchromesh gearboxes (STL 345, 346) but all soon reverted to preselective gearboxes. STL 346 had experimental air brakes which were replaced by the standard Lockheed type in August 1935. STL 352 had its Daimler D128 gearbox replaced by the new AEC D132 unit soon after delivery and the others were soon treated similarly. The design was adopted as standard from the spring of 1934. In 1938 STLs 253, 263 and 290 were converted experimentally to run with synchromesh gearboxes, which were still fitted at the end of 1939; they were reclassified 1/4STL.

The STL2 body was a first step towards the more curvaceous design which grew to full flower in the STL5 (see page 88) and introduced the more rounded rear end which remained a feature of the standard STL until 1939. The front was not a thing of beauty, the styling being merely a sloped version of the STL1. The four angular transitions between the different parts of the body and the rather clumsy looking angled front upper deck windows are clearly shown in this official picture of STL 203, the earliest of the first main run of preselector STLs. London's Transport Museum

There were 350 STLs with bodies of a fundamentally similar design to that carried by STL 444 at Raynes Park, with a mixture of crash and preselective gearboxes. Earlier examples, such as this, had route number indicator boxes with glass of the same size as the route number and a thick beading separating the lower deck side panels. Later examples had a full depth glass, masked top and bottom and a slimmer beading similar to the STL5 parked behind. STL 444 was among the first to be fitted with the new AEC preselective gearbox. J. Higham

The first order placed by the LPTB was for a further hundred similar vehicles which were delivered between March and June 1934, the order again being split half and half crash (STL 353–402; 6STL3) and preselective, with fluid flywheels (STL 403–452; 7STL3/2). The petrol engines were again A145 type recovered from LTs. By this time, the Board had decided to standardise on the Wilson preselective gearbox and the units fitted to the 7STLs were AEC's own design, the D132. The next 150, delivered between June and October 1934, also had A145 petrol engines recovered from LTs and all were fitted with the D132 preselective gearbox and fluid flywheel (STL 453–552, 559–608; 7STL3/2). These had some minor changes to the bodywork, the most noticeable being the full depth glass on the route number boxes, masked at top and bottom, and a thinner aluminium beading between the lower deck panels instead of the earlier wooden type. Eleven of the 7STLs were equipped with Sinclair traction couplings in December 1934 and January 1935, continuing the experiment started on STL 252 (STL 470, 473, 474, 477, 479, 481–483, 485, 487 and 489). They reverted to standard preselective transmission in about November or December 1935 but the experiment continued on STL 431 for a time.

The rear of STL 420 in Crystal Palace Parade shows the more rounded profile which replaced the severely upright lines of the STL1 body and was to remain the basic styling for all subsequent standard STLs. The Central Bus livery in this period comprised a silver roof, white upper deck and lower deck window pillars, red main body panels and black dividing bands between the roof and the upper deck windows and at cantrail level.
The Omnibus Society

The final version of the 'sloping body' design was the STL3/2, which had a full-depth glass in the number indicator box, masked in black above and below the route number. This had a surprisingly beneficial effect on its appearance. Willesden's STL 384, at work on route 18 at Euston, had a crash gearbox and was therefore omitted from the programme of conversion to oil engines in 1939. J. Higham

The five Regents acquired from Chas. H. Pickup were allocated to Croydon while still in their original open top condition to work on route 254, but STL 553 is on route 59 far from home at Camden Gardens under the shadow of the North London Railway.
J.F. Higham Collection

The missing numbers were applied to six unusually interesting AEC Regents acquired from Independents Charles H. Pickup (STL 553–556, 12STL8 and 557, 1/12STL8) and Brickwood (STL 558; 13STL9). The Pickup Regents had been the first of the type to operate in London and were famously unique in having 53-seat open-top bodywork with enclosed staircases, by Park Royal. They had A140 petrol engines and crash gearboxes, STL 557 differing from the others in having Lockheed brakes as fitted on the LGOC type. After a brief spell at Old Kent Road, these five buses were sent to Croydon garage for a time to replace the last of the O-type Tilling petrol-electrics operating on route 254 (later renumbered 64) where a low bridge determined the need for open toppers. The route was eventually altered to avoid the bridge and the Pickups were then fitted with new Chiswick top decks.

Still on route 59, STL 553 has now had a standard Chiswick top deck grafted onto the Park Royal body, giving this untidy mis-match between the six-bay lower deck and five-bay upper. The glass rainshields over the lower deck opening windows have been retained, making another odd contrast with the less elaborate upper deck. D.W.K. Jones

Former Redline Birch-bodied STL 558, as modified by Chiswick in 1934 with open staircase and board and stencil indicators, was transferred from Harrow Weald to Catford in November 1936 where it could be seen running alongside open staircase STs. Unlike the STs, STL 558 had fluid transmission and a preselective gearbox. D.W.K. Jones

STL 558 had Daimler preselective transmission and triple servo brakes and was fitted with a second-hand Birch Bros. body from a Daimler CF6, built in 1930 with open staircase. This had been lengthened and the staircase enclosed and it was in this condition that it joined London Transport's fleet. Following inspection at Chiswick Works when it was found that the body needed major renovation, it was rebuilt with an open staircase and route boards, instead of the roller blinds with which it had been acquired. Roller blinds were again fitted in 1939, but this time were the Board's standard size.

Twelve other STLs were delivered new to London Transport in April and May 1934 but, as they were intended for Country Buses, did not receive numbers until 1935 when they became STL 1044B–1055B (11STL7). These had standard provincial speci- fication chassis with AEC A165 8.8 litre oil engines and crash gearboxes and forty-eight seat forward-entrance lowbridge bodies by Weymann of Addlestone to their standard metal-framed design. They were bought to replace the PS-type at Godstone garage on route 410, which passed under a low bridge at Oxted. They were always known as the 'Godstone STLs'.

The standard Weymann metal-framed lowbridge body gives BPF269 (later STL 1045B) a distinctive non-London look. Apart from the overall design, the glass rainshields above the windows were a feature not to be found on any of its LPTB contemporaries. The limitations of the compressed between-decks panels have been skilfully overcome to allow the insertion of a full set of route and destination indicators. Ken Glazier collection

The cheerful lower deck interior of a 'Godstone' STL reveals other non-standard features, especially in the use of polished walnut for the window pillars, the design of the seats, the colourful moquette, the moulded glass covers on the lights and the green patterned covering applied to the interior panels. As the staircase had to land at right angles to the upper deck gangway, it extended further across the saloon than was normal, blocking the forward view from the offside, although that to the nearside was little better because of the high bulkhead. London's Transport Museum

The STL5 introduced at the end of 1934 was an evolutionary leap in the development of double-deck styling and introduced the design which was to remain the standard, with refinements, until 1939. The smooth uninterrupted line of its front profile in a gentle slope from roof to dash was the most notable improvement and the total effect was now of a neat well-proportioned and uncluttered vehicle. STL 804 at Victoria is in the original condition with its sidelamps set into the cantrail band and with no nearside driver's mirror. The knobbed rod projecting from the front mudguard was a device, fashionable for a time, intended to help the driver line up the bus with the kerb. G.H.F. Atkins

The first purely London Transport design, which applied from STL 609 onward, marked a major improvement in appearance which was carried through as the basis of all buses in the class until 1939. The main difference was at the front where the slope was less pronounced but followed a smooth profile from roof to bonnet instead of the partly angular shape of earlier designs. The dashboard was also more rounded and the cab and nearside bulkhead windows curved down to meet the bottom of the saloon windows. The side lamps were sited in the black relief band between the decks and there were a few other minor changes. The interior finish was also brighter with the light yellow of the ceiling being extended half way down the window pillars. The mechanical specification, which now became standard, included the new A171 7.7 litre oil engine, preselective gearbox and fluid transmission. STL 609–758 were classified 9STL5 and a further similar batch, nominally STL 759–958, 1/9STL5. Fifteen of the latter were fitted with new style tubular framed seats and were classified 1/9STL5/2. The number batches in this period were nominal because the changeover from one design of body to the next did not take place cleanly at a given number, the allocation of numbers depending on the order in which chassis became available for bodying.

Between December 1936 and May 1938, full-fronted STL 857 was numbered STF 1 and operated experimentally from Hackney garage. It is seen here at The Chippenham, Shirland Road, on route 6. Behind the line of the driver's cab the body was more or less a standard STL but the large number of opening windows is noteworthy. Apart from the obvious major differences at the front, the black lining was extended around the windows at the front to join up, so that the silver of the roof extended down to meet the red of the between-decks panels and the front lower deck pillars were red. J. Higham

One of this batch, STL 857, was the subject of an experiment with a new body design which to some extent reflected fashion trends outside London. It was fully-fronted with its radiator concealed behind a decorative grille and a much more pronounced curve to the front profile which in some respects foreshadowed the RT. The front upper deck and driver's cab windows curved downwards towards the front pillars in a style which enjoyed a short vogue at the time. The number of opening windows was increased to five each side upstairs and four down. The internal finish was similar to the later STL11 bodies, with double panelling and tubular metal-framed seats. It entered service in November 1936 and was soon renumbered STF 1 but reverted to STL 857 in May 1938 when it was converted to half cab. It received a standard body in May 1939 and its original body was mounted on the chassis of STL 1167, remaining distinctive because of its curvature and large number of opening windows.

A number of experiments were carried out on this batch. Two hundred had rubber engine mountings, air brakes were fitted to STL 738, 741–744, 754, 757–760 and an air-operated gearbox to STL 760 in June 1937. The latter was replaced with a Miller fully automatic gearbox in November 1937 which it retained until November 1939, an experiment of particular significance in connection with the development later of the Routemaster. STLs 688, 691, 701–703 were converted to direct injection combustion in September 1936 and ran in this condition until April 1938. Many other technical experiments also took place.

Chiswick design influence was asserted over Country Buses in 1936 when the standard STL was modified with forward entrances to meet the operational requirements of the department. From this angle, in North Street Bromley, STL 1030B looks little different from an STL5, but the staircase can be seen in the first and second bays and the rearmost bay is part of the seated area. Ken Glazier collection

The first significant variation from the basic rear-entrance fifty-six seater was a batch of eighty-five for the Country Bus department, delivered between January and May 1935, to which were added a further four in July (STL 959B–1043B, 1056B–1059B; 10STL6). These retained the basic profile of the STL5 but, in deference to Country Bus policy at the time, had forward entrances and only forty-eight seats. The entrances were doorless and the saloon bulkhead was angled towards the rear, making the lower step wider. In the absence of an open rear platform, an emergency exit was required on the lower deck and this took the form of a hinged door in the centre of the rear wall, as already adopted on single-deckers. The seating capacity of these eighty-nine vehicles was increased to fifty-two by placing seats over the rear wheel arches in the lower deck during 1939, with STL 1039 completed in February 1940.

Unlike the Godstone STLs the STL6 bodies did not have platform doors on their wide forward entrances. The angled bulkhead was a none-too-successful attempt to reduce draughts in the lower saloon. This official photograph of STL 994 taken at Reigate gives a good overview of the neat and elegant lines of the standard STL body. Snook & Son/Ken Glazier collection

On the STL11 body the destination indicator was above the number and route displays, the sidelamps were moved to lower deck waist level and the moulding above the lower deck windows was flattter and less prominent. STL 1132, at Putney Common, was one of the first of the type, being delivered to the rebuilt Chelverton Road garage in February 1936. J. Higham

An improved version of the STL5 body, classified STL11, was specified for (nominally) STL 1060–1259, 1264–1463 and 1514–1613, built between March and September 1936, except STL 1603 whose chassis was used for engineering training and did not receive a body until April 1938. These had fully lined panelling throughout and the new tubular framed seats, which were now adopted as standard. After the first fifty bodies, the destination indicator was moved to a position above the intermediate and route number displays, where it remained on all subsequent STLs. STL 1264 onwards had a slightly less powerful version of the 7.7 litre engine, rated at 108 bhp, and were classified 3/9STL11.

The numbers STL 1260–1263 were reserved for four specially built short wheelbase chassis whose specification was otherwise the same as the contemporary standard STLs

This early wartime view at Victoria shows short-wheelbase STL 1262 with the Birch body inherited from DST 4 (see page 79). It now has a new ST-type rounded cab and its roof route number box and separate destination indicator have been removed in favour of a standard size composite box. The position of the former roof box can be located by the narrow replacement panel in the centre of the front dome. D.W.K. Jones

The body of DST 3 was used in combination with a special short wheelbase Regent chassis to create STL 1260, which looked at first glance like a standard ST as did STL 1261 and 1263. The three points of recognition which revealed its more modern provenance were the thicker centre of the rear wheel, the flatter section of the front wheel centres and the 1936-issue registration number. STL 1260 and 1261 are seen together at Edmonton Station (today's Edmonton Green) running from Tottenham garage to which three of the four were allocated from the start. D.A. Ruddom collection

The second batch of Country Bus STLs had Weymann metal-framed bodies based on the STL11 design and could also be distinguished by the radiused inner corners of the front upper deck windows. STL 1478B, on route 313 in Cecil Road, Enfield, was the only one of the batch to be allocated to a northern area garage. D.A. Ruddom collection

(14STL10). They were intended to carry the bodies of DST 1–3 and 5, whose chassis had been scrapped. STL 1260, 1261 and 1263 were fitted with the ST-style bodies from DST 1–3 while STL 1262 took the Dodson body which had been DST 5.

STL 1464B–1513B were a second batch of Country Buses of the same basic layout as the first but with metal-framed bodywork by Weymann (1/10STL6/1), with the revised indicator layout adopted on the STL11. They could also be distinguished by the front upper deck windows which were radiused at the four top corners. They went into service between July and December 1936. During August and September 1939 a body float was created for the STL6 and STL6/1 types by replacing the bodies of four of the former and two of the latter with standard rear-entrance STL14/1s from Central Area stock. These were the first STL bodies to change livery from red to green. The buses concerned were STL 975B, 993B, 1001B, 1003B, 1465B and 1477B.

All standard STLs built from October 1936 onwards had roof-mounted route number boxes. A total of 687 nominally numbered in the ranges STL 1614–2013 and 2189–2515 had Chiswick-built bodies classified STL12, STL14 or STL14/1. The intention had been to adopt the STL12 design, which incorporated steel, rather than ash, for the wheel arches and underframe but production problems restricted the number built to only six in the first batch and ninety-four in the second. The remainder had the earlier type underframe and were classified STL14 or 14/1 but were identical in external appearance. The neatly designed route number box could be opened from inside the upper saloon when the number had to be changed, a considerable improvement on the design used for the Bluebirds STs and LTs.

Some of the buses in these two batches varied from the standard specification. STL 1642, 1654, 1657, 1661, 1668 and 1670 were delivered without engines and were fitted with modified direct injection units as part of the continuing comparative tests with the indirect injection type. Although experimental vehicles were not normally given different codes, these were classified 5/9STL. After experimental service at Hanwell garage, the engines were replaced at first overhaul and the buses reclassified 4/9STL. Twenty-five of the first batch were fitted with Widney Stewart PYP winding gear on their opening windows but these were troublesome and no further STLs were so fitted. STL 2343, delivered in November 1937, had a modified nearside front wing assembly with a curved projection forward from the bulkhead running neatly into the all-rubber mudguard. This was later tried on the 10T10 class and became standard on the RT family. The body was transferred to STL 2434 in 1939. The chassis of STL 2513–2515 were fitted experimentally with a new A182 8.8 litre direct injection oil engine, which incorporated a geared timing chain, the same type as fitted to RT 1 in its ST 1140 guise.

From October 1936 onwards all new STLs had a roof route number box, the Chiswick-built bodies built between then and May 1938 being coded STL12 or STL14. STL 1932, seen at Victoria station, was an STL14 which differed from the STL12 in having timber rather than metal underframes. G.H.F. Atkins

Like the NSs they replaced, the STL13 tunnel buses had a domed roof and more tapered rear end to avoid contact with the walls or roof of Blackwall Tunnel. They also reverted to having the complete set of route and destination indicators between the decks. STL 1825 ran for a short time at Holloway but was photographed on Blackheath after transfer to Athol Street. The intermediate point blind is one of the rear displays from an NS, masked to exclude the destination, fitted as a temporary arrangement until the correct type could be made. J.F. Higham

The upper deck of a tunnel STL, showing the sharply curved roof and the rearrangement of the seating at the head of the stairs, with an additional double on the offside and two single seats one behind the other instead of side-by-side. London's Transport Museum

Forty from the first batch had bodywork designed for working through Blackwall Tunnel and had inward sloping roofs, to avoid hitting the tunnel roof, and a narrower rear end to give adequate clearance from the walls on the tunnel's sharp bends (STL13). They also reverted to the STL11 style of indicator layout, without roof route number. Internally, the staircase had to curve at the top, which reduced their overall capacity to 55 and caused the upper deck seating to be re-arranged. They were fitted with steel-reinforced tyres to protect them when rubbing against the kerbs in the narrow roadway of the tunnel. They entered service in March and April 1937 initially at Holloway and Hackney garages while Athol Street was made ready, the first operating on route 108 on 24th March 1937. Camberwell also received an allocation for their share of route 108, until the whole batch was concentrated at Athol Street in January 1938.

Concurrently with the Chiswick-built buses, a batch of 175 was built by Park Royal Coachworks Ltd using their own patented metal-framed construction but to the standard STL profile (STL 2014–2188; 4/9STL15). They were hardly distinguishable externally from the Chiswick version, the only difference being a vertical moulding down each window pillar. Internally they could be identified readily by their rounded window cappings and the design of the panels below the windows which ran in a continuous unbroken sweep down to the cove panels. They went into service between February and September 1937 as part of the normal replacement programme and were not confined to any specific garages.

The last 132 STLs were a further development of the classic design, which now reached its zenith. The original order was for 115 vehicles, which were to have been RTs but AEC were not ready to start volume production of the new model and London Transport decided to have one more batch of STLs. A further seventeen were added to meet the needs of the Country Bus department and were intended initially to be a temporary allocation pending the production of a further batch of fifty forward-entrance vehicles. In the event thirty-nine were painted green, the first new rear-entrance buses assigned to the department by London Transport. STL 2516–2647 (15STL16) had an improved mechanical specification, including the A173 direct injection oil engine, which extensive trials had shown to be more economical and long lasting than the indirect injection type. The enhanced specification also included flexible engine mountings, R.P. automatic brake adjusters and automatic chassis lubrication.

The Chiswick-built bodywork was similar to the STL12 and 14 types but had detailed improvements which anticipated the RT specification. The main external differences were the lower quarter of the driver's windscreen, which could be opened, a longer radiator shell on which the registration plate was carried and disc trims on both front and rear wheels. Platform handrails were covered in Doverite plastic and the grabrail above the luggage compartment under the stairs was flat in section and deeper than the usual tubular rail. This type was also used on the first RTs. Internally they were similar to the most recent STLs but the seat toprails were of thinner section. The six which had the last six bodies were fitted experimentally with hand-built rubber mudguards, which were more bulbous and it was therefore necessary to eliminate the inward curve of the body and the rearward sweep of the mudguard (STL 2621, 2642, 2643, 2645, 2646 and 2647; 1/15STL16/1). They entered service between March and September 1939, the red ones mainly at Hanwell with sixteen going to newly opened Alperton, and the Country Bus ones to Northfleet and Dartford between May and August. Although the green examples were numbered indiscriminately between 2517 and 2638, their bodies were in three distinct number blocks of five, twelve and twenty-two.

In the summer of 1939, all petrol engined STLs with preselective transmission except STL 50 and 558, were converted to oil, leaving 287 with petrol engines and crash gearboxes. They were given the same flexibly mounted A173 engine as the 15STLs and were simultaneously fitted with automatic brake adjusters which brought them close to the latest mechanical standard. They were recoded 16STL18, with variants depending on their original classification (see summary below). The first conversion, as a prototype, was STL 493 in February 1939 and the main programme ran from March to November. STL 493, 533 and 536 started work at Chalk Farm on 28th March and the last into service was STL 289 at Willesden on 27th November. Other garages to receive them were Camberwell and Sutton. A further major programme to convert 1,916 STLs to direct injection A173 specification was delayed by the outbreak of war.

Another change to the earlier Chiswick-built STLs numbered below 609 took place as they went through overhaul during 1938 and 1939. The large staircase window on the offside was replaced by a narrower window and a plain panel on which a route number stencil holder was installed.

The outbreak of war on 3rd September 1939 had a widespread effect on the allocation of STLs, including the immediate loan of 258 by Central Buses to Country Buses which proved to be a pointer to future events. In the Central Area, petrol-engined vehicles were replaced with oilers as far as possible and this brought STLs to a number of new garages, notably Streatham (which received a large number of the new 15STL16s displaced from Hanwell), Kingston and Uxbridge. 15STL16s were also used for the resumed Green Line service to Grays from 1st November 1939.

Chassis:	AEC Regent 661 (petrol) or 0661 (oil)
Engine:	AEC A140 6-cylinder 6.1 litre 95 bhp petrol (STL 1–130, 153–252); AEC A145 6-cylinder 7.4 litre 130 bhp petrol (STL 253–552, 559–608); AEC A162

The 15STL16 type of 1939 was the high point in STL design and paved the way for the RT. Externally very similar to the earlier roof box designs, the STL16 benefited from a longer radiator, with registration plate mounted on its grille in line with the dumbirons, and the application of wheel trim discs front and back. STL 2565 is at London Bridge working from Hanwell garage where the majority of the red ones were allocated. The Omnibus Society

6-cylinder 7.4 litre petrol (STL 553–558); AEC A171 6-cylinder 7.7 litre 95 bhp indirect injection oil (STL 342–352, 609–1043, 1056–1641, 1643–1653, 1655, 1656, 1658–1660, 1662–1667, 1669, 1671–2515); AEC A173 6-cylinder 7.7 litre 95 bhp direct injection oil (STL 1642, 1654, 1657, 1661, 1668, 1670, 2516–2647)

Transmission: AEC D124 4 speed crash (1–49, 51–130; 153–202, 253, 263, 290, 292–341, 353–402, 553–557, 1044–1055); Daimler D128 4 speed direct selection preselective (STL 50, 203–252, 254–262, 264–289, 291, 342–352, 558); AEC D132 4 speed direct selection preselective (STL 403–552, 559–1043, 1056–2647)

Chassis codes[1,2]: 1STL (STL 1–49, 158, 171, 172; 2STL (153–157, 159–170, 173–202); 3STL (STL 50, 203–252; 4STL[3] (253–291, 403–405); 5STL (342–352); 6STL (292–341, 353–402); 7STL (STL 406–552, 559–608); 8STL (STL 51–130); 9, 1/9, 2/9, 3/9, 4/9STL (STL 609–958, 1060–1259, 1264–1463, 1514–2515); 10STL (STL 959–1043, 1056–1059); 1/10STL (STL 1464–1513); 11STL (STL 1044–1055); 12STL (STL 553–556); 1/12STL (STL 557); 13STL (STL 558); 14STL (STL 1260–1263); 15STL (STL 2516–2647, except STL 2621, 2642, 2643, 2645–2647, 1/15STL)

Bodywork: LGOC or LPTB (Chiswick) (STL 1–50, 153–552, 559–1043, 1056–1261, 1263–1463, 1514–2013, 2189–2647; Park Royal/Chiswick (STL 553–557); Park Royal (STL 2014–2188); Tilling or Dodson (STL 51–130); Weymann (1044–1055, 1464–1513; Birch (STL 558); Dodson (STL 1262)

Capacity: H30/26R except: STL 553–557 O30/26R[7]; STL 1044–1055 L26/22FD; STL 959–1043, 1056–1059, 1464–1513 H29/19F[4]; STL13 type Tunnel buses (see list) H30/25R

Body codes[1,2]: STL1 (STL 1–50[6], 153–202); STL2 (STL 203–252); STL3 (STL 292–341, 353–402); STL3/1 (STL 342–352); STL3/2 (STL 253–291, 403–552, 559–608); STL4 (51–130); STL5 (STL 608–744, 746–856, 858–887, 889–910, 912–915, 917, 918, 920–941, 943–958, 1064, 1067, 1073); STL5/2 (STL888, 911, 916, 919, 942, 1061, 1071, 1074, 1091, 1094, 1102, 1105, 1108, 1112, 1128); STL6 (STL 959–1043, 1056–1059); STL6/1[5] (STL 1464–1513); STL7 (STL 1044–1055); STL8 (STL 553–558); STL9 (STL 559); STL10 (STL 1260–1263); STL11 (STL 1060, 1062, 1063, 1065, 1066, 1068–1070, 1072, 1075–1090, 1092, 1093, 1095–1101, 1103, 1104, 1106, 1107, 1109–1111, 1113–1127, 1130–1259, 1264–1463, 1514–1602, 1604–1618, 1620–1626, 1628, 1630, 1632, 1634, 1635, 1638); STL12 (STL 1603, 1847, 1915, 1922, 1926, 1935, 1951, 2348, 2432, 2437, 2439, 2441, 2442, 2444, 2446, 2449, 2451–2453, 2455–2458, 2460, 2462–2515 STL13 (tunnel buses – see fleet list); STL14 (STL 745, 1129, 1619, 1627, 1629, 1631, 1633, 1636, 1637, 1639–1808, 1810–1813, 1815–1817, 1819–1822, 1824, 1826, 1829, 1831–1834, 1836–1840, 1859, 1863, 1869, 1870, 1873, 1877–1883, 1885–1914, 1916–1921, 1923–1925, 1927–1934, 1936–1950, 1952–2005, 2007–2013, 2189–2202, 2204, 2205, 2207); STL14/1 (STL 2203, 2206, 2208–2347, 2349–2431, 2433–2436, 2438, 2440, 2443, 2445, 2447, 2448, 2450, 2454, 2459, 2461; STL15 (STL 2014–2189); STL16 (STL 2516–2647, except STL 2621, 2642, 2643, 2645, 2646 and 2647 STL16/1)

Built: 1932–1939
Number in stock: 1.7.33: 155   31.12.39: 2,625

[1] The codes shown for vehicles first licensed before the introduction of the coding system in 1934 are those which would have applied at the date of acquisition or manufacture had the coding system existed at the time. Although anachronistic, this method is used to identify the form of the vehicles either when acquired or when first licensed. Subsequent changes are shown only when they represent a significant alteration to the specification or the introduction of new features.

[2] STL 203–252 reclassified 16STL18/1 when fitted with oil engines and modernised in 1939. STL 254–262, 264–289, 291 reclassified 1/16STL18 when fitted with oil engines and modernised in 1939. STL 403–552, 559–608 reclassified 2/16STL18 when fitted with oil engines and modernised in 1939

[3] STL 253, 263, 290 reclassified 1/4STL in 1938

[4] STL 959–1043, 1056–1059 converted to H29/23F in 1938/1939

[5] STL 975, 993, 1001, 1003, 1465 and 1477 converted to STL14/1 in August/September 1939.

[6] STL 50 later reclassified STL1/1

[7] STL 553–557 became H30/26R between May and September 1934.

STL		STL		STL		* Date into stock	STL		* Date into stock
1	GX5324	73	YY5373	167	JJ4380		239	AGX589	6.11.33
2	JJ4340	74	YY5374	168	AGX518		240	AGX582	23.10.33
3	JJ4364	75	YY5375	169	AGX520		241	AGX596	11.11.33
4	JJ4341	76	YY5376	170	AGX508		242	AGX566	2.10.33
5	JJ4353	77	YY5377	171	AGX502		243	AGX567	3.10.33
6	JJ4344	78	YY5378	172	AGX507		244	AGX577	13.10.33
7	JJ4346	79	YY5379	173	AGX504		245	AGX581	1.11.33
8	JJ4360	80	YY5380	174	AGX514		246	AGX580	31.10.33
9	JJ4354	81	JJ6281	175	AGX517		247	AGX569	23.9.33
10	JJ4361	82	JJ6282	176	AGX515		248	AGX586	30.10.33
11	GX5400	83	JJ6283	177	AGX516		249	AGX593	10.11.33
12	JJ4365	84	JJ6284	178	AGX533	† 31.7.33	250	AGX578	5.10.33
13	JJ4337	85	JJ6285	179	AGX535	† 31.7.33	251	AGX587	31.10.33
14	JJ4342	86	JJ6286	180	AGX522	† 31.7.33	252	AGX579	19.10.33
15	JJ4357	87	JJ6287	181	AGX523	6.7.33	253	AUC546	4.1.34
16	GX5330	88	JJ6288	182	AGX521	7.7.33	254	AUC512	23.11.33
17	GX5399	89	JJ6289	183	AGX519		255	AUC539	12.12.33
18	GX5329	90	JJ6290	184	AGX530	† 31.7.33	256	AUC542	27.12.33
19	JJ4366	91	JJ6291	185	AGX525	10.7.33	257	AUC548	3.1.34
20	GX5328	92	JJ6292	186	AGX532	† 31.7.33	258	AUC544	2.1.34
21	JJ4362	93	JJ6293	187	AGX524	11.7.33	259	AUC538	11.12.33
22	JJ4355	94	JJ6294	188	AGX531	12.7.33	260	AUC522	30.11.33
23	GX5335	95	JJ6295	189	AGX527	12.7.33	261	AUC513	25.11.33
24	JJ4332	96	JJ6296	190	AGX529	10.7.33	262	AUC510	21.11.33
25	JJ4358	97	JJ6297	191	AGX528	11.7.33	263	AUC511	21.11.33
26	JJ4335	98	JJ6298	192	AGX544	† 3.8.33	264	AUC507	21.11.33
27	GX5336	99	JJ6299	193	AGX526	7.7.33	265	AGX595	15.11.33
28	JJ4338	100	JJ6300	194	AGX536	† 3.8.33	266	AGX591	16.11.33
29	JJ4331	101	JJ6301	195	AGX541	† 31.7.33	267	AUC533	9.12.33
30	GX5398	102	JJ6302	196	AGX534	† 2.8.33	268	AUC518	28.11.33
31	JJ4343	103	JJ6303	197	AGX538	† 31.7.33	269	AUC514	24.11.33
32	GX5334	104	JJ6304	198	AGX537	† 31.7.33	270	AGX594	10.11.33
33	JJ4359	105	JJ6305	199	AGX543	† 2.8.33	271	AUC519	29.11.33
34	JJ4348	106	JJ6306	200	AGX539	† 31.7.33	272	AGX599	17.11.33
35	JJ4336	107	JJ6307	201	AGX540	† 31.7.33	273	AUC506	18.11.33
36	JJ4345	108	JJ6308	202	AGX542	† 2.8.33	274	AUC505	17.11.33
37	JJ4350	109	JJ6309	203	AGX547	3.8.33	275	AUC537	11.12.33
38	JJ4339	110	JJ6310	204	AGX557	13.9.33	276	AUC516	2.12.33
39	JJ4351	111	AGF821	205	AGX548	9.9.33	277	AUC517	24.11.33
40	JJ4352	112	AGF822	206	AGX552	28.8.33	278	AUC524	5.12.33
41	JJ4347	113	AGF823	207	AGX545	19.8.33	279	AUC543	13.12.33
42	JJ4371	114	AGF824	208	AGX546	19.8.33	280	AUC520	16.12.33
43	JJ4349	115	AGF825	209	AGX559	30.8.33	281	AUC525	6.12.33
44	JJ4356	116	AGF826	210	AGX549	28.8.33	282	AUC536	27.12.33
45	JJ4367	117	AGF827	211	AGX556	20.9.33	283	AUC526	8.12.33
46	JJ4368	118	AGF828	212	AGX554	1.9.33	284	AUC547	28.12.33
47	JJ4372	119	AGF829	213	AGX583	25.10.33	285	AUC527	5.12.33
48	JJ4369	120	AGF830	214	AGX584	24.10.33	286	AUC532	15.12.33
49	JJ4370	121	AGF831	215	AGX558	6.9.33	287	AUC541	19.12.33
50	JJ4363	122	AGF832	216	AGX560	5.9.33	288	AUC540	18.12.33
51	YY5351	123	AGF833	217	AGX585	26.10.33	289	AUC545	1.1.34
52	YY5352	124	AGF834	218	AGX551	9.9.33	290	AUC551	6.1.34
53	YY5353	125	AGF835	219	AGX574	27.9.33	291	AUC549	30.12.33
54	YY5354	126	AGF836	220	AGX564	7.9.33	292	AUC550	28.12.33
55	YY5355	127	AGF837	221	AGX561	2.9.33	293	AUC560	29.12.33
56	YY5356	128	AGF838	222	AGX563	16.9.33	294	AUC559	8.1.34
57	YY5357	129	AGF839	223	AGX562	21.9.33	295	AUC556	17.1.34
58	YY5358	130	AGF840	224	AGX553	12.9.33	296	AUC552	11.1.34
59	YY5359	153	AGX505	225	AGX555	23.8.33	297	AUC554	29.12.33
60	YY5360	154	AGX510	226	AGX598	14.11.33	298	AUC553	29.12.33
61	YY5361	155	AGX513	227	AGX588	4.11.33	299	AUC555	16.1.34
62	YY5362	156	JJ4378	228	AGX575	13.10.33	300	AUC561	16.1.34
63	YY5363	157	AGX506	229	AGX568	21.9.33	301	AUC558	2.2.34
64	YY5364	158	AGX501	230	AGX571	26.9.33	302	AUC566	8.2.34
65	YY5365	159	JJ4376	231	AGX572	7.10.33	303	AUC562	4.1.34
66	YY5366	160	AGX503	232	AGX565	5.10.33	304	AUC577	15.2.34
67	YY5367	161	AGX550	233	AGX592	9.11.33	305	AUC578	6.2.34
68	YY5368	162	JJ4379	234	AGX570	28.9.33	306	AUC569	22.1.34
69	YY5369	163	AGX509	235	AGX573	23.9.33	307	AUC567	10.1.34
70	YY5370	164	AGX511	236	AGX590	7.11.33	308	AUC568	9.2.34
71	YY5371	165	JJ4377	237	AGX576	29.9.33	309	AUC579	16.1.34
72	YY5372	166	AGX512	238	AGX597	13.11.33	310	AUC570	9.1.34

STL		* Date into stock	STL		* Date into stock	STL		* Date into stock
311	AUC571	12.1.34	383	AXM631	22.3.34	455	AYV619	22.6.34
312	AUC572	27.1.34	384	AUC521	9.4.34	456	AYV630	5.7.34
313	AUC573	25.1.34	385	AXM642	10.4.34	457	AYV614	13.6.34
314	AUC574	5.2.34	386	AXM643	6.4.34	458	AYV621	22.6.34
315	AUC592	7.2.34	387	AXM644	26.3.34	459	AYV613	14.6.34
316	AUC583	31.1.34	388	AXM645	7.4.34	460	AYV609	27.6.34
317	AUC586	20.1.34	389	AXM646	6.4.34	461	AYV622	29.6.34
318	AUC585	26.1.34	390	AXM649	13.4.34	462	AYV617	19.6.34
319	AUC588	29.1.34	391	AXM648	11.4.34	463	AYV642	12.7.34
320	AUC580	12.2.34	392	AXM647	29.3.34	464	AYV620	21.6.34
321	AUC600	12.2.34	393	AXM652	12.4.34	465	AYV643	10.7.34
322	AUC589	29.1.34	394	AXM653	30.4.34	466	AYV618	20.6.34
323	AUC587	19.1.34	395	AXM698	24.5.34	467	AYV641	10.7.34
324	AUC584	27.1.34	396	AXM661	24.4.34	468	AYV628	27.6.34
325	AUC593	23.1.34	397	AUC598	17.4.34	469	AYV651	20.7.34
326	AUC590	14.2.34	398	AXM612	19.4.34	470	AYV644	12.7.34
327	AUC594	24.1.34	399	AXM651	16.4.34	471	AYV649	16.7.34
328	AUC595	26.2.34	400	AXM659	25.4.34	472	AYV646	13.7.34
329	AUC597	3.2.34	401	AXM662	21.4.34	473	AYV624	25.6.34
330	AXM658	12.4.34	402	AXM656	26.4.34	474	AYV623	23.6.34
331	AUC599	13.2.34	403	AXM666	30.4.34	475	AYV645	11.7.34
332	AUC596	23.2.34	404	AXM667	23.4.34	476	AYV627	26.6.34
333	AXM677	28.4.34	405	AXM655	24.4.34	477	AYV634	6.7.34
334	AXM607	24.2.34	406	AXM668	1.5.34	478	AYV632	4.7.34
335	AXM601	22.2.34	407	AXM657	12.5.34	479	AYV652	19.7.34
336	AXM606	21.2.34	408	AXM674	7.5.34	480	AYV655	26.7.34
337	AXM603	17.2.34	409	AXM663	23.5.34	481	AYV640	7.7.34
338	AXM602	16.2.34	410	AXM664	2.5.34	482	AYV626	25.6.34
339	AXM609	20.2.34	411	AXM673	7.5.34	483	AYV636	5.7.34
340	AXM608	19.2.34	412	AXM675	5.5.34	484	AYV629	4.7.34
341	AXM604	15.2.34	413	AXM676	15.5.34	485	AYV639	9.7.34
342	AUC557	28.12.33	414	AXM669	8.5.34	486	AYV631	3.7.34
343	AUC591	24.1.34	415	AXM665	3.5.34	487	AYV638	7.7.34
344	AUC563	14.2.34	416	AXM672	3.5.34	488	AYV635	6.7.34
345	AUC581	26.1.34	417	AXM671	10.5.34	489	AYV650	18.7.34
346	AUC564	25.1.34	418	AXM685	10.5.34	490	AYV648	17.7.34
347	AUC565	1.2.34	419	AXM681	11.5.34	491	AYV659	24.7.34
348	AUC582	27.1.34	420	AXM682	14.5.34	492	AYV665	13.8.34
349	AUC575	3.2.34	421	AXM684	15.5.34	493	AYV653	19.7.34
350	AUC576	22.1.34	422	AXM670	4.5.34	494	AYV654	20.7.34
351	AXM613	20.4.34	423	AXM680	16.5.34	495	AYV647	16.7.34
352	AXM654	19.4.34	424	AXM683	10.5.34	496	AYV666	14.8.34
353	AXM620	7.3.34	425	AXM678	17.5.34	497	AYV658	23.7.34
354	AXM624	19.3.34	426	AXM679	9.5.34	498	AYV670	20.8.34
355	AXM625	13.3.34	427	AYV610	14.6.34	499	AYV656	23.7.34
356	AXM633	19.3.34	428	AXM687	24.5.34	500	AYV688	29.8.34
357	AXM614	5.3.34	429	AXM688	25.5.34	501	AYV678	23.8.34
358	AXM611	28.2.34	430	AXM689	25.5.34	502	AYV674	14.8.34
359	AXM621	5.4.34	431	AYV637	9.7.34	503	AYV669	20.8.34
360	AXM632	15.3.34	432	AXM690	19.5.34	504	AYV675	17.8.34
361	AXM622	8.3.34	433	AXM691	22.5.34	505	AYV686	24.8.34
362	AXM615	1.3.34	434	AXM686	23.5.34	506	AYV689	27.8.34
363	AXM610	27.2.34	435	AXM692	30.5.34	507	AYV690	1.9.34
364	AXM619	21.3.34	436	AXM697	28.5.34	508	AYV682	24.8.34
365	AXM617	9.3.34	437	AYV611	13.6.34	509	AYV681	22.8.34
366	AXM638	3.4.34	438	AYV608	16.6.34	510	AYV697	29.8.34
367	AXM627	12.3.34	439	AXM696	29.5.34	511	AYV698	4.9.34
368	AXM636	5.4.34	440	AXM699	2.6.34	512	AYV657	25.7.34
369	AXM628	23.3.34	441	AXM693	26.5.34	513	AYV683	21.8.34
370	AXM616	3.3.34	442	AXM700	1.6.34	514	AYV671	14.8.34
371	AXM623	28.3.34	443	AXM695	2.6.34	515	AYV660	1.8.34
372	AXM618	6.3.34	444	AYV601	1.6.34	516	AYV661	1.8.34
373	AXM629	16.3.34	445	AXM694	1.6.34	517	AYV662	1.8.34
374	AXM630	20.3.34	446	AYV604	11.6.34	518	AYV667	1.8.34
375	AXM640	18.4.34	447	AYV602	9.6.34	519	AYV663	15.8.34
376	AXM641	3.4.34	448	AYV607	8.6.34	520	AYV687	30.8.34
377	AXM639	23.3.34	449	AYV612	15.6.34	521	AYV664	1.8.34
378	AXM626	10.3.34	450	AYV603	5.6.34	522	AYV694	1.9.34
379	AXM637	4.4.34	451	AYV605	6.6.34	523	AYV676	21.8.34
380	AXM634	17.3.34	452	AYV606	7.6.34	524	AYV672	20.8.34
381	AXM635	4.4.34	453	AYV633	5.7.34	525	AYV668	15.8.34
382	AXM650	14.4.34	454	AYV625	26.6.34	526	AYV704	7.9.34

STL		* Date into stock	STL		* Date into stock	STL		* Date into stock
527	AYV701	8.9.34	599	AYV745	13.10.34	671	BLH731	14.12.34
528	AYV707	12.9.34	600	AYV746	17.10.34	672	BLH730	13.12.34
529	AYV679	21.8.34	601	AYV764	15.10.34	673	BLH736	19.12.34
530	AYV673	16.8.34	602	AYV758	16.10.34	674	BLH728	14.12.34
531	AYV685	22.8.34	603	AYV756	26.10.34	675	BLH735	18.12.34
532	AYV680	18.8.34	604	AYV762	16.10.34	676	BLH724	10.12.34
533	AYV677	22.8.34	605	AYV759	22.10.34	677	BLH745	28.12.34
534	AYV691	25.8.34	606	AYV757	6.11.34	678	BLH771	18.1.35
535	AYV725	21.9.34	607	AYV761	17.10.34	679	BLH739	19.12.34
536	AYV705	10.9.34	608	AYV763	22.10.34	680	BLH742	27.12.34
537	AYV706	12.9.34	609	AYV766	18.10.34	681	BLH743	31.12.34
538	AYV703	7.9.34	610	AYV772	16.11.34	682	BLH737	22.12.34
539	AYV700	28.9.34	611	AYV769	6.11.34	683	BLH746	29.12.34
540	AYV695	4.9.34	612	AYV774	15.11.34	684	BLH747	1.1.35
541	AYV716	15.9.34	613	AYV770	14.11.34	685	BLH748	3.1.35
542	AYV684	25.8.34	614	AYV775	15.11.34	686	BLH749	2.1.35
543	AYV696	6.9.34	615	AYV773	7.11.34	687	BLH744	31.12.34
544	AYV692	31.8.34	616	AYV779	16.11.34	688	BLH764	14.1.35
545	AYV708	13.9.34	617	AYV787	22.11.34	689	BLH750	2.1.35
546	AYV693	28.8.34	618	AYV768	5.11.34	690	BLH759	10.1.35
547	AYV714	14.9.34	619	AYV767	18.2.35	691	BLH752	4.1.35
548	AYV710	14.9.34	620	AYV776	16.11.34	692	BLH754	5.1.35
549	AYV699	11.9.34	621	AYV771	14.11.34	693	BLH751	3.1.35
550	AYV702	5.9.34	622	AYV788	26.11.34	694	BLH753	4.1.35
551	AYV709	18.9.34	623	AYV783	17.11.34	695	BLH756	8.1.35
552	AYV715	17.9.34	624	BLH702	26.11.34	696	BLH758	9.1.35
553	GW1744	8.11.33	625	AYV777	15.11.34	697	BLH757	8.1.35
554	GW1224	8.11.33	626	AYV780	28.12.34	698	BLH755	7.1.35
555	GW1785	8.11.33	627	BLH717	8.12.34	699	BLH761	11.1.35
556	GX167	8.11.33	628	BLH711	30.11.34	700	BLH768	17.1.35
557	GY839	8.11.33	629	AYV789	21.11.34	701	BLH765	15.1.35
558	GW2294	1.12.33	630	AYV792	24.11.34	702	BLH763	12.1.35
559	AYV750	5.10.34	631	BLH703	26.11.34	703	BLH762	12.1.35
560	AYV719	27.9.34	632	AYV781	17.11.34	704	BLH770	17.1.35
561	AYV721	10.10.34	633	BLH740	21.12.34	705	BLH766	16.1.35
562	AYV727	20.9.34	634	BLH716	5.12.34	706	BLH767	16.1.35
563	AYV712	19.9.34	635	AYV785	20.11.34	707	BLH769	18.1.35
564	AYV735	19.10.34	636	AYV793	28.11.34	708	BXD414	19.3.35
565	AYV718	21.9.34	637	AYV782	17.11.34	709	BLH775	4.2.35
566	AYV711	22.9.34	638	AYV778	16.11.34	710	BLH772	21.1.35
567	AYV723	24.9.34	639	AYV786	21.11.34	711	BLH773	21.1.35
568	AYV726	22.9.34	640	BLH701	22.11.34	712	BLH784	21.2.35
569	AYV722	24.9.34	641	BLH738	20.12.34	713	BLH776	20.2.35
570	AYV720	25.9.34	642	AYV790	22.11.34	714	BLH777	22.2.35
571	AYV732	25.9.34	643	BLH709	29.11.34	715	BLH774	20.2.35
572	AYV733	26.9.34	644	AYV784	19.11.34	716	BLH782	22.2.35
573	AYV713	27.9.34	645	BLH712	3.12.34	717	BLH785	19.2.35
574	AYV724	26.9.34	646	AYV791	22.11.34	718	BLH786	19.2.35
575	AYV728	28.9.34	647	BLH705	24.11.34	719	BLH778	21.2.35
576	AYV743	11.10.34	648	BLH733	18.12.34	720	BLH779	26.2.35
577	AYV741	6.10.34	649	BLH706	28.11.34	721	BLH790	28.2.35
578	AYV734	29.9.34	650	BLH708	28.11.34	722	BLH795	5.3.35
579	AYV738	8.10.34	651	BLH704	24.11.34	723	BLH796	4.3.35
580	AYV729	3.10.34	652	BLH707	30.11.34	724	BLH780	4.3.35
581	AYV730	1.10.34	653	BLH710	1.12.34	725	BLH787	23.2.35
582	AYV731	1.10.34	654	BLH715	4.12.34	726	BLH781	25.2.35
583	AYV739	3.10.34	655	BLH718	11.12.34	727	BLH791	26.2.35
584	AYV740	4.10.34	656	BLH719	6.12.34	728	BLH783	19.2.35
585	AYV736	2.10.34	657	BLH720	7.12.34	729	BLH792	1.3.35
586	AYV760	19.10.34	658	BLH722	8.12.34	730	BLH788	27.2.35
587	AYV744	5.10.34	659	BLH723	11.12.34	731	BLH789	28.2.35
588	AYV751	8.10.34	660	BLH732	18.12.34	732	BXD408	11.3.35
589	AYV753	4.10.34	661	BLH713	3.12.34	733	BLH794	4.3.35
590	AYV749	18.10.34	662	BLH714	5.12.34	734	BXD421	21.3.35
591	AYV737	9.10.34	663	BLH725	12.12.34	735	BXD404	8.3.35
592	AYV752	9.10.34	664	BLH726	15.12.34	736	BLH797	6.3.35
593	AYV742	18.10.34	665	BLH741	21.12.34	737	BLH793	27.2.35
594	AYV765	31.10.34	666	BLH729	12.12.34	738	BXD402	6.3.35
595	AYV747	10.10.34	667	BLH734	17.12.34	739	BXD405	9.3.35
596	AYV754	11.10.34	668	BLH721	6.12.34	740	BXD403	8.3.35
597	AYV755	26.10.34	669	BLH727	12.12.34	741	BXD418	20.3.35
598	AYV748	12.10.34	670	BLH760	11.1.35	742	BXD451	17.6.35

STL		* Date into stock	STL		* Date into stock	STL		* Date into stock
743	BXD416	19.3.35	815	CGJ77	7.10.35	887	CGJ29	15.11.35
744	BXD417	20.3.35	816	BXD493	4.7.35	888	CGJ23	25.11.35
745	DGX260	24.11.36	817	BXD472	17.6.35	889	BXD588	21.8.35
746	BXD413	12.3.35	818	BXD507	12.7.35	890	BXD589	20.8.35
747	BXD412	15.3.35	819	BXD478	25.6.35	891	BXD605	8.10.35
748	BXD406	9.3.35	820	BXD494	3.7.35	892	BXD616	26.10.35
749	BXD409	13.3.35	821	BXD481	10.7.35	893	BXD602	26.8.35
750	BXD411	13.3.35	822	BXD510	17.7.35	894	BXD618	3.9.35
751	BXD415	16.3.35	823	BXD475	18.6.35	895	BXD613	12.11.35
752	BXD407	11.3.35	824	BXD495	9.7.35	896	BXD604	2.9.35
753	BXD410	14.3.35	825	BXD496	2.8.35	897	BXD620	22.10.35
754	BXD420	21.3.35	826	BXD479	27.6.35	898	BXD596	3.9.35
755	BXD422	22.3.35	827	BXD482	1.7.35	899	BXD617	1.11.35
756	BXD419	22.3.35	828	BXD483	8.7.35	900	BXD607	9.10.35
757	BXD424	3.4.35	829	BXD497	12.7.35	901	BXD621	4.9.35
758	BXD423	4.4.35	830	BXD488	28.6.35	902	CGJ43	3.10.35
759	BXD425	16.5.35	831	BXD518	29.7.35	903	BXD614	16.10.35
760	BXD441	1.6.35	832	BXD579	25.7.35	904	CGJ22	1.11.35
761	BXD455	4.6.35	833	BXD509	24.7.35	905	CGJ28	11.11.35
762	BXD426	16.5.35	834	BXD499	12.8.35	906	BXD606	28.10.35
763	BXD431	24.5.35	835	BXD490	5.7.35	907	CGJ30	14.11.35
764	BXD443	30.5.35	836	BXD505	11.7.35	908	CGJ44	19.9.35
765	BXD449	3.6.35	837	BXD515	13.7.35	909	CGJ14	5.9.35
766	BXD444	29.5.35	838	BXD610	5.10.35	910	BXD599	22.8.35
767	BXD437	3.6.35	839	BXD585	31.7.35	911	CGJ34	22.11.35
768	BXD445	29.5.35	840	BXD491	3.7.35	912	CGJ51	30.10.35
769	BXD473	19.6.35	841	BXD492	5.7.35	913	BXD619	24.10.35
770	BXD466	14.6.35	842	BXD512	15.7.35	914	CGJ19	12.9.35
771	BXD442	30.5.35	843	BXD508	24.8.35	915	CGJ12	7.11.35
772	BXD434	23.5.35	844	BXD498	6.7.35	916	CGJ36	5.12.35
773	BXD432	23.5.35	845	BXD580	22.7.35	917	CGJ24	29.10.35
774	BXD436	25.5.35	846	BXD506	11.7.35	918	BXD615	18.9.35
775	BXD435	20.5.35	847	BXD516	16.7.35	919	CGJ33	22.11.35
776	BXD433	24.5.35	848	BXD519	26.7.35	920	CGJ56	20.9.35
777	BXD430	23.5.35	849	BXD611	7.11.35	921	CGJ54	16.10.35
778	BXD452	21.6.35	850	BXD520	23.7.35	922	CGJ55	25.9.35
779	BXD438	31.5.35	851	BXD514	24.7.35	923	CGJ35	21.11.35
780	BXD461	22.6.35	852	BXD581	30.7.35	924	CGJ50	13.11.35
781	BXD439	27.5.35	853	BXD592	6.9.35	925	CGJ62	26.9.35
782	BXD440	25.5.35	854	BXD513	19.7.35	926	CGJ42	14.9.35
783	BXD446	1.6.35	855	BXD591	17.8.35	927	CGJ38	22.10.35
784	BXD429	22.5.35	856	BXD583	1.8.35	928	CGJ59	17.9.35
785	BXD428	22.5.35	857	BXD582	6.11.35	929	CGJ63	30.9.35
786	BXD457	17.6.35	858	BXD517	18.7.35	930	CGJ67	23.9.35
787	BXD456	12.6.35	859	BXD595	2.9.35	931	CGJ16	9.9.35
788	BXD448	31.5.35	860	BXD598	29.8.35	932	CGJ69	1.10.35
789	BXD450	1.6.35	861	CGJ20	10.9.35	933	CGJ25	8.11.35
790	BXD462	24.6.35	862	BXD603	23.8.35	934	CGJ52	25.10.35
791	BXD453	4.6.35	863	BXD587	21.8.35	935	CGJ74	18.10.35
792	BXD447	31.5.35	864	BXD597	30.8.35	936	CGJ60	18.9.35
793	BXD484	28.6.35	865	CGJ11	12.9.35	937	CGJ57	16.9.35
794	BXD468	14.6.35	866	BXD590	16.8.35	938	CGJ49	4.11.35
795	BXD460	24.6.35	867	BXD577	20.7.35	939	CGJ61	26.9.35
796	BXD458	15.6.35	868	BXD594	28.8.35	940	CGJ53	24.10.35
797	BXD454	7.6.35	869	CGJ18	11.9.35	941	CGJ58	21.9.35
798	BXD464	25.6.35	870	CGJ13	5.11.35	942	CGJ41	26.11.35
799	BXD469	15.6.35	871	BXD578	31.7.35	943	CGJ64	28.9.35
800	BXD465	17.6.35	872	BXD586	13.8.35	944	CGJ48	3.10.35
801	BXD459	18.6.35	873	BXD584	27.7.35	945	CGJ39	15.11.35
802	BXD476	19.6.35	874	CGJ15	4.9.35	946	CGJ45	11.9.35
803	BXD467	13.6.35	875	BXD593	31.8.35	947	CGJ65	27.9.35
804	BXD463	13.6.35	876	CGJ17	6.9.35	948	CGJ40	20.11.35
805	BXD480	26.6.35	877	CGJ37	19.11.35	949	CGJ31	30.9.35
806	BXD474	20.6.35	878	CGJ27	17.10.35	950	CGJ46	10.10.35
807	BXD470	14.6.35	879	BXD609	9.11.35	951	CGJ47	13.9.35
808	BXD489	26.6.35	880	CGJ32	6.11.35	952	CGJ68	5.10.35
809	BXD485	27.6.35	881	CGJ21	5.9.35	953	CGJ70	31.10.35
810	BXD471	21.6.35	882	BXD608	18.11.35	954	CGJ72	11.10.35
811	BXD486	2.7.35	883	BXD612	2.10.35	955	CGJ75	11.10.35
812	BXD511	17.7.35	884	BXD601	22.8.35	956	CGJ66	24.9.35
813	BXD487	1.7.35	885	CGJ26	16.11.35	957	CGJ71	2.11.35
814	BXD477	26.6.35	886	BXD600	26.8.35	958	CGJ73	12.10.35

STL		*Date into stock	STL		*Date into stock	STL		*Date into stock
959	BLH816	25.1.35	1031	BLH891	3.5.35	1103	CGJ126	2.1.36
960	BLH817	5.2.35	1032	BLH885	30.4.35	1104	CGJ111	15.1.36
961	BLH830	7.2.35	1033	BLH897	11.5.35	1105	CGJ105	6.12.35
962	BLH834	14.2.35	1034	BLH875	26.4.35	1106	CGJ94	21.12.35
963	BLH826	14.2.35	1035	BLH899	13.5.35	1107	CGJ152	20.1.36
964	BLH827	5.2.35	1036	BLH882	25.4.35	1108	CGJ97	2.12.35
965	BLH824	14.2.35	1037	BLH883	26.4.35	1109	CGJ100	30.12.35
966	BLH831	8.2.35	1038	BLH900	10.5.35	1110	CLE35	6.2.36
967	BLH822	8.2.35	1039	BLH886	1.5.35	1111	CGJ99	11.12.35
968	BLH835	11.2.35	1040	BLH887	1.5.35	1112	CGJ108	6.12.35
969	BLH818	26.1.35	1041	BLH898	17.5.35	1113	CGJ107	29.1.36
970	BLH823	5.2.35	1042	BLH888	8.5.35	1114	CGJ96	19.12.35
971	BLH828	9.2.35	1043	BLH890	3.5.35	1115	CGJ106	31.12.35
972	BLH819	4.2.35	b 1044	BPE221	† .4.34	1116	CLE85	5.3.36
973	BLH820	7.2.35	b 1045	BPF269	† .4.34	1117	CGJ95	3.2.36
974	BLH832	13.2.35	b 1046	BPF270	† .4.34	1118	CGJ133	13.1.36
975	BLH825	11.2.35	b 1047	BPF288	† .4.34	1119	CGJ139	16.1.36
976	BLH821	7.2.35	b 1048	BPF289	† .4.34	1120	CGJ113	31.1.36
977	BLH825	7.2.35	b 1049	BPF391	† .5.34	1121	CGJ114	14.1.36
978	BLH833	13.2.35	b 1050	BPF397	† .5.34	1122	CGJ124	7.1.36
979	BLH836	14.2.35	b 1051	BPF416	† .5.34	1123	CGJ131	3.1.36
980	BLH849	5.4.35	b 1052	BPF417	† .5.34	1124	CLE17	23.1.36
981	BLH837	12.2.35	b 1053	BPF456	† .5.34	1125	CGJ150	17.1.36
982	BLH838	12.2.35	b 1054	BPF457	† .5.34	1126	CGJ120	11.1.36
983	BLH839	18.2.35	b 1055	BPF458	† .5.34	1127	CLE12	9.1.36
984	BLH851	6.4.35	1056	BLH503	17.7.35	1128	CGJ110	29.11.35
985	BLH840	18.2.35	1057	BLH504	10.7.35	1129	DGX216	11.11.36
986	BLH859	29.4.35	1058	BLH501	15.7.35	1130	CGJ125	1.1.36
987	BLH847	30.3.35	1059	BLH502	15.7.35	1131	CLE13	18.2.36
988	BLH842	29.3.35	1060	CLE37	12.2.36	1132	CLE29	3.2.36
989	BLH843	1.4.35	1061	CGJ76	28.11.35	1133	CLE26	28.1.36
990	BLH860	12.4.35	1062	CGJ138	16.1.36	1134	CGJ147	15.1.36
991	BLH850	28.3.35	1063	CGJ122	4.1.36	1135	CGJ135	6.1.36
992	BLH844	10.4.35	1064	CGJ78	19.10.35	1136	CGJ121	8.1.36
993	BLH845	26.3.35	1065	CGJ116	10.1.36	1137	CLE11	21.1.36
994	BLH865	12.4.35	1066	CGJ84	4.2.36	1138	CGJ140	8.1.36
995	BLH853	9.4.35	1067	CGJ79	21.10.35	1139	CGJ153	17.1.36
996	BLH848	3.4.35	1068	CGJ83	13.2.36	1140	CLE46	4.2.36
997	BLH855	2.4.35	1069	CGJ109	29.1.36	1141	CGJ119	14.1.36
998	BLH841	26.3.35	1070	CGJ83	4.2.36	1142	CLE22	31.1.36
999	BLH852	29.3.35	1071	CGJ104	3.12.35	1143	CGJ132	16.1.36
1000	BLH846	27.3.35	1072	CGJ134	14.1.36	1144	CGJ136	3.1.36
1001	BLH854	2.4.35	1073	CGJ81	15.10.35	1145	CGJ145	10.2.36
1002	BLH856	3.4.35	1074	CGJ89	28.11.35	1146	CLE14	15.2.36
1003	BLH857	3.4.35	1075	CGJ102	11.12.35	1147	CGJ141	18.1.36
1004	BLH862	12.4.35	1076	CGJ85	20.12.35	1148	CGJ154	20.12.35
1005	BLH863	9.4.35	1077	CGJ90	28.12.35	1149	CLE21	27.1.36
1006	BLH869	15.4.35	1078	CGJ86	2.1.36	1150	CGJ144	12.2.36
1007	BLH861	6.4.35	1079	CGJ128	8.1.36	1151	CGJ142	10.1.36
1008	BLH864	18.4.35	1080	CGJ129	7.1.36	1152	CGJ148	12.2.36
1009	BLH868	10.4.35	1081	CLE30	28.1.36	1153	CLE38	11.2.36
1010	BLH866	13.4.35	1082	CGJ127	6.1.36	1154	CGJ149	15.2.36
1011	BLH870	24.4.35	1083	CLE45	6.2.36	1155	CGJ155	14.2.36
1012	BLH889	2.5.35	1084	CGJ101	16.12.35	1156	CLE23	31.1.36
1013	BLH871	15.4.35	1085	CGJ117	13.1.36	1157	CLE41	27.1.36
1014	BLH867	17.4.35	1086	CGJ112	31.12.35	1158	CGJ156	22.1.36
1015	BLH881	25.4.35	1087	CGJ112	22.1.36	1159	CLE43	7.2.36
1016	BLH884	18.5.35	1088	CGJ91	14.12.35	1160	CLE15	28.1.36
1017	BLH873	17.4.35	1089	CGJ118	10.1.36	1161	CGJ151	14.2.36
1018	BLH872	11.4.35	1090	CGJ82	20.12.35	1162	CGJ157	17.2.36
1019	BLH876	29.4.35	1091	CGJ143	30.11.35	1163	CLE42	12.2.36
1020	BLH877	24.4.35	1092	CLE20	28.1.36	1164	CLE16	31.1.36
1021	BLH893	8.5.35	1093	CGJ137	9.1.36	1165	CLE18	23.1.36
1022	BXD526	14.5.35	1094	CGJ130	16.12.35	1166	CLE44	14.2.36
1023	BLH895	7.5.35	1095	CGJ123	6.1.36	1167	CLE31	31.1.36
1024	BLH878	24.4.35	1096	CGJ93	19.12.35	1168	CLE32	30.1.36
1025	BLH879	25.4.35	1097	CGJ115	21.1.36	1169	CLE52	10.2.36
1026	BLH874	4.5.35	1098	CGJ88	23.12.35	1170	CLE24	1.2.36
1027	BLH880	18.4.35	1099	CGJ92	23.12.35	1171	CLE28	22.1.36
1028	BLH892	7.5.35	1100	CGJ146	13.2.36	1172	CLE40	30.1.36
1029	BLH896	8.5.35	1101	CGJ98	16.12.35	1173	CLE50	10.3.36
1030	BLH894	9.5.35	1102	CGJ103	9.12.35	1174	CLE27	28.1.36

STL		* Date into stock	STL		* Date into stock	STL		* Date into stock
1175	CLE25	20.1.36	1247	BXD992	24.3.36	1319	CGF536	28.4.36
1176	CLE73	20.2.36	1248	BYE312	26.3.36	1320	CGF540	27.4.36
1177	CLE75	10.2.36	1249	BLT355	12.3.36	1321	CLO39	30.4.36
1178	CLE60	6.2.36	1250	CLE96	24.2.36	1322	CLX511	30.4.36
1179	CLE84	5.2.36	1251	BXH467	26.3.36	1323	CLX512	8.5.36
1180	CLE67	21.2.36	1252	BXA618	9.3.36	1324	CLX516	8.5.36
1181	CLE88	7.2.36	1253	BXD695	28.2.36	1325	CLX513	30.4.36
1182	CLE93	25.2.36	1254	BXL215	18.3.36	1326	CLX530	6.5.36
1183	BXX973	12.3.36	1255	BUV785	14.3.36	1327	CLX522	5.5.36
1184	CLE54	7.2.36	1256	BUW576	10.3.36	1328	CLX517	8.5.36
1185	CLE48	5.2.36	1257	BXA886	9.3.36	1329	CLX518	8.5.36
1186	BXD401	29.2.36	1258	BXH603	24.3.36	1330	CLX519	8.5.36
1187	CLE55	21.2.36	1259	BXF31	26.3.36	1331	CLX526	4.5.36
1188	CLE49	8.2.36	1260	CLE33	7.4.36	1332	CLX523	11.5.36
1189	CLE53	20.2.36	1261	CLE39	6.6.36	1333	CLX520	8.5.36
1190	CLE64	13.2.36	1262	CLE34	23.9.36	1334	CXX143	18.6.36
1191	CLE86	11.2.36	1263	CLE36	4.3.36	1335	CLX521	4.5.36
1192	CLE80	5.3.36	1264	BYL812	27.3.36	1336	CLX524	5.5.36
1193	CLE61	27.2.36	1265	BXU721	18.3.36	1337	CLX527	5.5.36
1194	CLE94	26.2.36	1266	BXO55	16.3.36	1338	CLX525	5.5.36
1195	CLE59	24.2.36	1267	BYH255	27.3.36	1339	CLX528	6.5.36
1196	CLE56	24.2.36	1268	BXN540	18.3.36	1340	CLX577	18.5.36
1197	CLE62	22.2.36	1269	BXN355	19.3.36	1341	CLX529	6.5.36
1198	CLE68	19.2.36	1270	CLX514	1.5.36	1342	CLX531	7.5.36
1199	CLE51	7.2.36	1271	BXU722	23.3.36	1343	CLX591	20.5.36
1200	CLE47	26.2.36	1272	BXU715	17.3.36	1344	CLX532	8.5.36
1201	CLE63	7.2.36	1273	BXY318	20.3.36	1345	CLX542	18.5.36
1202	CLE57	20.2.36	1274	BXO54	28.2.36	1346	CLX533	7.5.36
1203	CLE70	17.2.36	1275	BXU752	20.3.36	1347	CLX587	22.5.36
1204	CLE87	4.3.36	1276	BYH256	6.4.36	1348	CLX582	19.5.36
1205	CLE82	4.3.36	1277	BYH912	6.4.36	1349	CLX580	19.5.36
1206	CLE83	7.3.36	1278	BYK791	7.4.36	1350	CLX536	13.5.36
1207	BUW575	14.3.36	1279	BYH679	30.3.36	1351	CLX593	25.5.36
1208	CLE69	19.2.36	1280	BXW307	19.3.36	1352	CLX539	14.5.36
1209	CLE78	21.2.36	1281	BYE589	31.3.36	1353	CLX540	14.5.36
1210	CLE71	15.2.36	1282	BXU800	21.3.36	1354	CLX579	15.5.36
1211	BUW785	17.3.36	1283	BYH254	25.3.36	1355	CLX534	8.5.36
1212	CLE65	24.2.36	1284	BXV161	20.3.36	1356	CLX581	18.5.36
1213	CLE66	2.3.36	1285	BYF360	25.3.36	1357	CLX537	13.5.36
1214	CLE77	18.2.36	1286	BXW136	31.3.36	1358	CXX111	5.6.36
1215	CLE58	25.2.36	1287	BYM557	6.4.36	1359	CLX595	25.5.36
1216	CLE72	24.2.36	1288	BYL960	26.3.36	1360	CLX583	20.5.36
1217	BLY145	14.3.36	1289	CLX515	1.5.36	1361	CLX578	15.5.36
1218	BXB845	19.3.36	1290	BYM556	31.3.36	1362	CLX535	9.5.36
1219	CLE81	12.3.36	1291	BYM554	30.3.36	1363	CLX586	21.5.36
1220	BXH409	27.3.36	1292	BYN974	9.4.36	1364	CLX592	23.5.36
1221	BXA711	6.3.36	1293	BYN760	7.4.36	1365	CLX589	22.5.36
1222	BLD98	3.3.36	1294	BYO913	14.4.36	1366	CLX584	20.5.36
1223	CLE79	6.3.36	1295	BYN920	7.4.36	1367	CLX541	16.5.36
1224	BUL279	13.3.36	1296	BYX961	23.4.36	1368	CLX538	14.5.36
1225	CLE74	18.2.36	1297	BYR802	14.4.36	1369	CLX576	15.5.36
1226	CLE76	20.2.36	1298	BYP4	18.4.36	1370	CXX130	11.6.36
1227	BLN618	10.3.36	1299	BYP480	9.4.36	1371	CLX585	20.5.36
1228	BUC516	13.3.36	1300	BYP481	16.4.36	1372	CXX106	26.5.36
1229	BUL48	16.3.36	1301	BYO986	14.4.36	1373	CXX104	28.5.36
1230	CLE91	27.2.36	1302	BYU319	20.4.36	1374	CLX597	26.5.36
1231	BYM463	15.4.36	1303	BYU167	17.4.36	1375	CXX109	2.6.36
1232	CLE95	26.2.36	1304	BYU385	20.4.36	1376	CLX590	21.5.36
1233	CLE90	3.3.36	1305	BYT696	17.4.36	1377	CLX596	26.5.36
1234	BUL347	16.3.36	1306	BYU164	20.4.36	1378	CXX114	15.6.36
1235	BUW595	24.3.36	1307	CGC197	28.4.36	1379	CXX107	27.5.36
1236	BLO239	9.3.36	1308	BYU392	21.4.36	1380	CXX125	5.6.36
1237	BLC45	11.3.36	1309	BYU844	22.4.36	1381	CXX108	2.6.36
1238	BLN216	16.4.36	1310	BYU845	21.4.36	1382	CLX594	25.5.36
1239	CLE92	2.3.36	1311	CLF503	28.4.36	1383	CLX588	23.5.36
1240	BLC518	11.3.36	1312	BYV557	22.4.36	1384	CXX139	15.6.36
1241	CLE89	5.3.36	1313	BYY701	4.5.36	1385	CXX101	28.5.36
1242	BXX857	12.3.36	1314	BYY835	23.4.36	1386	CXX102	27.5.36
1243	BXN283	16.3.36	1315	CGU762	29.4.36	1387	CXX118	2.6.36
1244	BGF545	27.2.36	1316	CGO129	29.4.36	1388	CXX115	3.6.36
1245	BXH468	23.3.36	1317	BYX39	23.4.36	1389	CXX103	27.5.36
1246	BGO161	27.7.36	1318	BYX979	4.5.36	1390	CXX116	8.6.36

STL		* Date into stock	STL		* Date into stock	STL		* Date into stock
1391	CXX113	28.5.36	1463	CXX212	7.7.36	1535	CXX228	28.7.36
1392	CXX110	3.6.36	1464	CXX451	18.6.36	1536	CXX237	20.8.36
1393	CXX112	29.5.36	1465	CXX452	25.6.36	1537	CXX242	28.7.36
1394	CXX120	6.6.36	1466	CXX453	23.6.36	1538	CXX229	18.8.36
1395	CXX119	9.6.36	1467	CXX454	7.7.36	1539	CXX233	29.7.36
1396	CXX105	29.5.36	1468	CXX455	24.10.36	1540	CXX231	21.8.36
1397	CXX124	5.6.36	1469	CXX456	20.7.36	1541	CXX240	19.8.36
1398	CXX122	3.6.36	1470	CXX457	31.10.36	1542	CXX236	24.7.36
1399	CXX127	10.6.36	1471	CXX458	3.10.36	1543	CXX241	13.8.36
1400	CXX126	8.6.36	1472	CXX459	27.10.36	1544	CXX251	21.8.36
1401	CXX117	29.5.35	1473	CXX460	29.10.36	1545	CXX246	11.8.36
1402	CXX121	4.6.36	1474	CXX461	17.7.36	1546	CXX247	17.8.36
1403	CXX254	10.8.36	1475	CXX462	21.8.36	1547	CXX252	23.7.36
1404	CXX128	10.6.36	1476	CXX463	24.9.36	1548	CXX253	19.8.36
1405	CXX129	9.6.36	1477	CXX464	4.7.36	1549	CXX245	27.7.36
1406	CXX123	9.6.36	1478	CXX465	3.12.36	1550	CXX266	12.8.36
1407	CXX133	8.6.36	1479	CXX466	25.8.36	1551	CXX255	26.8.36
1408	CXX131	4.6.36	1480	CXX467	11.6.36	1552	CXX260	21.8.36
1409	CXX132	4.6.36	1481	CXX468	19.8.36	1553	CXX265	12.8.36
1410	CXX134	11.6.36	1482	CXX469	22.7.36	1554	CXX259	24.8.36
1411	CXX135	11.6.36	1483	CXX470	1.7.36	1555	CXX261	26.8.36
1412	CXX141	16.6.36	1484	CXX471	1.12.36	1556	CXX262	29.8.36
1413	CLE209	13.6.36	1485	CXX472	6.10.36	1557	CXX263	14.8.36
1414	CLE210	12.6.36	1486	CXX473	1.10.36	1558	CXX264	24.8.36
1415	CXX140	17.6.36	1487	CXX474	7.12.36	1559	CXX280	28.8.36
1416	CXX147	22.6.36	1488	CXX475	26.11.36	1560	CXX274	14.8.36
1417	CXX179	24.6.36	1489	CXX476	28.10.36	1561	CXX268	30.7.36
1418	CXX144	18.6.36	1490	CXX477	23.11.36	1562	CXX284	27.8.36
1419	CXX137	19.6.36	1491	CXX478	9.7.36	1563	CXX267	30.7.36
1420	CXX208	7.7.36	1492	CXX479	20.10.36	1564	CXX269	26.8.36
1421	CXX145	17.6.36	1493	CXX480	31.7.36	1565	CXX279	25.8.36
1422	CXX138	16.6.36	1494	CXX481	16.7.36	1566	CXX275	24.8.36
1423	CXX146	18.6.36	1495	CXX482	5.9.36	1567	CXX276	17.8.36
1424	CXX136	15.6.36	1496	CXX483	24.7.36	1568	CXX277	15.8.36
1425	CXX149	25.6.36	1497	CXX484	10.10.36	1569	CXX278	7.9.36
1426	CXX142	16.6.36	1498	CXX485	17.9.36	1570	CXX306	17.9.36
1427	CXX148	19.6.36	1499	CXX486	13.8.36	1571	CXX298	14.9.36
1428	CXX176	22.6.36	1500	CXX487	28.8.36	1572	CXX285	31.8.36
1429	CXX181	24.6.36	1501	CXX488	30.7.36	1573	CXX281	27.8.36
1430	CXX150	22.6.36	1502	CXX489	3.9.36	1574	CXX290	2.9.36
1431	CXX184	29.6.36	1503	CXX490	9.9.36	1575	CXX282	3.9.36
1432	CXX201	3.7.36	1504	CXX491	18.9.36	1576	CXX293	9.9.36
1433	CXX177	23.6.36	1505	CXX492	12.11.36	1577	CXX283	3.9.36
1434	CXX187	2.7.36	1506	CXX493	5.11.36	1578	CXX287	28.8.36
1435	CXX182	25.6.36	1507	CXX494	14.11.36	1579	CXX299	9.9.36
1436	CXX178	23.6.36	1508	CXX495	17.11.36	1580	CXX286	28.8.36
1437	CXX180	29.6.36	1509	CXX496	12.11.36	1581	CXX292	2.9.36
1438	CXX186	1.7.36	1510	CXX497	9.11.36	1582	CXX302	7.9.36
1439	CXX185	13.7.36	1511	CXX498	19.11.36	1583	CXX291	4.9.36
1440	CXX183	26.6.36	1512	CXX499	7.11.36	1584	CXX307	15.9.36
1441	CXX188	2.7.36	1513	CXX500	31.10.36	1585	CXX304	15.9.36
1442	CXX189	30.6.36	1514	CXX225	19.8.36	1586	CXX322	21.9.36
1443	CXX192	11.7.36	1515	CXX218	18.7.36	1587	CXX288	5.9.36
1444	CXX196	1.7.36	1516	CXX217	10.8.36	1588	CXX294	9.9.36
1445	CXX191	9.7.36	1517	CXX213	11.7.36	1589	CXX303	26.9.36
1446	CXX190	29.6.36	1518	CXX216	28.7.36	1590	CXX295	28.9.36
1447	CXX193	18.7.36	1519	CXX226	27.7.36	1591	CXX300	17.9.36
1448	CXX194	24.7.36	1520	CXX219	14.8.36	1592	CXX296	28.9.36
1449	CXX195	7.7.36	1521	CXX221	29.7.36	1593	CXX301	24.9.36
1450	CXX205	8.7.36	1522	CXX214	1.9.36	1594	CXX289	4.9.36
1451	CXX206	9.7.36	1523	CXX215	25.8.36	1595	CXX308	10.9.36
1452	CXX197	3.7.36	1524	CXX224	14.7.36	1596	CXX309	11.9.36
1453	CXX202	6.7.36	1525	CXX227	16.7.36	1597	CXX325	18.9.36
1454	CXX207	9.7.36	1526	CXX223	21.7.36	1598	CXX323	18.9.36
1455	CXX209	17.7.36	1527	CXX220	28.7.36	1599	CXX321	21.9.36
1456	CXX203	14.7.36	1528	CXX222	22.8.36	1600	CXX320	23.9.36
1457	CXX210	8.7.36	1529	CXX235	20.8.36	1601	CXX297	23.9.36
1458	CXX199	30.6.36	1530	CXX230	15.8.36	1602	CXX310	13.10.36
1459	CXX198	2.7.36	1531	CXX234	18.8.36	1603	ELP293	26.4.38
1460	CXX200	7.7.36	1532	CXX238	20.8.36	1604	CXX328	24.9.36
1461	CXX211	10.7.36	1533	CXX239	14.8.36	1605	CXX315	25.9.36
1462	CXX204	10.7.36	1534	CXX232	20.7.36	1606	CXX333	25.9.36

STL		* Date into stock	STL		* Date into stock	STL		* Date into stock
1607	CXX311	9.9.36	1679	DGX210	13.11.36	1751	DGX292	5.1.37
1608	CXX312	11.9.36	1680	DGX209	12.11.36	1752	DGX293	8.1.37
1609	CXX314	14.9.36	1681	DGX217	23.11.36	1753	DGX298	31.12.36
1610	CXX313	16.9.36	1682	DGX208	21.11.36	1754	DGX295	5.1.37
1611	CXX316	22.9.36	1683	DGX211	9.11.36	1755	DGX296	7.1.37
1612	CXX305	22.9.36	1684	DGX212	2.12.36	1756	DGX297	14.1.37
1613	CXX324	16.9.36	1685	CXX375	3.11.36	1757	DGX299	31.12.36
1614	CXX332	1.10.36	1686	DGX193	16.11.36	1758	DGX301	6.1.37
1615	CXX329	30.9.36	1687	CXX376	10.11.36	1759	DGX302	2.1.37
1616	CXX326	2.10.36	1688	DGX254	24.11.36	1760	DGX303	4.1.37
1617	CXX318	29.9.36	1689	CXX377	3.11.36	1761	DGX304	15.1.37
1618	CXX317	7.10.36	1690	CXX379	4.11.36	1762	DGX305	1.1.37
1619	CXX319	15.10.36	1691	CXX378	2.11.36	1763	DGX306	4.1.37
1620	CXX327	30.9.36	1692	DGX191	29.10.36	1764	DGX307	12.1.37
1621	CXX335	8.10.36	1693	DGX192	5.11.36	1765	DGX308	20.1.37
1622	CXX331	7.10.36	1694	DGX214	23.11.36	1766	DGX309	12.1.37
1623	CXX334	1.10.36	1695	CXX381	2.11.36	1767	DGX310	16.1.37
1624	CXX341	5.10.36	1696	DGX215	18.11.36	1768	DGX311	18.1.37
1625	CXX330	16.10.36	1697	CXX380	3.12.36	1769	DGX312	21.1.37
1626	CXX338	8.10.36	1698	DGX218	20.11.36	1770	DGX313	15.1.37
1627	CXX337	16.10.36	1699	DGX194	20.11.36	1771	DGX314	18.1.37
1628	CXX339	29.9.36	1700	DGX219	4.12.36	1772	DGX315	21.1.37
1629	CXX336	15.10.36	1701	DGX250	3.12.36	1773	DGX316	15.1.37
1630	CXX340	5.10.36	1702	DGX195	19.11.36	1774	DGX317	22.1.37
1631	CXX351	9.10.36	1703	DGX245	28.11.36	1775	DGX325	20.1.37
1632	CXX342	6.10.36	1704	DGX246	26.11.36	1776	DGX330	19.1.37
1633	CXX361	31.10.36	1705	DGX247	24.11.36	1777	DGX326	19.1.37
1634	CXX343	6.10.36	1706	DGX248	4.12.36	1778	DGX331	22.1.37
1635	CXX344	2.10.36	1707	DGX251	26.11.36	1779	DGX332	23.1.37
1636	CXX352	14.10.36	1708	DGX252	30.11.36	1780	DGX333	25.1.37
1637	CXX374	17.11.36	1709	DGX249	28.11.36	1781	DGX338	28.1.37
1638	CXX345	7.10.36	1710	DGX255	16.12.36	1782	DGX339	29.1.37
1639	CXX346	12.10.36	1711	DGX256	7.12.36	1783	DGX342	28.1.37
1640	CXX359	4.11.36	1712	DGX265	17.12.36	1784	DGX340	27.1.37
1641	CXX347	14.10.36	1713	DGX257	30.11.36	1785	DGX349	1.2.37
1642	CXX366	27.10.36	1714	DGX261	1.12.36	1786	DGX341	26.1.37
1643	CXX348	9.10.36	1715	DGX294	12.1.37	1787	DGX345	30.1.37
1644	CXX349	22.10.36	1716	DGX262	15.12.36	1788	DGX346	1.2.37
1645	CXX365	20.10.36	1717	DGX323	25.1.37	1789	DGX350	29.1.37
1646	CLE19	27.10.36	1718	DGX258	28.11.36	1790	DGX359	3.2.37
1647	CXX363	19.10.36	1719	DGX263	1.12.36	1791	DGX358	3.2.37
1648	CXX372	5.11.36	1720	DGX264	9.12.36	1792	DGX356	2.2.37
1649	CXX360	2.12.36	1721	DGX275	10.12.36	1793	DLU11	5.2.37
1650	CXX356	19.10.36	1722	DGX259	11.12.36	1794	DLU14	4.2.37
1651	CXX350	28.10.36	1723	DGX266	7.12.36	1795	DLU16	12.2.37
1652	CXX358	23.10.36	1724	DGX267	9.12.36	1796	DGX360	6.2.37
1653	CXX355	12.10.36	1725	DGX268	19.12.36	1797	DLU13	12.2.37
1654	CXX368	22.10.36	1726	DGX269	5.12.36	1798	DLU20	15.2.37
1655	CXX362	16.10.36	1727	DGX270	8.12.36	1799	DGX357	2.2.37
1656	CXX354	21.10.36	1728	DGX271	28.12.36	1800	DLU15	11.2.37
1657	CXX367	29.10.36	1729	DGX272	17.12.36	1801	DLU32	18.2.37
1658	DGX196	6.11.36	1730	DGX273	8.12.36	1802	DLU29	17.2.37
1659	CXX357	20.10.36	1731	DGX276	12.12.36	1803	DLU21	10.9.37
1660	DGX197	14.11.36	1732	DGX277	11.12.36	1804	DLU17	5.2.37
1661	CXX369	26.10.36	1733	DGX278	10.12.36	1805	DLU33	25.2.37
1662	CXX364	21.10.36	1734	DGX279	14.12.36	1806	DLU30	16.2.37
1663	DLU172	9.7.37	1735	DGX280	14.12.36	1807	DLU22	13.2.37
1664	CXX353	26.10.36	1736	DGX283	16.12.36	1808	DLU34	22.2.37
1665	DGX198	6.11.36	1737	DGX274	22.12.36	t 1809	DLU48	15.3.37
1666	CXX373	30.10.36	1738	DGX324	14.1.37	1810	DLU36	17.2.37
1667	DGX213	19.11.36	1739	DLU40	24.2.37	1811	DLU31	16.2.37
1668	CXX371	23.10.36	1740	DLU292	6.5.37	1812	DLU41	19.2.37
1669	DGX199	11.11.36	1741	DGX281	21.12.36	1813	DLU35	17.2.37
1670	CXX370	28.10.36	1742	DGX284	29.12.36	t 1814	DLU188	4.3.37
1671	DGX200	7.11.36	1743	DGX282	15.12.36	1815	DLU44	18.2.37
1672	DGX201	10.11.36	1744	DGX286	18.12.36	1816	DLU42	19.2.37
1673	DGX202	9.11.36	1745	DGX287	28.12.36	1817	DLU193	1.3.37
1674	DGX203	16.11.36	1746	DGX285	18.12.36	t 1818	DLU189	13.3.37
1675	DGX204	17.11.36	1747	DGX288	1.1.37	1819	DLU195	25.2.37
1676	DGX207	18.11.36	1748	DGX289	21.12.36	1820	DLU194	2.3.37
1677	DGX205	13.11.36	1749	DGX290	22.12.36	1821	DLU49	27.2.37
1678	DGX206	12.11.36	1750	DGX291	29.12.36	1822	DLU45	23.2.37

STL		*Date into stock	STL		*Date into stock	STL		*Date into stock
t 1823	DLU190	13.3.37	1895	DLU272	1.5.37	1967	DLU156	20.5.37
1824	DLU205	3.3.37	1896	DLU255	9.4.37	1968	DLU164	2.6.37
t 1825	DLU191	8.3.37	1897	DLU273	23.4.37	1969	BXT431	3.6.37
1826	DLU197	1.3.37	1898	DLU256	15.4.37	1970	DLU166	24.5.37
t 1827	DLU206	5.3.37	1899	DLU254	15.4.37	1971	DLU165	3.6.37
t 1828	DLU207	6.3.37	1900	DLU293	10.5.37	1972	DLU167	2.6.37
1829	DLU210	2.3.37	1901	DLU278	27.4.37	1973	DLU171	4.6.37
t 1830	DLU196	9.3.37	1902	DLU260	19.4.37	1974	DLU168	25.5.37
1831	DLU208	3.3.37	1903	DLU261	17.4.37	1975	BXU697	5.6.37
1832	DLU198	24.2.37	1904	DLU274	26.4.37	1976	BYR792	2.6.37
1833	DLU199	23.2.37	1905	DLU258	16.4.37	1977	BUW565	4.6.37
1834	DLU200	23.2.37	1906	DLU296	7.5.37	1978	BXW938	5.6.37
t 1835	DLU201	15.3.37	1907	DLU263	20.4.37	1979	CGK320	7.6.37
1836	DLU202	26.2.37	1908	DLU275	27.4.37	1980	CGW270	16.6.37
1837	DLU203	25.2.37	1909	DLU264	22.4.37	1981	CLT303	1.7.37
1838	DLU204	27.2.37	1910	DLU279	29.4.37	1982	BYY149	7.6.37
1839	DLU50	26.2.37	1911	DLU270	30.4.37	1983	CGU628	15.6.37
1840	DLU192	27.2.37	1912	DLU265	21.4.37	1984	BYX384	4.6.37
t 1841	DLU209	15.3.37	1913	DLU257	16.4.37	1985	CGF772	7.6.37
t 1842	DLU242	30.3.37	1914	DLU262	19.4.37	1986	CGK953	8.6.37
t 1843	DLU216	17.3.37	1915	DLU294	11.5.37	1987	CLN408	28.6.37
t 1844	DLU213	9.3.37	1916	DLU308	20.5.37	1988	CGX49	22.6.37
t 1845	DLU211	15.3.37	1917	DLU298	19.5.37	1989	CLM970	24.6.37
t 1846	DLU212	16.3.37	1918	DLU276	30.4.37	1990	CGU38	15.6.37
1847	DLU214	19.5.37	1919	DLU290	5.5.37	1991	CGY212	17.6.37
t 1848	DLU218	17.3.37	1920	DLU269	28.4.37	1992	CGW269	16.6.37
t 1849	DLU215	10.3.37	1921	DLU271	5.5.37	1993	CGX48	16.6.37
t 1850	DLU219	16.3.37	1922	DLU300	11.5.37	1994	CUV501	7.7.37
t 1851	DLU217	18.3.37	1923	DLU281	8.5.37	1995	CLN413	28.6.37
t 1852	DLU224	22.3.37	1924	DLU301	21.5.37	1996	CXU346	12.7.37
t 1853	DLU225	3.4.37	1925	DLU152	24.5.37	1997	CGO914	14.6.37
t 1854	DLU221	20.3.37	1926	DLU146	14.5.37	1998	CLN740	29.6.37
t 1855	DLU232	31.3.37	1927	DLU286	3.5.37	1999	CGU222	19.6.37
t 1856	DLU222	16.3.37	1928	DLU287	6.5.37	2000	CGY208	17.6.37
t 1857	DLU227	19.3.37	1929	DLU282	3.5.37	2001	CLO846	29.6.37
t 1858	DLU226	31.3.37	1930	DLU306	25.5.37	2002	CLW777	5.7.37
1859	DLU220	14.4.37	1931	DLU302	10.5.37	2003	CGY607	21.6.37
t 1860	DLU228	18.3.37	1932	DLU283	5.5.37	2004	CLO847	25.6.37
t 1861	DLU229	5.4.37	1933	DLU291	4.5.37	2005	CLX700	5.7.37
t 1862	DLU223	23.3.37	1934	DLU148	26.5.37	2006	DYL846	22.7.37
1863	DLU239	12.4.37	1935	DLU140	19.5.37	2007	CGY428	22.6.37
t 1864	DLU236	1.4.37	1936	DLU299	27.5.37	2008	CGY663	22.6.37
t 1865	DLU230	2.4.37	1937	DLU145	15.5.37	2009	CLN401	24.6.37
t 1866	DLU237	30.3.37	1938	DLU139	15.5.37	2010	CLU366	2.7.37
t 1867	DLU235	30.3.37	1939	DLU141	13.5.37	2011	CLX21	2.7.37
t 1868	DLU295	7.4.37	1940	DLU295	27.5.37	2012	CLW82	1.7.37
1869	DLU252	15.4.37	1941	DLU304	13.5.37	2013	CLF885	22.6.37
1870	DLU231	13.4.37	1942	DLU159	1.6.37	2014	DGX253	19.1.37
t 1871	DLU240	6.4.37	1943	DLU142	26.5.37	2015	DGX300	29.1.37
t 1872	DLU238	6.4.37	1944	DLU297	20.5.37	2016	DGX319	3.2.37
1873	DLU268	22.4.37	1945	DLU303	10.5.37	2017	DGX320	8.2.37
t 1874	DLU241	7.4.37	1946	DLU155	22.5.37	2018	DGX321	11.2.37
t 1875	DLU234	25.3.37	1947	DLU143	24.5.37	2019	DGX318	4.2.37
t 1876	DLU243	6.4.37	1948	DLU147	1.6.37	2020	DGX322	12.2.37
1877	DLU246	9.6.37	1949	DLU307	2.6.37	2021	DGX327	13.2.37
1878	DLU289	8.6.37	1950	DLU305	7.5.37	2022	DGX335	16.2.37
1879	DLU284	21.5.37	1951	DLU138	14.5.37	2023	DGX328	16.2.37
1880	DLU248	10.6.37	1952	DLU150	2.6.37	2024	DGX329	11.2.37
1881	DLU247	6.5.37	1953	DLU151	27.5.37	2025	DGX337	25.2.37
1882	DLU259	14.6.37	1954	DLU144	25.5.37	2026	DLU12	9.3.37
1883	DLU249	4.5.37	1955	DLU149	22.5.37	2027	DGX351	2.3.37
t 1884	DLU244	6.4.37	1956	DLU163	31.5.37	2028	DGX343	10.3.37
1885	DLU267	20.5.37	1957	DLU153	31.5.37	2029	DGX336	22.2.37
1886	DLU253	14.4.37	1958	CGP272	14.6.37	2030	DGX344	22.2.37
1887	DLU245	12.4.37	1959	DLU157	3.6.37	2031	DGX334	18.2.37
1888	DLU280	29.4.37	1960	DLU161	21.5.37	2032	DGX347	5.3.37
1889	DLU266	24.4.37	1961	DLU160	4.6.37	2033	DGX352	2.3.37
1890	DLU251	17.4.37	1962	DLU162	31.5.37	2034	DGX353	1.3.37
1891	DLU277	28.4.37	1963	DLU154	28.5.37	2035	DGX348	6.3.37
1892	DLU249	13.4.37	1964	DLU158	1.6.37	2036	DGX354	4.3.37
1893	DLU285	30.4.37	1965	DLU170	14.5.37	2037	DGX355	6.3.37
1894	DLU250	10.4.37	1966	DLU169	26.5.37	2038	DLU23	2.4.37

STL		* Date into stock	STL		* Date into stock	STL		* Date into stock
2039	DLU18	22.3.37	2111	DLU110	8.6.37	2183	DYL835	26.8.37
2040	DLU38	17.3.37	2112	DLU111	3.6.37	2184	DYL836	25.8.37
2041	DLU24	15.3.37	2113	DLU112	4.6.37	2185	DYL837	27.8.37
2042	DLU25	12.3.37	2114	DLU113	5.6.37	2186	DYL838	28.8.37
2043	DLU39	16.3.37	2115	DLU114	4.6.37	2187	DYL839	25.8.37
2044	DLU19	10.3.37	2116	DLU115	14.6.37	2188	DYL840	25.8.37
2045	DLU37	16.3.37	2117	DLU116	21.6.37	2189	CLF886	21.6.37
2046	DLU26	12.3.37	2118	DLU117	10.6.37	2190	CLH881	23.6.37
2047	DLU43	7.4.37	2119	DLU118	11.6.37	2191	CLL355	23.6.37
2048	DLU27	19.3.37	2120	DLU119	9.6.37	2192	CLN407	25.6.37
2049	DLU28	13.3.37	2121	DLU120	10.6.37	2193	CUU997	3.7.37
2050	DLU46	5.4.37	2122	DLU121	17.6.37	2194	CXR252	8.7.37
2051	DLU47	7.4.37	2123	DLU122	17.6.37	2195	CXL823	9.7.37
2052	DLU53	8.4.37	2124	DLU123	15.6.37	2196	CXO566	8.7.37
2053	DLU54	13.4.37	2125	DLU124	12.6.37	2197	CXR641	12.7.37
2054	DLU51	18.3.37	2126	DLU125	15.6.37	2198	CLX652	10.7.37
2055	DLU52	18.3.37	2127	DLU126	22.6.37	2199	CLR387	26.6.37
2056	DLU55	3.4.37	2128	DLU127	18.6.37	2200	CXO903	6.7.37
2057	DLU56	23.3.37	2129	DLU128	25.6.37	2201	CXR251	6.7.37
2058	DLU57	20.3.37	2130	DLU129	22.6.37	2202	CXR254	7.7.37
2059	DLU58	23.3.37	2131	DLU130	25.6.37	2203	CYL465	11.7.37
2060	DLU59	31.3.37	2132	DLU131	24.6.37	2204	CYH783	13.7.37
2061	DLU60	25.3.37	2133	DLU132	22.6.37	2205	CYT677	13.7.37
2062	DLU61	31.3.37	2134	DLU133	3.7.37	2206	CYF598	14.7.37
2063	DLU62	20.4.37	2135	DLU134	26.6.37	2207	CYL841	13.7.37
2064	DLU63	17.4.37	2136	DLU135	3.7.37	2208	CYT711	15.7.37
2065	DLU64	14.4.37	2137	DLU136	1.7.37	2209	CYT710	16.7.37
2066	DLU65	12.4.37	2138	DLU137	30.6.37	2210	CYR372	15.7.37
2067	DLU66	26.4.37	2139	DYL791	1.7.37	2211	DYL841	19.7.37
2068	DLU67	9.4.37	2140	DYL792	30.6.37	2212	CYU18	15.7.37
2069	DLU68	10.4.37	2141	DYL793	6.7.37	2213	CYU76	16.7.37
2070	DLU69	15.4.37	2142	DYL794	5.7.37	2214	CYU851	20.7.37
2071	DLU70	14.4.37	2143	DYL795	9.7.37	2215	DYL849	26.7.37
2072	DLU71	16.4.37	2144	DYL796	22.7.37	2216	DYL850	23.7.37
2073	DLU72	27.4.37	2145	DYL797	6.7.37	2217	DYL843	20.7.37
2074	DLU73	27.4.37	2146	DYL798	10.7.37	2218	DYL897	10.7.37
2075	DLU74	24.4.37	2147	DYL799	9.7.37	2219	DYL842	18.7.37
2076	DLU75	22.4.37	2148	DYL800	14.8.37	2220	DYL853	28.7.37
2077	DLU76	6.5.37	2149	DYL801	7.7.37	2221	DYL848	23.7.37
2078	DLU77	20.4.37	2150	DYL802	10.7.37	2222	DYL845	21.7.37
2079	DLU78	8.5.37	2151	DYL803	7.7.37	2223	DYL847	22.7.37
2080	DLU79	1.5.37	2152	DYL804	23.7.37	2224	DYL844	21.7.37
2081	DLU80	1.5.37	2153	DYL805	15.3.37	2225	DYL851	27.7.37
2082	DLU81	23.4.37	2154	DYL806	19.7.37	2226	DYL854	27.7.37
2083	DLU82	29.4.37	2155	DYL807	19.7.37	2227	DYL858	9.8.37
2084	DLU83	28.4.37	2156	DYL808	24.7.37	2228	DYL852	24.7.37
2085	DLU84	4.5.37	2157	DYL809	16.7.37	2229	DYL855	28.7.37
2086	DLU85	8.5.37	2158	DYL810	14.7.37	2230	DYL856	9.8.37
2087	DLU86	1.5.37	2159	DYL811	14.7.37	2231	DYL857	9.8.37
2088	DLU87	5.5.37	2160	DYL812	15.7.37	2232	DYL860	13.8.37
2089	DLU88	11.5.37	2161	DYL813	21.7.37	2233	DYL885	26.8.37
2090	DLU89	28.6.37	2162	DYL814	30.7.37	2234	DYL867	20.8.37
2091	DLU90	22.4.37	2163	DYL815	22.7.37	2235	DYL859	10.8.37
2092	DLU91	11.5.37	2164	DYL816	9.8.37	2236	DYL861	10.8.37
2093	DLU92	8.5.37	2165	DYL817	10.8.37	2237	DYL910	19.8.37
2094	DLU93	25.5.37	2166	DYL818	24.7.37	2238	DYL863	17.8.37
2095	DLU94	13.5.37	2167	DYL819	11.8.37	2239	DYL911	19.8.37
2096	DLU95	14.5.37	2168	DYL820	28.7.37	2240	DYL862	17.8.37
2097	DLU96	15.5.37	2169	DYL821	28.7.37	2241	DYL864	14.8.37
2098	DLU97	20.5.37	2170	DYL822	12.8.37	2242	DYL866	23.8.37
2099	DLU98	26.5.37	2171	DYL823	31.7.37	2243	DYL870	24.8.37
2100	DLU99	20.5.37	2172	DYL824	10.8.37	2244	DYL869	20.8.37
2101	DLU100	20.5.37	2173	DYL825	11.8.37	2245	DYL865	19.8.37
2102	DLU101	27.5.37	2174	DYL826	13.8.37	2246	DYL871	21.8.37
2103	DLU102	22.5.37	2175	DYL827	14.8.37	2247	DYL880	26.8.37
2104	DLU103	25.5.37	2176	DYL828	13.8.37	2248	DYL868	20.8.37
2105	DLU104	22.5.37	2177	DYL829	19.8.37	2249	DYL882	30.8.37
2106	DLU105	29.5.37	2178	DYL830	17.8.37	2250	DYL874	26.8.37
2107	DLU106	29.5.37	2179	DYL831	21.8.37	2251	DYL875	25.8.37
2108	DLU107	1.6.37	2180	DYL832	19.8.37	2252	DYL872	23.8.37
2109	DLU108	4.6.37	2181	DYL833	21.8.37	2253	DYL876	24.8.37
2110	DLU109	3.6.37	2182	DYL834	18.8.37	2254	EGO331	10.9.37

STL		* Date into stock	STL		* Date into stock	STL		* Date into stock
2255	DYL873	24.8.37	2327	EGO402	21.10.37	2399	EGO442	9.11.37
2256	DYL887	31.8.37	2328	EGO378	4.10.37	2400	EGO444	10.11.37
2257	DYL883	30.8.37	2329	EGO361	25.9.37	2401	EGO477	29.11.37
2258	DYL888	31.8.37	2330	EGO380	7.10.37	2402	EGO446	12.11.37
2259	DYL884	30.8.37	2331	EGO399	19.10.37	2403	EGO456	8.12.37
2260	DYL877	25.8.37	2332	EGO381	12.10.37	2404	EGO450	15.11.37
2261	DYL878	28.8.37	2333	EGO372	5.10.37	2405	EGO453	13.11.37
2262	DYL881	27.8.37	2334	EGO362	24.9.37	2406	EGO447	18.11.37
2263	DYL879	27.8.37	2335	EGO398	13.10.37	2407	EGO457	13.12.37
2264	DYL886	1.9.37	2336	EGO373	1.10.37	2408	EGO449	13.12.37
2265	DYL890	7.9.37	2337	EGO382	16.10.37	2409	EGO454	7.12.37
2266	DYL889	1.9.37	2338	EGO374	1.10.37	2410	EGO459	15.12.37
2267	DYL891	9.9.37	2339	EGO383	8.10.37	2411	EGO473	26.11.37
2268	DYL892	3.9.37	2340	EGO386	12.10.37	2412	EGO460	20.11.37
2269	DYL893	8.9.37	2341	EGO394	11.10.37	2413	EGO455	23.11.37
2270	DYL894	4.9.37	2342	EGO375	2.10.37	2414	EGO469	24.11.37
2271	EGO332	3.9.37	2343	EGO385	6.10.37	2415	EGO466	22.11.37
2272	DYL898	13.9.37	2344	EGO395	2.11.37	2416	EGO461	11.12.37
2273	DYL901	11.9.37	2345	EGO422	30.10.37	2417	EGO470	14.12.37
2274	EGO334	6.9.37	2346	EGO400	20.10.37	2418	EGO471	25.11.37
2275	DYL899	2.9.37	2347	EGO390	9.10.37	2419	EGO467	7.12.37
2276	DYL895	6.9.37	2348	EGO397	8.1.38	2420	EGO463	19.11.37
2277	DYL902	31.8.37	2349	EGO387	15.10.37	2421	EGO474	10.12.37
2278	DYL900	7.9.37	2350	EGO389	15.10.37	2422	EGO472	6.12.37
2279	DYL903	2.9.37	2351	EGO396	21.10.37	2423	EGO475	25.11.37
2280	DYL896	3.9.37	2352	EGO403	19.10.37	2424	EGO468	23.11.37
2281	EGO333	9.9.37	2353	EGO388	14.10.37	2425	EGO480	1.12.37
2282	EGO338	13.9.37	2354	EGO413	28.10.37	2426	EGO476	26.11.37
2283	EGO335	15.9.37	2355	EGO401	18.10.37	2427	EGO478	29.11.37
2284	EGO336	11.9.37	2356	EGO392	13.10.37	2428	EGO464	24.11.37
2285	EGO339	14.9.37	2357	EGO393	11.10.37	2429	EGO479	30.11.37
2286	EGO337	8.9.37	2358	EGO429	3.11.37	2430	EGO483	14.12.37
2287	EGO342	9.11.37	2359	EGO404	22.10.37	2431	EGO465	27.11.37
2288	EGO349	17.9.37	2360	EGO406	20.10.37	2432	EGO487	17.12.37
2289	EGO340	13.9.37	2361	EGO407	23.10.37	2433	EGO481	30.11.37
2290	EGO341	14.9.37	2362	EGO408	27.10.37	2434	EGO484	4.12.37
2291	EGO354	23.9.37	2363	EGO414	27.10.37	2435	EGO488	4.12.37
2292	EGO343	16.9.37	2364	EGO423	17.11.37	2436	EGO485	3.12.37
2293	EGO347	18.9.37	2365	EGO409	22.10.37	2437	ELP108	18.12.37
2294	EGO350	20.9.37	2366	EGO410	25.10.37	2438	EGO482	6.12.37
2295	EGO345	16.9.37	2367	EGO421	26.10.37	2439	ELP102	31.12.37
2296	EGO348	17.9.37	2368	EGO415	25.10.37	2440	EGO486	2.12.37
2297	EGO370	4.10.37	2369	EGO428	20.11.37	2441	ELP103	4.1.38
2298	EGO344	21.9.37	2370	EGO411	30.10.37	2442	ELP104	21.12.37
2299	EGO352	20.9.37	2371	EGO416	5.11.37	2443	EGO489	1.12.37
2300	EGO363	29.9.37	2372	EGO439	8.11.37	2444	ELP114	20.12.37
2301	EGO355	22.9.37	2373	EGO436	2.12.37	2445	ELP106	9.12.37
2302	EGO356	22.9.37	2374	EGO412	23.10.37	2446	ELP109	3.1.38
2303	EGO353	23.9.37	2375	EGO433	1.11.37	2447	ELP107	8.12.37
2304	EGO351	20.9.37	2376	EGO425	26.10.37	2448	ELP101	2.12.37
2305	EGO346	15.9.37	2377	EGO426	3.11.37	2449	ELP105	4.1.38
2306	EGO364	29.9.37	2378	EGO417	29.10.37	2450	ELP112	15.12.37
2307	EGO358	22.9.37	2379	EGO418	29.10.37	2451	ELP111	20.12.37
2308	EGO376	5.10.37	2380	EGO419	2.11.37	2452	ELP115	3.1.38
2309	EGO366	6.10.37	2381	EGO451	16.11.37	2453	ELP110	17.12.37
2310	EGO371	8.10.37	2382	EGO438	16.11.37	2454	ELP117	16.12.37
2311	EGO367	30.9.37	2383	EGO440	13.11.37	2455	ELP118	11.1.38
2312	EGO357	21.9.37	2384	EGO458	27.11.37	2456	ELP120	10.1.38
2313	EGO420	5.11.37	2385	EGO431	6.11.37	2457	ELP119	11.1.38
2314	EGO405	16.10.37	2386	EGO424	22.11.37	2458	ELP123	12.1.38
2315	CLH173	25.9.37	2387	EGO432	1.11.37	2459	ELP113	11.12.37
2316	EGO359	24.9.37	2388	EGO430	17.11.37	2460	ELP116	28.12.37
2317	CLH861	27.9.37	2389	EGO427	4.11.37	2461	ELP121	16.12.37
2318	EGO391	9.10.37	2390	EGO462	19.11.37	2462	ELP129	3.1.38
2319	CLH885	27.9.37	2391	EGO445	12.11.37	2463	ELP124	5.1.38
2320	EGO369	18.10.37	2392	EGO434	15.11.37	2464	ELP133	7.1.38
2321	EGO365	28.9.37	2393	EGO441	4.11.37	2465	ELP126	30.12.37
2322	EGO384	7.10.37	2394	EGO435	9.12.37	2466	ELP125	31.12.37
2323	EGO379	2.10.37	2395	EGO437	11.11.37	2467	ELP138	23.4.38
2324	EGO377	14.10.37	2396	EGO443	8.11.37	2468	ELP128	6.1.38
2325	EGO368	30.9.37	2397	EGO448	11.11.37	2469	ELP122	5.1.38
2326	EGO360	28.9.37	2398	EGO452	18.11.37	2470	ELP136	1.2.38

STL		* Date into stock	STL		* Date into stock	STL		* Date into stock
2471	ELP127	30.12.37	2531	FJJ691	4.5.39	g 2591	FJJ751	25.5.39
2472	ELP130	6.1.38	2532	FJJ692	5.6.39	2592	FJJ752	31.5.39
2473	ELP131	1.1.38	g 2533	FJJ693	18.5.39	2593	FJJ753	13.6.39
2474	ELP144	5.2.38	g 2534	FJJ694	19.5.39	2594	FJJ754	7.6.39
2475	ELP132	21.12.37	2535	FJJ695	13.5.39	g 2595	FJJ755	31.5.39
2476	ELP142	17.1.38	g 2536	FJJ696	27.5.39	2596	FJJ756	8.6.39
2477	ELP154	15.1.38	2537	FJJ697	22.6.39	2597	FJJ757	2.8.39
2478	ELP134	4.1.38	2538	FJJ698	22.6.39	2598	FJJ758	15.6.39
2479	ELP135	10.2.38	g 2539	FJJ699	24.4.39	2599	FJJ759	12.6.39
2480	ELP150	28.1.38	2540	FJJ700	4.5.39	g 2600	FJJ760	22.6.39
2481	ELP143	14.1.38	g 2541	FJJ701	24.5.39	2601	FXT49	6.6.39
2482	ELP137	24.1.38	2542	FJJ702	28.4.39	2602	FXT50	14.6.39
2483	ELP139	9.2.38	g 2543	FJJ703	17.5.39	2603	FXT51	10.6.39
2484	ELP148	24.1.38	2544	FJJ704	3.3.39	2604	FXT52	19.6.39
2485	ELP147	13.1.38	2545	FJJ705	11.5.39	g 2605	FXT53	23.6.39
2486	ELP151	28.2.38	2546	FJJ706	14.4.39	2606	FXT54	3.6.39
2487	ELP141	12.1.38	2547	FJJ707	6.5.39	2607	FXT55	20.6.39
2488	ELP140	7.1.38	g 2548	FJJ708	2.5.39	g 2608	FXT56	27.6.39
2489	ELP146	13.1.38	g 2549	FJJ709	29.4.39	g 2609	FXT57	24.6.39
2490	ELP152	12.2.38	2550	FJJ710	12.4.39	2610	FXT58	27.7.39
2491	ELP145	7.2.38	2551	FJJ711	11.5.39	g 2611	FXT59	29.6.39
2492	ELP168	14.2.38	g 2552	FJJ712	26.5.39	g 2612	FXT60	3.7.39
2493	ELP156	5.2.38	g 2553	FJJ713	28.4.39	2613	FXT61	17.6.39
2494	ELP167	14.2.38	2554	FJJ714	13.4.39	g 2614	FXT62	22.6.39
2495	ELP162	5.2.38	2555	FJJ715	15.4.39	g 2615	FXT63	11.7.39
2496	ELP153	5.2.38	2556	FJJ716	15.4.39	g 2616	FXT64	6.7.39
2497	ELP165	5.2.38	2557	FJJ717	9.5.39	g 2617	FXT65	14.7.39
2498	ELP157	12.2.38	g 2558	FJJ718	16.5.39	g 2618	FXT66	26.6.39
2499	ELP164	28.2.38	g 2559	FJJ719	28.4.39	g 2619	FXT67	13.7.39
2500	ELP171	8.2.38	2560	FJJ720	25.4.39	g 2620	FXT68	5.7.39
2501	ELP163	7.2.38	2561	FJJ721	17.4.39	2621	FXT69	15.8.39
2502	ELP172	9.2.38	2562	FJJ722	29.4.39	2622	FXT70	31.7.39
2503	ELP158	5.2.38	g 2562	FJJ722	29.4.39	g 2623	FXT71	12.7.39
2504	ELP173	28.2.38	2563	FJJ723	25.4.39	2624	FXT72	19.7.39
2505	ELP159	11.2.38	2564	FJJ724	27.3.39	2625	FXT73	31.7.39
2506	ELP169	7.2.38	2565	FJJ725	11.4.39	g 2626	FXT74	8.7.39
2507	ELP160	15.2.38	2566	FJJ726	27.3.39	g 2627	FXT75	1.7.39
2508	ELP170	8.2.38	2567	FJJ727	27.3.39	2628	FXT76	20.7.39
2509	ELP149	25.1.38	2568	FJJ728	9.3.39	2629	FXT77	22.7.39
2510	ELP161	11.2.38	2569	FJJ729	6.3.39	g 2630	FXT78	30.6.39
2511	ELP166	5.2.38	2570	FJJ730	9.3.39	g 2631	FXT79	28.6.39
2512	ELP155	15.2.38	2571	FJJ731	25.3.39	2632	FXT80	15.7.39
2513	ELP174	30.3.38	2572	FJJ732	6.3.39	g 2633	FXT81	7.7.39
2514	ELP176	9.5.38	2573	FJJ733	29.3.39	g 2634	FXT82	10.7.39
2515	ELP175	30.3.38	2574	FJJ734	17.3.39	2635	FXT83	1.8.39
2516	FJJ676	5.5.39	2575	FJJ735	31.3.39	2636	FXT84	25.7.39
g 2517	FJJ677	15.5.39	2576	FJJ736	5.4.39	2637	FXT85	31.7.39
2518	FJJ678	17.3.39	2577	FJJ737	18.7.39	g 2638	FXT86	4.7.39
2519	FJJ679	3.6.39	2578	FJJ738	4.4.39	2639	FXT87	29.7.39
2520	FJJ680	19.4.39	2579	FJJ739	3.4.39	2640	FXT88	26.7.39
2521	FJJ681	20.4.39	2580	FJJ740	3.4.39	2641	FXT89	21.7.39
g 2522	FJJ682	20.5.39	2581	FJJ741	5.4.39	2642	FXT90	4.8.39
2523	FJJ683	9.6.39	2582	FJJ742	5.4.39	2643	FXT91	16.8.39
2524	FJJ684	1.6.39	2583	FJJ743	5.4.39	2644	FXT92	24.7.39
g 2525	FJJ685	25.5.39	2584	FJJ744	3.4.39	2645	FXT93	18.8.39
2526	FJJ686	12.5.39	2585	FJJ745	5.4.39	2646	FXT94	21.8.39
2527	FJJ687	22.4.39	2586	FJJ746	26.4.39	2647	FXT95	28.8.39
2528	FJJ688	14.6.39	2587	FJJ747	18.4.39			
2529	FJJ689	29.3.39	2588	FJJ748	26.4.39			
2530	FJJ690	5.5.39	2589	FJJ749	21.4.39			
			2590	FJJ750	2.6.39			

* Where there is no date given in the 'Date into stock' column, the vehicle was acquired on vesting day, 1st July 1933 from the LGOC or one of the other Underground Group companies. These included STL 51–130 which were operated by Tilling but had been owned by LGOC. These were immediately placed on formal loan to Tilling until the company was acquired by the Board on 1st October 1933.
† Month of first licensing, more precise date not available
b Lowbridge body
g STL16 type painted green (all STL6, 6/1 and 7 were green until 1939 – see above)
t Tunnel body

Q

Among the first new vehicle purchases authorised by the LPTB in 1933 were four double-deck AEC Qs, two for Central Bus operation (Q 2, 3; 2Q2) and two for Country Buses (Q 4, 5; 3Q3). At the time of the order there was still no oil engine available for the Q and all four were therefore petrol-engined. Their transmission was the newly adopted standard preselective gearbox and fluid flywheel, of AEC design on the Country Buses and Daimler on the Central Bus pair. The 2Q2s had Metro-Cammell patented metal-framed bodywork based on the AEC registered design, with STL components used for the route and destination indicators and rear emergency exit window. When new they had fixed front windows but these were replaced by half-drops at an unknown date. The entrance was ahead of the front axle, which would have allowed a seating capacity of 60 but this was not exploited as the Board's standard 56 was adopted. Internally they were finished to London Transport's current standard including wooden backed seats, covered in the contemporary green moquette, bare lamp bulbs and painted woodwork. The chassis of Q 2 arrived at Chiswick on 21st November 1933 but the completed vehicle was not received until 30th May 1934, five days after Q 3. The two vehicles were licensed at Harrow Weald, for operation on route 114, on 5th and 6th July respectively. They were re-allocated to Middle Row in January 1935, to be tried on the busy in-town route 52, and stayed there until July 1937 when the experiment was abandoned. They were then repainted green and transferred to Leatherhead for operation on route 406.

The 3Q3s were bodied by Weymann of Addlestone, using the same Metro-Cammell patented method of construction. They differed from the 2Q2s in details of styling but more significantly in having centre entrances, a position then being adopted as standard by the Country Bus department. Their capacity was also held at 56, although in this case it was higher than Reigate's normal standard of 48. The seating capacity was reduced to 53 in May 1939 (Q 4) and July 1939 (Q 5). The internal finish was markedly different from the Q2s and resembled that of the 'Godstone' STLs, with polished walnut mouldings on windows and ceiling, moulded lamp shades, brightly patterned green moquette and patterned 'Rexine' on the side panels. The seats were Ackles and Pollock lightweight tubular framed models with double curved high backs. Upper deck seating was in conventional forward-facing pairs, with a single alongside the stairwell and a bench for five across the back. Downstairs there were four forward facing pairs of doubles and, in front of the stairs, a longitudinal seat on each side with a forward-facing double ahead of the front axle. They carried Green Line fleet names when new but never operated as coaches, the fleet names being amended before they entered service at Leatherhead on route 406 in August 1934.

The last AEC Q bought by London Transport (Q 188; 7Q7) was intended as the forerunner of a small fleet of double-deck coaches for the busy east London routes operated by Romford (London Road) garage. It was unique in being a three-axle version, a wheel arrangement which the Board apparently favoured at the time for coach use, as it had also been specified for the LTCs and there was a proposal to use LTs on the Romford routes as an interim measure until new vehicles were available. The chassis specification differed from the 2Q and 3Qs in having the AEC A170 oil engine but the transmission was the same as the 3Qs. Some sources suggest that Q 188 was fitted with a French designed Cotal electrically operated epicyclic unit, which would have been much in advance of the contemporary preselectors, but official records do not support this. The fifty-one seat bodywork was by Park Royal and was in some respects a double-deck development of the 6Q6 with some details of the design influenced by STF 1, the front profile being smoothly curved from skirt to roof. An appearance of extra length and sleekness was given to the upper-deck by arranging the windows in pairs as double length bays, separated by a slim pillar painted black. Internally it foreshadowed the RT in having rounded window cappings with polished finishers and

The Central Bus double-deck Qs had open doorways ahead of the front wheels, platform doors on buses being banned by the Metropolitan Police. Their Metro-Cammell metal-framed bodywork was based on AEC's own preferred design which, as can be seen on Q 2 climbing up from Burnt Oak station, had styling which was ultra-modern for its day. The Board's slavish adherence to a standard route and destination blind layout led to the inclusion of an intermediate point display above the entrance, barely a foot away from the front blind. Q 2 spent most of its Central Bus life on route 52 working from Middle Row garage. Capital Transport collection

To accommodate the sliding doors on the Country Bus version, the entrance was placed behind the front wheels and this became the standard arrangement on the department's buses in the 1930s. The basic design shown on BPJ224 (later Q 5) was the same as the Central Bus vehicles but Weymann of Addlestone supplied the bodies. The rear end incorporated a standard London Transport type emergency exit window on the upper deck and a centrally placed hinged door downstairs.

opening windows operated by winding gear, the handles placed centrally above the windows. All seats were forward facing, except for a longitudinal bench downstairs opposite the stairwell. Four were singles alongside the rear wheel arches. The chassis of Q 188 was delivered on 19th May 1936 and was sent for bodying in July but the completed vehicle was not taken into stock until 1st February 1937. It then languished while negotiations took place with the Trade Union which proved ultimately to be abortive. It spent seven weeks at Reigate in September and October 1937 but was not licensed for service until 1st June 1938. It then went to Hertford for operation as a bus on route 310, where the other double-deckers were also transferred at the same time.

All five were transferred to Grays in the wake of the fleet redeployment which took place when the 15STL16s were delivered in July 1939. They were all delicensed on the outbreak of war and were still in store at the end of 1939.

Chassis:	AEC 'Q' 762 (Q 2–5); AEC Q O763 (Q 188)
Engine:	AEC A167 6-cylinder 7.4 litre 110 bhp petrol (Q 2–5); AEC A170 7.7 litre 6-cylinder 95bhp oil (Q 188)
Transmission:	Daimler D129 4-speed preselective with fluid flywheel (Q 2,3); AEC D133 4-speed direct selection preselective with fluid flywheel (Q 4,5,188)
Bodywork:	Metro-Cammell (Q 2,3); Weymann (Q 4,5); Park Royal (Q 188)
Capacity:	H56F (Q 2,3); H56CD (Q 4,5); DPH51CD (Q 188)
L.T. code:	2Q2 (Q 2,3); 3Q3 (Q 4,5); 7Q7 (Q 188)
Built:	1934 (Q 2–5); 1937 (Q 188)
Number built:	5
Number in stock:	1.7.33: Nil 31.12.39: 5

Q		Date into stock	Q		Date into stock	Q		Date into stock
2	AYV615	30.5.34	4	BPG507	5.34	188	DGO500	1.2..37
3	AYV616	25.5.34	5	BPF224	5.34			

Features worthy of note in this view of Q 5 passing Kingston Bus Station are the position of the staircase rising above the engine; the longitudinal seat over the front of the engine and front wheel; and the sidelamps at cantrail level differing from the Central Bus version which had them below the windscreen. The Surrey registration was applied because responsibility for Country Bus vehicles remained at Reigate until the end of 1935. J.F. Higham

The lower deck of the Park Royal body on Q 188 was similar in design and layout to the 6Q6 coaches from the same manufacturer while the design as a whole was influenced by STF 1 (STL 857) and foreshadowed the RT, particularly in its internal finish. Originally intended as a Green Line coach it was advertising that service when photographed in Cecil Road, Enfield operating ignominiously as a bus. Ken Glazier collection

The similarity of the Leyland-bodied STD to the Chiswick STL was striking but there were several telltale clues to their different provenance, apart from the radiator and dumbirons. The black beading above the upper deck windows was slimmer, giving the impression of a deeper roof, and the corresponding beading between the decks was replaced by the typical Leyland inverted gutter style. Among other differences, the signalling window at the rear of the lower deck was significantly foreshortened and the route number stencil placed in a correspondingly higher position. STD 38 was one of the standard vehicles with crash gearbox and Leyland's famously misnamed 'silent third'. J.F. Higham

STD

In 1937, London Transport decided to accelerate the replacement of the obsolescent NS class and placed a then record order for 786 buses and coaches, of which 672 were double-deckers. As the Board was barred by statute from building more than 527 bodies a year, it was necessary to find alternative suppliers for some of the work. Leyland was chosen to share the body contract and the opportunity was taken to purchase complete buses so that an alternative source for chassis could also be tested.

The one hundred Leylands (STD 1–100) were nominally based on the standard TD4 and TD4c model Titan chassis but London Transport's specification required a number of modifications based on the standards of the contemporary STL. This included low geared steering, the worm and nut column assembly being supplied by AEC, revised dumb-irons so that the towing arrangements could be interchangeable with the STL, the removal of the autovac from the front bulkhead to a position under the bonnet and the provision of STL-type driving pedals. The standardisation with the STL did not extend to the gearbox, which on the first ninety was the standard Leyland crash unit, with its famous 'silent third' (1STD1). The last ten were fitted with Lysholm-Smith torque converter ('gearless') transmission (2STD1/1). These could be identified by the presence of the torque converter header on the front bulkhead. Apparently, this transmission system was not satisfactory to London Transport and these ten buses had standard gearboxes fitted at their first overhaul or soon afterwards, when they were reclassified 1STD1/1.

The bodywork was also the standard Leyland metal framed product modified in detail to resemble the latest style of roof-box STL. Leyland borrowed STL 1217 to study the detailed design of the Chiswick body and the finished product was a fairly good copy. The differences most easily detected were the smaller 'signalling' window on the offside staircase panel, the curved moulding at waist level, the sharper down-curve of the driver's cab window and the absence of an equivalent curve on the front bulkhead. Interestingly, the standard Leyland body which was the basis for the STD had been developed by Leyland in 1936 from London Transport's specification for trolleybuses. The 2STD1/1s had only 55 seats while fitted with torque converters.

The first Titan received at Chiswick was STD 91, the first of the torque converter examples, which arrived on 18th March 1937. It then spent over a month at Chiswick before being returned to Leyland, where it stayed for another month, during which time it is believed the transmission was fitted with a positive neutral. It did not enter service until July. Meanwhile, delivery of the standard type began with STD 1 and 2 on 5th April 1937 and the first to be licensed was STD 6 on 21st April 1937. The entire batch was allocated to Hendon where it fulfilled the total needs of the garage. On 1st September 1939, in anticipation of the imminent outbreak of the Second World War, thirteen of the class were placed on loan to the Country Bus department for use in the movement of evacuees and other wartime emergency activities. They were delicensed on 30th September and remained in store at various Country Bus garages until being relicensed for service on 1st November. With the reduction of services, Hendon needed fewer vehicles and those not required were allocated to Cricklewood for route 16, STD 13 going as a 'pilot' on 17th October. It was followed by twenty-three more on 1st November, although subsequent movements reduced the total to fourteen by the end of the year.

STD 92 was one of the ten fitted with torque converters, immediately identifiable from this angle by the converter header attached to the front bulkhead. The deeper valance above the bonnet is another feature which distinguished the STDs from STLs. Ken Glazier collection

Chassis:	Leyland Titan TD4 modified (STD 1–90); Titan TD4c (STD 91–100)						
Engine:	Leyland six cylinder 8.6 litre direct injection 94 bhp;						
Transmission:	Leyland four speed crash (helical third speed) (STD 1–90); Lysholm-Smith torque converter (STD 91–100[1])						
Bodywork:	Leyland						
L.T. codes:	1STD1 (1–90); 2STD1/1 (91–100[1])						
Capacity:	H30/26R (STD 1–90); H29/26R (STD 91–100 [1])						
Built:	1937						

Number built
  (by 31.12.39): 100
Number in stock: 1.7.33: Nil   31.12.39: 100

[1] At first overhaul torque converters were replaced by standard gearboxes, the seating capacity was increased to H30/26R and the classification altered to 1STD1/1.

STD		Date into stock	STD		Date into stock	STD		Date into stock
1	DLU311	5.4.37	35	DLU345	30.4.37	69	DLU379	20.5.37
2	DLU312	5.4.37	36	DLU346	24.4.37	70	DLU380	28.5.37
3	DLU313	15.4.37	37	DLU347	1.5.37	71	DLU381	25.5.37
4	DLU314	15.4.37	38	DLU348	1.5.37	72	DLU382	25.5.37
5	DLU315	17.4.37	39	DLU349	1.5.37	73	DLU383	25.5.37
6	DLU316	15.4.37	40	DLU350	1.5.37	74	DLU384	25.5.37
7	DLU317	15.4.37	41	DLU351	6.5.37	75	DLU385	28.5.37
8	DLU318	22.4.37	42	DLU352	5.5.37	76	DLU386	25.5.37
9	DLU319	17.4.37	43	DLU353	5.5.37	77	DLU387	26.5.37
10	DLU320	17.4.37	44	DLU354	5.5.37	78	DLU388	27.5.37
11	DLU321	17.4.37	45	DLU355	5.5.37	79	DLU389	26.5.37
12	DLU322	17.4.37	46	DLU356	5.5.37	80	DLU390	26.5.37
13	DLU323	17.4.37	47	DLU357	7.5.37	81	DLU391	26.5.37
14	DLU324	17.4.37	48	DLU358	6.5.37	82	DLU392	1.6.37
15	DLU325	24.4.37	49	DLU359	6.5.37	83	DLU393	1.6.37
16	DLU326	27.4.37	50	DLU360	7.5.37	84	DLU394	3.6.37
17	DLU327	27.4.37	51	DLU361	7.5.37	85	DLU395	3.6.37
18	DLU328	28.4.37	52	DLU362	7.5.37	86	DLU396	12.6.37
19	DLU329	24.4.37	53	DLU363	7.5.37	87	DLU397	12.6.37
20	DLU330	27.4.37	54	DLU364	8.5.37	88	DLU398	12.6.37
21	DLU331	28.4.37	55	DLU365	8.5.37	89	DLU399	12.6.37
22	DLU332	28.4.37	56	DLU366	8.5.37	90	DLU400	30.9.37
23	DLU333	29.4.37	57	DLU367	8.5.37	91	DLU401	18.3.37
24	DLU334	29.4.37	58	DLU368	8.5.37	92	DLU402	11.6.37
25	DLU335	29.4.37	59	DLU369	8.5.37	93	DLU403	15.6.37
26	DLU336	29.4.37	60	DLU370	20.5.37	94	DLU404	17.6.37
27	DLU337	29.4.37	61	DLU371	8.5.37	95	DLU405	21.6.37
28	DLU338	5.5.37	62	DLU372	8.5.37	96	DLU406	15.6.37
29	DLU339	29.4.37	63	DLU373	8.5.37	97	DLU407	21.6.37
30	DLU340	30.4.37	64	DLU374	8.5.37	98	DLU408	23.6.37
31	DLU341	30.4.37	65	DLU375	8.5.37	99	DLU409	24.6.37
32	DLU342	30.4.37	66	DLU376	20.5.37	100	DLU410	2.7.37
33	DLU343	30.4.37	67	DLU377	20.5.37			
34	DLU344	30.4.37	68	DLU378	20.5.37			

Facing page top **At first glance this could be the upper deck of a 1937-series STL but closer examination reveals a number of differences which show it to be an STD. The window pillars are chunkier and flatter in profile, there is a thicker line of beading above the windows, the window openers are not recessed into the beading and the vertical rail joining the front centre pillar to a short grab-rail was an embellishment not found on the STL. Most notably, the linings are Rexine-covered throughout, rather than painted.** London's Transport Museum

Facing page bottom **On the lower deck of the Leyland body, the front bulkhead is again distinctively different. The centre pillar is much wider than on the Chiswick bodies, almost a pre-echo of the post-war RTWs, and the front window sills do not curve downwards which, although perhaps neater, did restrict the forward view for front seat passengers. Also at the front the seats are on a shallow pedestal.** London's Transport Museum

RT

The RT was a development of the AEC Regent chassis as used in the STL class but with an engine design strongly influenced by Leyland practice, following London Transport's operation of the one hundred 1937 Leyland Titans.

The successful and economical operation of these direct injection pot cavity units led London Transport to specify similar 8.8 litre engines for the 10T10s, which were built by AEC under licence from Leyland. London Transport's policy had turned towards having large engines, with a derated power output to improve fuel economy and engine life, and the engine chosen for the new RT was therefore a 9.6-litre unit which developed 100bhp at 1,800rpm.

Design of the new bus had started in 1937 and a prototype chassis was built and delivered to London Transport on 23rd May 1938, formally becoming the Board's property on 30th June. Other new features of the chassis were the use of air pressure to operate both brakes and gears and a much lower bonnet and radiator. The new engine was not yet ready and the chassis was fitted instead with a similar but lower rated 8.8 litre unit at first. The body of TD 111 was mounted on the chassis and in this heavily disguised form, numbered ST 1140, it entered trial service from Hanwell (HW) garage on route 18C (Hanwell Garage–Wembley Empire Pool) on 13th July 1938. After the completion of trial running on 31st December 1938, the chassis returned to Chiswick to receive its newly designed body and it may have been at this time that the new A185 9.6 litre engine was fitted.

The new body was mounted on the chassis on 27th March 1939 and the complete vehicle was numbered RT 1. The body was of composite construction and the rear overhang was self-supporting, the chassis frame being cut off behind the rear wheels. As built it had 56 seats but this took it over the gross laden weight limit and the capacity was reduced to 55 by replacing the double seat on the nearside opposite the stairs with a single. In this condition it was shown to the Press on 13th July 1939 and entered public service on route 22 from Chelverton Road garage on 9th August.

Meanwhile two orders for 150 and 188 production chassis had been placed but the outbreak of war led to the suspension of the second order indefinitely. Production of the first of the 150 started almost immediately and the first three chassis received their bodies on 28th December 1939. The production batch differed from RT 1 in having the rear overhang supported on an extension of the chassis frame in the conventional manner. Eleven had been taken into stock by the end of 1939.

Chassis:	AEC Regent III O661
Engine:	AEC A180 6-cylinder 8.8 litre direct injection (while operating as ST 1140); AEC A185 6-cylinder direct injection 9.6 litre 100 bhp oil
Transmission:	AEC D140 4-speed air-operated preselective with fluid flywheel.
Bodywork:	LPTB (Chiswick)
Capacity:	H29/26R (RT 1); H30/26R (remainder)
L.T. codes:	1RT1 (RT 1): 2RT2 (remainder)
Built:	1939
Number built (by 31.12.1939):	11
Number in stock	1.7.33: Nil 31.12.39: 11

RT		Date into stock	RT		Date into stock	RT		Date into stock
1	EYK396	* 27.3.39	20	FXT195	28.12.39	43	FXT218	29.12.39
15	FXT190	28.12.39	37	FXT212	30.12.39	44	FXT219	29.12.39
16	FXT191	28.12.39	38	FXT213	30.12.39	47	FXT222	30.12.39
19	FXT194	28.12.39	39	FXT214	29.12.39			

* First entered stock as ST 1140 30.6.38

RT 1 approaches the stand at Aldwych on its press demonstration trip in July 1939.
Members of the trade and national press were taken on a trip to Hampstead Heath.
The new bus entered passenger service on route 22 the following month.

MINOR TYPES

This list shows those double-deckers acquired from Independents which did not fit into any of the larger classes. It is therefore presented in a condensed form which lists the details separately under individual headings for each chassis make, arranged alphabetically.

The lists under each heading are arranged in numerical order of fleet numbers with those vehicles which remained unnumbered until withdrawn shown at the end of each list.

Identity	Chassis model	Body make	Seats	Acquired from	New	Date Into stock	Date out of stock
DAIMLER							
MF8001	Y	Hickman	O22/20R	B.B.P. Omnibus Co Ltd	1924	15.12.33	20.6.34
GUY							
* YW7829	FCX	Dodson	O34/28RO	Charles H. Pickup, Camberwell	1928	10.11.33	17.5.34
* UC3213	FCX	Dodson	H34/28RO	The City Motor Omnibus Company Ltd	1928	7.11.34	20.7.35
* YX1833	FCX	Dodson	H34/28RO	The City Motor Omnibus Company Ltd	1928	7.11.34	23.7.35
* YU7375	FCX	Dodson	H34/28RO	The City Motor Omnibus Company Ltd	1927	7.11.34	24.7.35
* YU4431	FCX	Dodson	H34/28RO	The City Motor Omnibus Company Ltd	1927	7.11.34	24.7.35
* YX4101	FCX	Dodson	H34/28RO	The City Motor Omnibus Company Ltd	1928	7.11.34	22.7.35
* YT8954	FCX	Dodson	H34/28RO	The City Motor Omnibus Company Ltd	1927	7.11.34	20.7.35
* YU7838	FCX	Dodson	H34/28RO	The City Motor Omnibus Company Ltd	1928	7.11.34	20.7.35
* YX1834	FCX	Dodson	H34/28RO	The City Motor Omnibus Company Ltd	1928	7.11.34	23.7.35
* YX4098	FCX	Dodson	H34/28RO	The City Motor Omnibus Company Ltd	1928	7.11.34	20.7.35
* YX4100	FCX	Dodson	H34/28RO	The City Motor Omnibus Company Ltd	1928	7.11.34	23.7.35
TM1401	FCX	Dodson	H35/29RO	Eastern National Omnibus Co. Ltd	1927	1.9.33	10.34
* Numbered GS 15–25 respectively							
LEYLAND							
* XX9060	Leyland/ City 6-wheel	Dodson	H34/28RO	The City Motor Omnibus Company Ltd	1930	7.11.34	20.7.35
* GN5819	Leyland/ City 6-wheel	Ransomes	H34/28RO	The City Motor Omnibus Company Ltd	1931	7.11.34	20.7.35
* GO1559	Leyland/ City 6-wheel	Ransomes	H34/28RO	The City Motor Omnibus Company Ltd	1931	7.11.34	24.7.35
* GP127	Leyland/ City 6-wheel	Ransomes	H34/28RO	The City Motor Omnibus Company Ltd	1931	7.11.34	20.7.35
* GP4336	Leyland/ City 6-wheel	Ransomes	H34/28RO	The City Motor Omnibus Company Ltd	1931	7.11.34	22.6.35
* GP93	Leyland/ City 6-wheel	Ransomes	H34/28RO	The City Motor Omnibus Company Ltd	1931	7.11.34	22.6.35
† AGH149	Titanic TT1 (oil)	Dodson	H34/28RO	The City Motor Omnibus Company Ltd	1933	7.11.34	19.5.38
† AGH150	Titanic TT1 (oil)	Dodson	H34/28RO	The City Motor Omnibus Company Ltd	1933	7.11.34	19.5.38
† AGH151	Titanic TT1 (oil)	Dodson	H34/28RO	The City Motor Omnibus Company Ltd	1933	7.11.34	19.5.38
* Numbered LM 1–6							
† Numbered TC 1–3							
MAUDSLAY							
* EV3403	ML7c2	Dodson	H26/26R	Gordon Omnibus Co. Ltd, Leyton	1931	15.12.33	28.3.36
* Numbered MY 1							
SUNBEAM							
* JJ9235		Dodson	H36/28R	Westminster Omnibus Co. Ltd, Holloway	1933	10.7.34	16.5.35
* Numbered SM 1							
TILLING STEVENS							
PK4244	B10A2	Short Bros	O22/24R	London General Country Services Ltd	1928	1.7.33	5.35